*The Thames Torso Murders
of Victorian London*

ALSO BY R. MICHAEL GORDON

Alias Jack the Ripper:
Beyond the Usual Whitechapel Suspects
(McFarland, 2001)

The Thames Torso Murders of Victorian London

by R. Michael Gordon

To Don,
This is the first time this series
found its way to press. Hope it
was worth the wait.
Best Wishes
R. Michael Gordon
Nov. 29. 2010

McFarland & Company, Inc., Publishers

Jefferson, North Carolina, and London

Library of Congress Cataloguing-in-Publication Data

Gordon, R. Michael, 1952–
    The Thames torso murders of Victorian London / by
R. Michael Gordon.
        p.   cm.
    Includes bibliographical references and index.

    ISBN-13: 978-0-7864-1348-5
    softcover : 50# alkaline paper ∞

    1. Serial murders— England — London — History —19th century.
    2. Serial murders— England — London — History —19th Century.
    I. Title.
HV6535.G6L65349   2002
364.15'23'09421109034 — dc21   2002006628

British Library cataloguing data are available

Manufactured in the United States of America

Cover photographs ©2002 Corbis Images and Art Today

*McFarland & Company, Inc., Publishers
    Box 611, Jefferson, North Carolina 28640
        www.mcfarlandpub.com*

For Elizabeth Jackson and four unknown women who met their fates in the East End of Victorian London under the shadow of a serial killer who may one day be discovered to have been "Jack the Ripper."

They now rest as the shadows fall.

Acknowledgments

Any work on the Torso Murder Series must surely rest on the shoulders of those men of London's famous police force — Scotland Yard — who worked so hard many years ago to solve these murders. And, although no one suspect was ever brought to trial for these deaths, it cannot be said to have been due to any lack of effort on the part of the inspectors and beat constables who spent years investigating and tracking down leads in this series of murders. To them must go my thanks and primary acknowledgment. It is their work and the files they left behind which make this book possible, as we continue to search for more clues.

There are also several authors and researchers whose works on the Borough Poisoner and Ripper murders have been most helpful in understanding the history of these background cases. Primary of these are Paul Begg, Martin Fido, Keith Skinner, Philip Sugden, Hargrave L. Adam, Colin Wilson, George Weidenfeld, Stewart Evans, Donald Rumbelow, and Elizabeth Koper from the London Borough of Havering Central Library. Also, a heartfelt thank you to Debbie Gosling for her hard work and abilities to discover very interesting pieces of history related to these cases, as well as her suggestion for a motive in these cases. I was constantly amazed.

I would also like to thank the many individuals who have contributed their thoughts on these well-known cases on the Internet website *Ripper Casebook*. They have given no quarter and have asked for none in the quest to understand these most interesting series of crimes. A hearty well done as we continue to debate and uncover things which have in the past been only shadows.

A special thank you to the following for their personal encouragement and helpful comments concerning this work: Teresa Eidenbock, Robert

Urquidez (for his graphic contributions), Dr. Rudolph Campos, Jeanne Cartier and Gene Schwedler, Carole Fraser, Philip Gordon, Ruth Victoria Todd, John Hearn of California State University–Dominques Hills. And, finally, for their hard work and encouragement — Ginger Norton and David Duperre of Sedgeband Literary Associates.

I must also thank the men and women of the Metropolitan Police Service, Archives Branch, London, and especially Christine M. Thomas, for their research and records reviews.

Table of Contents

Introduction to Murder

For most readers of criminal history, when the words "East End of London" and "Serial Killer" come together they invariably think of "Jack the Ripper" and the "Autumn of Terror" in which those crimes were brought to the people of Victorian London in 1888–89. To be sure, the terror was quite real, as was the depraved sexual serial killer who hunted the back alleys of the East End searching for yet another victim for his ever ready blade.

During a central 13-week period, working in a single square mile of London centered on Whitechapel, the Ripper murdered six local prostitutes, mutilating most as he searched for body parts. The names of Martha Tabram, Annie Chapman, Mary Jane Kelly and the others have become well known to "Ripperologists" and casual readers alike. Few, however, remember the name Elizabeth Jackson, who died during a second series of murders in old London. And, whether it was the dramatic name given the killer in the Ripper series by an inflammatory press, or the closeness of the killings in time and place, or even perhaps the fact that no one was ever charged with those murders, what keeps this series in the minds of so many is hard to say. Whatever the reason, the fact remains that this is the case which seems to overshadow all others. It has even overshadowed one series which began before the Ripper series, lasted longer and was just as brutal in all respects as any Ripper murder ever was. That series of murders would be collectively known as the Thames Torso Murders or the Thames Dismemberment Murders. And, like the Ripper murders, it would occur for the most part in the East End of London, targeting local prostitutes.

The series began in 1887, fully one year before "Jack" began his work.

1

There would be a second in 1888 during the central Ripper series, two more in 1889 as the Ripper was slowing down, and then a long pause before a final torso would be found in 1902. And, despite many similarities in the Ripper and Torso murders, very few were willing to point to a single assassin as the prime suspect in both sets of crimes. In fact, it was official policy to view these crimes as fully separate events unlinked to any one killer and certainly not to the Ripper. Yet, there were similarities, such as the skills required, many of the wounds, the geographic area covered by the killer, the time frame and, of course, the selected victims, which do suggest that a closer inspection of these cases may very well show a connection. Serial killers do indeed change their killing styles, and situations sometimes dictate events not accounted for in murder plans. One such individual is the Zodiac killer in California, who has changed his technique so many times that some of his murders may even have looked like accidents. Serial killers do experiment with death. It is, after all, what they do best, and some go on for years.

Was this Torso series just one more manifestation of a madman who changed, seemingly at will, or an entirely different killer? Or was there some type of crossover? The question is asked: Just how many sexual serial killers were working London's East End in the late 1880s? If police theories at the time were correct, there were several, but was this a real working theory or public propaganda being used by a hard-pressed police force trying desperately to keep control? And, were these murders or something else?

Even those who felt they must write to the authorities and sign the name "Jack the Ripper" seemed unwilling to accept that the Ripper was responsible for the Torso Murders. As witnessed by one writer of a "Ripper" letter, no one wanted credit for these murders. "In the name of God hear me. I swear I did not kill the female whose body was found at Whitehall." No one ever wrote to the police claiming credit for the Torso Murders, at least none are to be found in the less than complete files located in the public record office.

One reason why the Torso Murders may have been officially downplayed can be seen in the geography of the two cases. In the Ripper series the women lived in an area of about 300 square yards and were, for the most part, killed in an area roughly one square mile. In the Torso series the victims were mostly unknown and could have come from any area of London, and the killing zone was at least 20 square miles. No police force in the world, then or now, could cover every possible area in the Torso series. In the Ripper series police resources were stretched to the maximum, and even that effort proved to be wholly unsuccessful. The Ripper was never caught in the act. It should also be recalled that, for the most part, the Ripper killed on the streets and alleys of the East End. This, of course, increased the possibility of his being caught. It also increased the thrill of the hunt. The Torso Killer never killed where the bodies were found and could have easily killed exclusively inside his preferred location, which seems to have moved around a bit even as he stayed in the general area of the East End. Some of the victims even had their bedclothes still hanging from their torsos or were wrapped up in them. The Torso Killer seemed to have more resources and greater mobility than the Ripper, thus his ability to strike in a larger area. Did he also keep track of the Ripper, and did he write any Ripper letters? And was he also responsible for some of the Ripper deaths? The record is silent on these questions, at least for now, but overlap is always a real possibility.

It was also important for the authorities to calm the population whenever it was possible. The public and official lie that the Ripper had been drowned in the Thames River or had been caught and placed in an asylum were examples of official propaganda aimed at calming the city and its potentially violent and mostly immigrant East End population. The police knew otherwise, as the hunt continued years after the final Ripper death. In point of fact, one document released from the files shows that the police felt the 1889 torso murder on Pinchin Street could very well have been done by the Ripper, even though the public had been told not to worry. That document was to be held back for 101 years, until 1990. It was also easier for the authorities to dismiss these cases as not as important as the Ripper murders because they were played out over a much longer period of time. Adding to the seeming lack of empathy in the press and public responses was the fact that only one Torso victim, Elizabeth Jackson, was ever identified. And she did not live in the Ripper's critical victim hunting zone, the 300 square yard area, at least not at the time of her death. It is much easier to dismiss a victim from one's mind if you don't know who they were or what they looked like. There were, after all, many distractions in the Victorian East End.

And what of the killer himself? What would drive an individual so hard that he could find no other release, save serial death? Only the most superficial information can be gleaned from the events themselves, and these are only educated guesses based on serial killer studies done over the past 20 or so years. Even after a century, most shadows still remain from these most interesting of cases.

He was a white male in his twenties, single at the time of the murders, living alone, or at least able to find a quiet place where he could do his "work." He was able to interact with other people, but only on a superficial level. His fear of women at all levels was the overriding force in all that he did, and the thought of killing and controlling them never left his mind. When he had finally taken control and fully destroyed their humanity he could at last feel a true power, and yet the feeling could not last. His self-hate could never be fully suppressed, no matter how many he killed.

If he had a job it could not have been of great value. It would not be allowed to keep him away from his real "work." And, to say the least, the Torso Killer was a coward, one who would not have been likely to attack another man. His victims were all small females who, in all likelihood, were asleep when death came. He was a sexual serial killer who would never have been able to consummate a normal relationship with any woman. He also kept very much to himself, never telling anyone of his crimes, and this may be the one major dividing line between the average murderer who brags about his deeds and the serial killer who lives, works and kills in a singular world all his own. He lives to kill in his twisted world, and none may enter and come out alive.

For whatever reasons, the Torso Murders would soon fade from the collective minds of London's population as other events rose to the forefront. As for the rest of the world, they would learn little in the shadow of the Ripper about "The Forgotten Serial Killer of Victorian London," who hunted the dark foggy streets of the East End from 1887 to 1902.

Chapter 1

London's Bloody History

One is forced to conclude that the Abyss is literally a huge man-killing machine...
Jack London — *The People of the Abyss*, 1903

AN OUTPOST CALLED LONDINIUM

London, England, first came to the attention of history as Londinium through Tacitus, a second century Roman writer and historian. The name itself is of Celtic origin and may mean "place of trading," but the actual meaning has been lost to history. It has been the political and economic center of the country, and then of an empire, from its earliest beginnings. Yet, when Julius Caesar (yes, the famous one who was stabbed in the back by his best friend) invaded England in 55 B.C., his reports somehow failed to mention this well-known trading post on the river. It is possible, however, that it was little more than a stopping off point at the time. So it was left to Tacitus to report that Roman "Londinium" was "a town of the highest repute and a busy emporium for trade and traders." By then the town could boast of its first bridge across the Thames, some 200 feet east of the well-known London Bridge of today's London. Its existence was recently confirmed by the discovery of massive wooden pilings of Roman age and origin that had been driven into the riverbed.

At the time the Romans built their "Londinium Bridge" the river was much wider, lower and a great deal shallower than the Thames we are familiar with today. Nevertheless, even in Roman times the river was required to transport a body or two along its muddy channel. Reports don't mention whether or not the victims were Pagan or Christian. But one

5

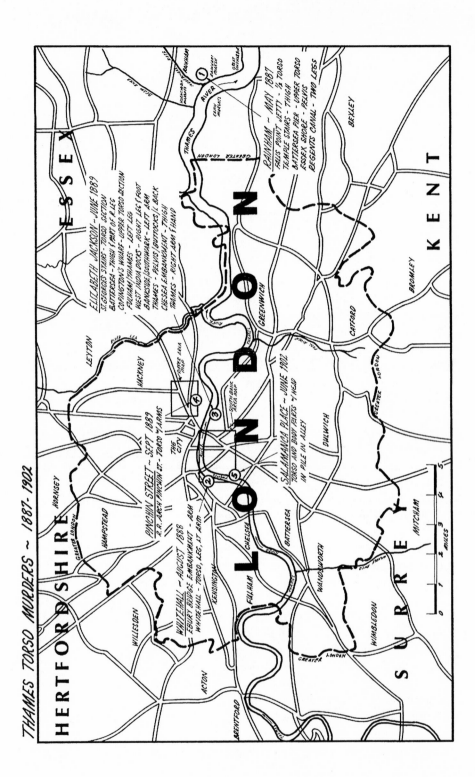

THAMES TORSO MURDERS ~ 1887-1902

HERTFORDSHIRE
ESSEX
KENT
SURREY
LONDON

ELIZABETH JACKSON ~ JUNE 1889
ST. GEORGES STAIRS - TORSO SECTION
BATTERSEA - THIGH & PART OF R. LEG
COPINGTON'S WHARF - UPPER TORSO SECTION
FULHAM / THAMES - LEFT LEG
WEST INDIA DOCKS - RIGHT LEG & FOOT
BANKSIDE (SOUTHWARK) - LEFT ARM
THAMES - PELVIS / BUTTOCKS / L. BACK
CHELSEA EMBANKMENT - THIGH
THAMES - RIGHT ARM & HAND

RAINHAM ~ MAY 1887
FALLS POINT - JETTY - 1/2 TORSO
TEMPLE STAIRS - THIGH
BATTERSEA PIER - UPPER TORSO
ESSEX SHORE - PELVIS
REGENTS CANAL - TWO LEGS

PINCHIN STREET ~ SEPT 1889
R.R. ARCH PINCHIN ST. - TORSO & ARMS

WHITEHALL ~ AUGUST 1888
EBURY BRIDGE EMBANKMENT - ARM
WHITEHALL - TORSO, LEG, LT. ARM

SALAMANCA PLACE ~ JUNE 1902
TORSO AND BODY PARTS + HEAD
IN PILE IN ALLEY

would expect both to have found their way into the slow moving waters of the "Bloody Thames."

Even under the Pax Romana (Roman Peace, which in reality was not all that peaceful except for the dead), Londoners would see their fair share of death and war first hand. In A.D. 60 the Pagan Queen Boadicea of the warring Iceni tribe attacked this northern Roman outpost and burned much of the town. Having beaten the mighty Roman legions in bloody battle, Boadicea promptly stormed and massacred the residents of London — Roman or not. It did not matter to her who they were as long as they had lived in London, and the river ran bright red with blood. The torsos were piled very high on that grim day! There is still a monument to the Queen of the Icenians near Parliament erected by the very people whom she chose to slaughter! The victory would not gain much for the Icenians however, as the Romans quickly rebuilt the town and, having learned from past battles, added a much-enlarged basilica. At the end of the 2nd century they would add a wall, which encircled (with the river at its southern end) an area of 325 acres. Some of that old Roman wall may still be seen to this day. Not far from that ancient wall, Victorian residents would later find some of the handiwork of the Thames Torso Killer.

With its interior lines secured from attack, the city soon rose to a population estimated at around 30,000. It was by the early 5th century a true city, and was by then an important military base for the Roman Empire until the Romans retreated and left the city and her traders to deal with the Anglo-Saxon invasion on their own. The town would soon fall to this newest invader.

Invasion and fire would continue to plague this trading city, as it was nearly completely destroyed by fire between 674 and 810 on three separate occasions. By the middle of the 9th century there was "a great slaughter" in London committed by the invading Danes, which was duly noted in the *Anglo-Saxon Chronicle* written in the late 10th century. But only after Alfred the Great, then king of the West Saxons, attacked the Danes in 886 and defeated them would the city once again be free. The city would stay relatively free until William I (popularly known as William the Conqueror) invaded England in 1066 and defeated the Saxons under King Harold at the famous Battle of Hastings. (It is a battle every British school child, including this writer, must study.) One month earlier, Bloody Harold had killed his brother Tostig in battle, so perhaps it was fitting that he too should be defeated. The powerful city, however, would still retain a moderate amount of independence. William (a man of Viking heritage) wisely decided to negotiate with the city with the "bloody reputation" rather than deplete his small forces even further in attempting to take the city by storm.

Indeed, he may not have believed he would be able to take the city by force, so it was a good decision. As for William, he would later die on a cold stone floor in a French monastery, stripped naked as his betrayers removed his property.

Throughout the Medieval period (roughly between the fall of Rome and the Renaissance), London would continue to grow (doubling the size of the old walled city) and prosper as city governments began to develop some of the roads and waterways still in use today. Traditions and a London way of life were starting to take hold. With these developments, however, came an increasing crime problem. It was indeed becoming a modern city as Londinium became London. It became the place to go if one wanted to do a brisk business in trade goods.

London, however, has always been a city in transition, even as it holds steadfast to long-held traditions. This was never more so than in the late Victorian period of the 1880s as the city passed its 1900th year. As Queen Victoria moved past her fiftieth year on the throne, the great city was once again in the grip of change. The city's central core was being rapidly depopulated to form a more complete political and commercial center. This very fast depopulation from 124,000 in 1841 to a little less than 60,000 by 1881 was only prologue to many other disruptions the population would be forced to live through. As more and more immigrants arrived, London became the most populated city on earth. The inner London boroughs, which surrounded the central city, ballooned from 1.8 million residents in 1841 to over 4.5 million by 1901. Death from one source or another would surely follow.

Widespread death, plague and other catastrophic events were not new to those who knew London's past. Indeed, plague was an intermittent threat, which had taken many lives. The so-called "Black Death" struck the city in 1348–49. It was indeed a deadly time. However, the most remembered of the plagues were to come in 1625 (when over 40,000 would perish) and again in 1664–65 (as another 75,000 died during "The Great Plague"). At one point in 1664 it was estimated that over 7000 had perished in a single week! One in seven had died as fires consumed the piles of bodies, and as the population once again struggled to endure. The city could not hold so many people so closely. Something had to give, and widespread death was the answer.

THE NEWS— July 6, 1665

Published for the
SATISFACTION & INFORMATION of the PEOPLE

By order from the Right Honourable the *Lord Arlington* principal
Secretary of State to His Majestie, I am commanded to publish

the following advertisement to satisfy all persons of the great
care of the Right Honourable the Lords of His Majesties most
Honourable Privy Council, for prevention of spreading of the
infection. Who by their order dated the one and thirtieth day of
May last past did authorize & require the Justices of the Peace
for the County of *Middlesex* and City and Libertie of *Westminster*, or any five of them, to treat with *James Angier, Esq.*, upon
his offers of certain Remedies and Medicaments for stopping the
contagion of the *Plague* and for disinfecting houses already
infected, etc.

Following closely on its latest plague came the infamous "Great Fire
of London" of 1666, which began in a small shop. It is commemorated by
"The Monument" placed very near where it began. It had been very dry
that year and a fire was not unexpected. During five days in September
almost four-fifths of the central city was consumed by the conflagration.
From eyewitness John Evelyn, a founding member of the Royal Society
(which would soon count among its members Sir Isaac Newton), we learn,
"…it burned both in breadth and length, the churches, public halls,
Exchange, hospitals, monuments and ornaments, leaping in a prodigious
manner from house to house and street to street, at great distances from
one another, for the heat had even ignited the air."

News reports at the time were, as would be expected, hard come by,
but *The London Gazette* did manage a press run for the period of "From
Monday, Septemb 3, to Monday, Septemp 10, 1666." The *Gazette* reported:
"Whitehall, Sept. 8. On the second instant, at one of the clock in the Morning, there hapned to break out, a sad in deplorable Fire in *Pudding-lane*
near *New Fish-street*, which falling out at that hour of night, and in a quarter of the Town so close built with wooden pitched houses spread itself so
far before day, and with such distraction to the inhabitants and Neighbours,
that care was not taken for the timely preventing the further diffusion of
it, by pulling down houses, as ought to have been; so that this lamentable
Fire in a short time became too big to be mastered by any Engines or working neer it." A thousand years of London's history went up in flames. The
fire had taken 13,000 homes, 87 local churches, the Royal Exchange and
most of the government buildings in the central city, yet only three would
die. It would be this fire which would mostly end the wood structures of
an older London, to be replaced by the brick and stone structures well
known today. The London known to William Shakespeare was gone forever. Strangely enough, many Londoners at the time did not view the fire
as all that bad. They felt that perhaps the fire had somehow cleansed the
city of whatever had caused the earlier plagues. The fire had probably

done just that, and in the process saving many lives in the future. London's heart was virtually destroyed, as was much history, but it would once again recover, and as it did it expanded in every direction.

Later, increasing the speed of this development was the horse drawn tramway system, known as the "poor man's bus," developed in the 1870s. Workers could now live farther away from the center of London in one of the outlying boroughs. However, this expansion was not so equally directed as far as economic growth was concerned. The East End of London would expand far faster in population than in the economic opportunities needed to support such a massive population growth. The growth had not been a natural one of local generation either. It had been more of an invasion by outside refugees, and the East End would suffer the brunt of that invasion.

THE LATE VICTORIAN EAST END

During the latter part of the 19th century on the continent of Europe, persecuted peoples were moving en masse away from nations and governments which saw them as less than desirable. Death and the destruction of homes and lives was the order of the day, creating many refugees. Many of these displaced people would eventually find their way to London, and for most that meant the crowded slums of the East End London ghettos. They were not welcomed by the "native" population, and it would not be an easy place to live.

The East End of London had, for a long time, been a place where caution and careful movement were to be held in high regard if one was to move safely along its cool dark passages. In the 1880s the East End could best be described as a giant killing field, not so much for the criminal element who owned the dark, filth soaked places (they were dangerous enough), but from the very environment itself.

On a visit to the East End while researching his classic 1903 work *The People of the Abyss*, Jack London described what he saw as he walked those damp, coal dust choked streets. "My first discovery was that empty houses were few and far between. Not one empty house could I find — a conclusive proof that the district was saturated...! True, the sanitation of the places I visited was wretched. From the imperfect sewage and drainage, defective traps, poor ventilation, dampness, and general foulness, I might expect my wife and babies speedily to be attacked by diphtheria, croup, typhoid, erysipelas, blood poisoning, bronchitis, pneumonia, consumption, and various kindred disorders. Certainly the death rate would be exceedingly high. So one is forced to conclude that the abyss is literally a huge man-killing machine...."

London himself was no stranger to poverty and depravation. He had been born out of wedlock to Flora Wellman and William Chaney in 1876. His mother would then marry widower John London, and Jack would take his name. London helped the family by working 10 hour days for 10¢ an hour in a San Francisco canning factory, and yet he still found time to read. There was little time, however, for formal education, and no money to pay for it. The poverty and exploitation he saw in the East End must have seemed quite familiar as he recalled his childhood, living and working on the waterfront of San Francisco Bay. The area's criminal element would have also seemed somewhat familiar to London as well.

Earlier, Arthur Morrison, a British writer whose articles appeared in the very popular *Strand* magazine, wrote a series of short stories about the East End. These stories were re-published in his 1894 book *Tales of Mean Streets*. They related events surrounding the general wife beating, street fights among the women and general drunkenness which prevailed among the lower class prostitutes of London. Morrison, who was born in Poplar, East End, but did not like to be reminded of the fact, tried to expose the tremendous degradation of the population among the working class poor of London. For the most part, his literary cries fell on deaf ears, as the upper classes of the West End continued on as usual. There were no reasons to do otherwise, since the government pursued a mostly hands-off policy in the ghettos of the East End.

The overcrowded and crime-ridden East End of the late 1880s could lay claim to nearly one million inhabitants, many of them newly arrived from Europe. Indeed, some 85 to 90 percent of the new arrivals were from the Continent, and many of them were Jewish. The Jewish centers around Whitechapel, Spitalfields and Mile End were fast becoming the most crowded ghetto in Europe, if not the world. In that small area as many as 15,000 people wandered the streets each day, homeless, sleeping "raw" out in the cold wherever they could find a place for the night. A "lucky" number, perhaps as many as 100,000, found shelter in one of the many workhouses scattered throughout the area. These workhouses offered a scant fare along with a filthy, infected mat to sleep on in a crowded room, but only after a full day's work on some meaningless task was completed. It would be a toss-up as to which "accommodation" would be the safest or cleanest.

In and around Whitechapel, central to the so-called "wicked quarter mile," lived over 90,000 people closely packed in. In the better areas of London the population could count 50 per acre. In Whitechapel the number was closer to 176. It was even worse in the crowded Bell Lane area, in which some 600 could be counted in a single acre. The noise, filth and smells of rotting debris were never far away, nor were the women who made their way in life as low-class prostitutes (estimated to number around 1200 by the local authorities). Many women found their way to the streets after losing a husband by death or abandonment. This lifestyle for many was the only way they could find to survive. For those men (or women, for that matter) with a few more pennies there were at least 60 brothels also serving the area. None of these houses, however, could be said to be safe or clean. But at least they were off the streets and out of the cold. It was a mixed blessing at best for all involved in the "trade."

> Conf. Memo— Police Commissioner Sir Charles Warren
>
> Oct. 25, 1888. There has been no return hitherto of the probable numbers of brothels in London, but during the last few months I have been tabulating the observations of Constables on their beats, and have come to the conclusion that there are 62 houses known to be brothels on the H or Whitechapel Divn and probably a great number of the houses which are more or less intermittently used for such purposes.

The Torso and Ripper victims were thought to have all been low-class prostitutes, but without identification of most of the Torso victims it is not much more than speculation on those murders. It must be said, however, that the one Torso victim who was identified was indeed a "lady of the night." Unlike with the Ripper's victims, it is impossible to discover if these were random targets of opportunity or women the killer had known for at least a short period of time. Certainly if these women had all been close friends or lived near the killer the risk of their deaths being linked by the authorities to one individual would have been great. And yet in the Ripper series all of the victims lived very close to the killer — one was even killed in the building he lived in at the time. It was a fact the police never picked up on during the intense investigation! The Torso Killer did, however, remove the heads and dispose of all, save one. That single head was cooked or boiled to remove any chance of identification. Was this a clue? Was he closely connected to this woman, thus the overwhelming need to hide her identity? With so many people coming up missing in that great city, a spare corpse or two would have been very hard to identify. It would be especially true if no one reported her as missing. Only the Ripper and Torso Killers were keeping a close eye on the prostitutes— a very close eye indeed.

For those with some kind of small income there were the many low-class common lodging houses spread throughout the area. For a few pennies (much the same as the cost of a low-class prostitute or a drink) a resident could purchase the use of a "bed" for the night. With as many as 230 rat and disease infested houses to choose from, an individual could move around a great deal, but many stayed in two or three familiar ones for long periods of time, off and on, as long as the money held out. Some of the less accommodating lodging houses could hold up to 70 at a time, but this could easily mean rooms full of filthy mats literally laid wall-to-wall. It would be from these lodging or "doss houses" that the Ripper would choose almost all of his victims. It was from one of these doss houses that the Torso Killer would choose his one identified victim as well. It is a loose, but arguably an important, connection. These killers knew the doss houses well, even though they may not have used them for their own accommodations, the Torso Killer least of all.

One hundred years earlier, much of the East End had been a prosperous area. Upper class merchants, many of the Jewish faith, had made Whitechapel their home. It was an area far enough away from the then crowded and potentially dangerous central London area to be safe from most street crime and disease, but close enough to the docks which lined the Thames River just to the south to allow easy access to trade and commerce. With massive immigration and a city-wide transition occurring, the East End was no longer safe, clean or uncrowded. It had become an unorganized slum badly in need of repair. In point of fact, it would take the bombing raids of Nazi Germany, off-target from the docks, to truly cause any renovations to be effected on the area. (Though the docks were the main target most of the time, Hitler did feel that by bombing the poor people of London he could force them to rise up against their country. History shows that he was wrong.) It would be the central city of London, as well as the East End, which would feel most of the onslaught of that war, as more than 30,000 would die. But that rather haphazard and unintended process of urban renewal was some 50 years into London's future at the time of the murders. There would be no such relief during the Victorian period, other than a large fire or two, mostly in the dock and warehouse areas.

Central to the haunts of the many prostitutes and their clients were the pubs, which seemed to be on just about every corner. In fact, many short passages held two or three such establishments in less than 100 yards. Whitechapel Road, which ran the greater length of the central East End area, could boast some 48 public houses along its dimly lit main passage. Many of these pubs never closed for any reason, even death or murder.

These often-crowded pubs would become a prime focus of investigation during the hunt, with the police placing plainclothesmen throughout the area.

To the obvious terrors of any crowded slum were added the moral values of these late 19th century occupants of the East End. Although the "Victorian Age" has the historical appeal of being considered proper and above board in many written works, this was clearly not the case in London's East End or, for that matter, the rest of London's hidden society. In 1875 the age of consent had been raised from 12 to 13 throughout Great Britain. It was not uncommon for a girl of 12 or 13 to be "with child" not long after her wedding day. As for the children who lived in the ghettos, there was a less than 50 percent chance that they would survive to see their fifth birthday. There were far too many ways to die in the East End during the late 1880s.

Adding to the true horrors of this Victorian ghetto was the almost common occurrence of incest within close families. Sex between brothers and sisters or fathers and daughters was common enough to be considered epidemic. It was also no surprise in that crowded social-economic environment to find prostitutes as young as fourteen, both male and female, working the streets of Whitechapel and Mile End. There was, of course, one final way to escape the daily terrors of London — suicide. For those who took their own lives— and there were many— suicide was not an end; it was, in their minds, the only escape. And yet, some three miles to the west and a world away, Queen Victoria sat on her gilded throne seemingly unconcerned until a serial killer or two came to town! Only then would those in power finally come to grips with the depravation "allowed" to fester so long in the East End. But even a serial killer could not change the minds of the rich of London's upper classes for long enough to affect any real long term improvements. After all, no serial killers were targeting any upper class women, and even during the terror to come in the next few years that fact was certain to all who cared to look.

A Death in Paris
on the Road to London

As fall moved towards winter in early November 1886, the people of Paris prepared themselves for the winds and snows they knew would soon blanket that great city. Along with the winter weather came floods of immigrants seeking new homes and jobs. Along with them came one who sought neither home nor trade. He had come only for death as he passed through Paris on his eventual way to London. And he had not been pushed out of his home. This man was on the run for other reasons.

The church at Montrouge in Paris had long been a place of quiet sanctuary for the locals, and would continue to be so for many more years to come. The quiet of the church, however, would be broken by the death of a suspected local prostitute whose mutilated body would be dumped on the doorstep of this same church. It was to be the signature of a demented serial killer just beginning his deadly work. At least it was the first such murder to be identified in the series. He may have earlier "worked" in Poland for a time, but that is, at this point, only speculation.

In the early morning hours of that cold November day a madman left his deadly calling card at Montrouge Church. The police were soon called to the scene to discover that the torso of a young woman had been deposited. The killer was nowhere to be seen. Upon further investigation they soon found that the head, right arm and both legs had been crudely cut off. These pieces of the body were nowhere to be seen, and it was obvious that the woman had been killed at another location and brought to the church for disposal. Indeed, it was possible that the left arm, with the hand still attached, was used as a tool in order to transport the torso. It was a crude but fully effective method. It was a method which would be used again.

Along with the missing limbs and head, the killer had seen fit to remove and carry off the victim's right breast and uterus. Other than the crudeness of the injuries, the Paris authorities had very little to go on. In fact, a detailed investigation would fail to uncover not only the killer, but the identity of the victim herself. And what would become a hallmark of the Torso Murders in England was also evident in this crime — the cause of death would never be discovered. It was also possible that the killer had simply tossed the missing body parts in the Seine River, as he would do in the Thames of London. No one would ever be brought to trial for the murder. There were simply no clues to go on at the time.

One possible clue to the killer's identity, however, may be found in an obscure and never published work by a British doctor named Thomas Dutton. Dr. Dutton, a personal friend of Ripper investigator Inspector Frederick Abberline, was reported to have written a work detailing his various ideas and thoughts on several criminal cases, including a few murders in Paris. In that work, titled *Chronicles of Crime,* he is reported to have written, "I have learned from a French doctor of a Russian junior surgeon, or feldscher, who was known to him in Paris about 1885–88. He was suspected of having killed and mutilated a "grisette" (prostitute) in Montmartre, but he left Paris before he could be arrested." This work by Dr. Dutton has since been lost or destroyed, depending on the source, and is therefore no longer available for confirmation. There is also a report in the *Encyclopedia of Murder*, by Colin Wilson, that a man named Chapman may have been involved. "Another chronicler declares positively that Chapman had decapitated a woman before he left Poland...." Perhaps he visited Paris as well!? We are left now with only speculation and loose ends—for the moment at least. Chapman, however, did leave Poland in a very big hurry!

As for the murder in Paris, it would become a prelude to future events soon to capture the imagination of the world. But Paris would not be the focal point of that morbid fascination with death. For whatever reason, the killer had chosen London to be his most productive work place, and he would be very productive.

1887

In 1887 Arthur Conan Doyle's first full length story, *A Study in Scarlet*, featuring a fictional detective named Sherlock Holmes, appeared in *Beeton's Christmas Annual*. It is too bad the great detective, or his creator, was unavailable to work on the Torso case at the time. Eighteen eighty-seven was also the year of Queen Victoria's Jubilee as England's reigning monarch, and the capital was prepared to put on a grand but dignified show. She had come to the throne upon the death of William IV on June 20, 1837. Later in 1837 she would make Buckingham Palace, in the heart of London, the primary residence of the royal family.

It was time to show the world how proper and civilized London was, and the Jubilee would be just the ticket. For many of the well-to-do living in or just visiting, London was a great world city with much to see and enjoy. In dramatic contrast, most of the "East-enders" were far too busy just trying to survive to be overly impressed with all of the royal fanfare, although many were on hand to enjoy the parades through the East End. It took their minds off of the daily struggle to stay alive. The Queen had even been welcomed in Whitechapel, but her stay lasted only a brief moment on her way back to the palace. The contrast, however, was never better expressed than in a published report found in the *Weekly Herald* of October 5, 1888: "The East End of London with its slums, its rookeries, its gin-palaces, its crowded population living in poverty, and not knowing where tomorrow's dinner will come from, has claims of the most pressing kind on the West End, where idleness and luxury are the temptations that assail virtue and charity, where in the gilded saloons, at the gaudy parties, in the ballroom and the theatre are wasted in empty show or worse, that wealth is entrusted to those who have it for dispensation of mercy, for feeding the hungry, clothing the naked and spreading truth where error holds sway."

The *Weekly Herald* could have also mentioned the East End opium dens, popular with the small Asian community, and the criminal gangs which also infected the area. It should be noted, however, that drug use among the Victorian population was not looked upon with universal disdain by any measure. Drug use at all levels of London society, although not fully accepted, was not universally condemned either. As for the gangs, they were a daily fact of life, preying on the people and businesses of the area. They were a cost of doing business, and business was good for a few. Many, however, lived on the edge of starvation, never really knowing when or from where their next meal would come.

American writer Jack London came right to the issue of starvation and depravity when he wrote, "They picked up stray crumbs of bread the size of peas, apple cores so black and dirty one would not take them to be apple cores, and these things these two men took into their mouths, and chewed them, and swallowed them...." This was the way of life for many in the East End slums, and a serial killer would have fit right in as just one more way to die. It was perhaps just a little faster, a little easier than starvation, but it was death nevertheless.

Attempting to hold things together was the Metropolitan Police. The force was established by Sir Robert Peel in 1829. It replaced the ancient system of parish constables and local watchmen with a single unified police force. These "bobbies," as they were called, after Sir Robert, numbered some 13,000 uniforms and plainclothesmen struggling to come to grips with a city undergoing a massive transition. There were far too many people coming into the city, and the city could not support those who had already arrived, let alone this latest influx. Adding to this population explosion was the natural suspicions many of these new people brought with them of police and authorities of any kind, no matter how well meaning the authorities may have been. Many of these people had barely escaped with their lives and had been able to save little of their property. Truly they were strangers in a strange land, keeping for the most part to themselves. Sir Robert's forces would have a very tough time gaining their trust, no matter what the circumstances. After the Ripper and Torso murders the public's already low confidence in the city's police forces would be greatly eroded. It would be quite some time before the Metropolitan Police would enjoy popular support in London. It would take a while longer in the East End!

Some areas of the central East End were not even safe for the police to patrol, so great was the danger of attack. One such avenue was Flower and Dean Street, which would become central to the Ripper murders. Scotland Yard Inspector Walter Dew would write, "So bad was the reputation of Flower and Dean Street that it was always 'double-patrolled' by the police. A single constable would have been lucky to reach the other end unscathed."

A Serial Killer's Method

By any standard of crime detection the Thames Torso Murder cases were sure to be difficult ones to solve. Crime detection in the late 19th century revolved around separating a small group of people — mostly known to the victim — and culling down suspects until only one remained. Despite the advances made since the turn of the century (the one before this last one) it is not much different in the 21st century. However, when the identity of the victim is unknown, the problem of detection greatly increases, to almost impossible odds. Just where do the authorities start their investigations to find their killer? This was the problem that faced local inspectors and the men of Scotland Yard during this series of crimes begun in 1887. And, despite the similarity in method and disposal, there was never any solid evidence linking all of these murders to a single killer.

The killer had gone to great lengths to cover his bloody tracks even as he continued his singular method. He always killed inside and not on the streets, as the Ripper had done with a majority of his victims. In point of fact, the Torso Killer seems to have murdered all of his victims in their beds. And that is exactly where Ripper victim Mary Jane Kelly was killed. The Torso Killer also cut up all of his victims (which "Jack" never did) into easy-to-carry parcels for transportation to his selected dumpsites. Cutting off arms and legs, as well as reducing some of the torsos, was this madman's standard practice. And he always removed the heads. Contrary to popular myth, the Ripper never removed a head, even though his ready blade cut very deeply and could have easily taken a head — or any other body part for that matter.

It would be the removal of the victims' heads which would most hinder the police investigation, as no one would be able to identify a torso — except one. The killer may not have been trying to hide his crimes; he was, however, trying to hide the identity of his victims. In contrast to the Torso series, the Ripper victims were relatively easy to identify and thus able to be tracked during their last days, hours and, at times, minutes. The Torso

Killer would completely destroy the identities of four out of five of his victims. Only Elizabeth Jackson would be proven to have fallen to his blade, and only when the tattoos on her arms were viewed by the few friends she had in the East End — and she had been with child at the time of her death. Was it the killer's child? If this was so, then how familiar was this killer to his victims? He may very well have lived with one or more of them for at least short periods of time. Or was it perhaps for only one night? That would have been enough. Whichever the case, not even Elizabeth Jackson could be tied to a viable suspect. Perhaps the killer never really needed to cut up his victims. He may have done it only for the pure pleasure he derived from the act of dismemberment itself.

But what of the remains? Would it not have been easier for this killer to simply bury his "pieces" or even burn them? The river may have sounded like a good place to dispose of his murderous bounty, but surely he was reading the many reports of body parts and torsos being discovered in and about the Thames. His method of hiding his crimes was simply not working. Was there something, or perhaps someone, preventing him from using other methods of disposal? Could he have had a helper — perhaps a woman?

What drove this man (I think we are on firm ground here that the killer was a man, even though the killer was never identified by any witness) to risk, even by some small measure, detection by his continued dumping of body parts into the river? Was there some part of him that wished he would be caught so that the demon that drove him could finally be silenced? Other serial killers have stated that they wished to be caught so as to end their nightmare. If that was the case in this series, then that part of the plan never worked. In any event, as far as the people of London were concerned this was to be the next series they would read about of torsos, torture and serial murder.

Chapter 2

Of Torsos, Torture and Serial Murder

It is a gut-wrenching thing to have to face the fact, daily, that I've destroyed not only the lives of my innocent victims, but pretty much my own life as well.
—convicted serial killer quoted in *Serial Murder* (2d ed.; Ronald H. Holmes and Stephen T. Holmes)

SOME CASES OF HISTORICAL INTEREST

Serial killers are not new to mankind's bloody history. And killers who chop up their victims and leave torsos around to be discovered are not new either. They are certainly not new to the people of England. To say the least, England has had more than its fair share of murderers. Indeed, it has been said that there is nothing the British enjoy more than a good, old-fashioned murder mystery. So it would not be too surprising to discover that some of the more interesting tales of serial murder have come from Great Britain. In fact, Victorian London seemed to be virtually filled with them, including the Thames Torso Killer, Jack the Ripper and the Lambeth Poisoner, to name but a few. It is even possible these days to pick up a copy of the latest murder guide to London at most local bookstores. And although Jack the Ripper got the most press coverage, he was by no means the first, nor the most productive, serial killer the people of England have ever known. And as history has shown, they do seem to pop up in England with seeming regularity. A few historical background cases are therefore presented here as backdrop to the Thames Torso Murders of Victorian London.

Burke and Hare — 1828

Other areas around the islands have also had interesting murder cases. One of the best known is the case of Burke and Hare out of Edinburgh, Scotland. William Burke and William Hare could best be described as Irish laborers who lived in the west of Edinburgh. The year was 1828 and the district they chose to call home was a dirty, sleazy area inhabited mostly by criminals and prostitutes. In fact, the men were living in a run-down lodging house with "two ladies of the night" named Nell Macdougal and Maggie Laird. The area suited them just fine, as the police were rarely in the area.

Always on the lookout for a bit of easy money Messrs. Burke and Hare would wait for one of the older lodgers to die from natural causes. Whenever this happy event occurred, the two men would take the unclaimed corpse to a local doctor of less than outstanding reputation named Knox. Dr. Knox paid a handsome price for the new dissection subject and asked very few questions. Before long the good doctor's demands for "medical supplies" exceeded local supply, so Burke and Hare decided to speed up the process a bit. It should be noted that poor laborers digging up bodies to sell to medical schools, as well as stripping the bodies of anything of value, was not all that uncommon at the time.

With a little murder for profit in effect, the men were soon able to supply Dr. Knox with 16 very fresh corpses in only nine months. Most of them were women. The money was coming in fast; however, the serial murder team moved a bit *too* fast, as they began to kill people who would be missed. In the past they had made sure their subjects would not be missed by any nosey relations. Before long, both men and the two women they lived with stood before the bar. But there was no honor among killers as Maggie Laird and William Hare turned "King's Evidence" and testified against Burke and Macdougal. In the end, the "lady" received a verdict of "not proven," while the greedy Mr. Burke took a short drop on the gallows in Edinburgh on January 28, 1829. It was a very well attended and very public hanging. As for the final location of William Burke's corpse? Well, it seems that Dr. Knox still needed fresh corpses for his medical studies, and, after all, this one was on the house.

Dr. Thomas Neill Cream — The Lambeth Poisoner — 1891/2

Doctor Cream was born in 1850 in Glasgow, Scotland. By the time he had celebrated his thirteenth birthday he had already shown signs of being a very troubled young man. His family had moved to Canada that year and the young boy did not like the move. He would later get over his feelings long enough to complete his medical education at McGill University, graduating with honors and becoming a doctor in 1876. His main interest in medicine does not, however, seem to have been fully altruistic. From his graduation through 1881 he appears to have had more interest in criminal activities than in being a doctor. He soon met Flora Brooks, and after a while she became pregnant. Her abortion by Cream nearly killed her. By 1881 he had "lost" four of his patients, including his formally healthy wife, under less than honest and very mysterious circumstances. He was also involved with blackmailing his patients, fraud, and even attempted murder.

In 1881 he found himself convicted of murder for poisoning one of his patients, a Mr. Stott, with strychnine, and was sentenced to life in prison. He would, however, spend only 10 years at Joliet Prison in Illinois before being released. He soon left the United States for Canada to pick up $16,000 from an inheritance, and arrived in London during the first week of October 1891. The "good doctor" wasted no time going to work finding and killing victims, almost as if he had some time to make up. On October 13 a young woman he had just met accepted a medicine from her new doctor friend, and thus Ellen Donworth became the first to die during Cream's new poison series. Nineteen-year-old Ellen was a well-known prostitute who lived on Duke Street, Westminster Bridge Road. Once again a serial killer had targeted prostitutes in London, even as the Ripper was ending his London series.

One week later the strychnine carrying Dr. Cream found and poisoned 26-year-old Matilda Clover, a prostitute who worked the same general area as Donworth. A few months later Cream attempted a duel serial murder on Emma Shrivell and Alice Marsh. Both were prostitutes who lived at 118 Stamford Street, a well-known house of prostitution. However, the dose given to each woman was not enough to kill them quickly. Both had time to get help, and they told the police what had happened before they slowly and painfully died. The police now had a very good description of the killer, and speculation ran wild that perhaps Jack the Ripper was trying a new method in his deadly game. Once again Londoners were aware of a serial killer working their city.

Unlike the Ripper, however, this killer enjoyed writing to the police and leaving a few clues along the way. He was even bold enough to inform the police where they could find the corpse of his latest victim. The only problem with the information was that his target, a young prostitute, had become suspicious and had not taken the little pills given to her by Cream. In fact, she had tossed them in the Thames. She would be very much alive and would prove to be an excellent witness, giving a very good description of the man, right down to his "cross-eyes" which could be viewed through his very thick glasses.

On June 3, 1892, some three weeks after the Lambeth Poisoner's "double event," Dr. Cream was arrested. He was tried and convicted of multiple murder in October of 1892, and saw the gallows on November 15 of that year. Before he died, however, he would play one last game on his executioners. As he dropped he could be heard to clearly state, "I am Jack the...."

Clearly he was not the Ripper, as he had been in an American prison at the time of the Ripper murders. He was just one more serial killer trying to take the mantle of Jack the Ripper for his own. Even serial killers have their "heroes." However, it could very well be that he did indeed write one or more of the later Ripper letters, "just for jolly."

Frederick Deeming — 1891/2

Very few serial killers operating during the Victorian period would ever confess to being Jack the Ripper in a written document. Frederick Deeming, however, would do just that. As this condemned killer waited in his cell for the hangman to do his work, he wrote his memoirs. And, although the authorities destroyed all of his letters, notes and memoirs, it has long been reported that within those prison papers he confessed to the Jack the Ripper murders. With those writings he became just one more serial killer waiting for death to attempt to mislead the police and become the most famous serial killer of all time. He could not, however, have been the Ripper, as he too was serving a prison sentence at the time of the Ripper murders. It should also be noted, for the record, that the confession Deeming wrote denied all of the murders he was surely responsible for, so the document did have a few provable lies within.

Deeming did, however, achieve a certain amount of fame within the halls of Scotland Yard. After his execution a plaster deathmask was made, and a copy was sent to Scotland Yard's Museum of Crime, better known as the Black Museum. For years after, whenever guests were shown the many articles of death inside the museum rooms, invariably the deathmask of Frederick Baily Deeming was identified as Jack the Ripper. The police knew better, as reported in the *Pall Mall Gazette* on April 8, 1892, "But so far the police are satisfied that the man now in custody in Australia is not the perpetrator of the Whitechapel crimes; indeed they have been unable to fix his residence in London at all except on the occasion when he visited the metropolis with Miss Mather...."

Deeming began his known murder spree with his own family, who lived in Dinham Villa, Rainhill, a small village near Liverpool in the north-west area of England. He murdered his four children and his first wife in his home and disposed of their corpses by burying them under the floor in the kitchen and covering it over with cement. Amazingly he seems to have completely gotten away with those crimes and simply left the area with his new second wife. Both soon moved to Australia.

It would be a short-lived migration for his "new bride," however, as she went missing within a month of her arrival. Deeming had murdered his second wife and had also sealed her into the floor of the home they had taken near Melbourne. With the authorities closing in, Deeming had made arrangements to marry a third woman when his second wife's body was discovered and he was arrested. It did not take long for the Australian court to convict him of the murder of his second wife. A few months after his conviction, investigators in England, contacted by Australian police, uncovered the remains of his family in Rainhill.

On the morning of May 23, 1892, Deeming was escorted to the gallows before a large and noisy crowd. Each one in the crowd at Melbourne Prison held a ticket to the hanging. And, after a long four minute reading of the proposed burial service by the chaplain, Deeming took his well-earned drop into the dark void. The official Australian crowd gave its loud and hearty approval.

The Blackout Jack the Ripper — 1942

Even during the darkest days of World War II, as London reeled from the nearly nightly bombing raids from Germany, a serial killer was, once again, at work. And he would work even faster than his namesake. On February 9, 1942, the body of Evelyn Hamilton was found, dumped during the early morning hours, inside an air-raid shelter in central London. Her scarf had been tied around her face to cover her mouth and nose so she could not scream, and she had been strangled. The victim this time was not a prostitute. In fact, she was an unmarried 42-year-old chemist on her way to a new job north of London in Lincolnshire who had simply picked up the wrong man from one of London's many pubs.

The next day German bombers returned, and so did the killer. That morning, 35-year-old prostitute and former show girl Mrs. Evelyn Oatley was found in her Soho apartment. Her naked corpse had been thrown onto her bed after she had been strangled. To complete the work, her killer had cut her throat and slashed the lower part of her body, splashing blood throughout the room. This time, however, the killer had left some vital evidence — his fingerprints.

As the blackouts and bombing raids continued, so did the killings. On February 13, the neighbors of Mrs. Margaret Lowe reported that she had "gone missing" from her apartment on Gosfield Street, Tottenham Court. When the police forced open the door they found a pile of woman's clothes near the foot of the bed and a great deal of blood around the room. Upon closer examination they found a black quilt which they removed from the bed to expose the naked corpse of Mrs. Lowe. She had been strangled by a silk stocking which was still tightly wound around her neck. Once again the killer had mutilated the lower part of the body, but he had added a new twist. Scattered around the room were three knives, a glass candlestick and a poker — all of which had been "used" on Mrs. Lowe, who had come to London as the war began to work as a prostitute. The police now had three victims in quick succession, and the killer was becoming more and more violent.

Even before detectives had finished their examination of the Lowe murder site they were called to yet another murder. This time the call was to an apartment in West London at Sussex Gardens, Paddington. There the inspectors found the body of Mrs. Doris Jouannet, the wife of a hotel manager. She had taken in one too many "male friends" while her husband was at work. Once again the victim had been thrown on a bed and left naked, except for an open, blood-stained bathrobe. She had been slashed a number of times in a manner described as a "sadistic frenzy." As before, the victim's scarf had been used to strangle this victim, and it was still in place. It had become the killer's trademark.

As it turned out, that night was to have been a "double event" when the killer attempted to attack another woman on the blacked-out streets of London. This time, however, the intended victim fought back with such force that she knocked the gas mask off of the killer's waist and ran. It would be the recovery of that gas mask and the subsequent matching of bloody fingerprints which would lead to 28-year-old Royal Air Force Airman Gordon Frederick Cummins. When his room was searched, the police found Margaret Lowe's cigarette case and a pen belonging to Doris Jouannet. The case for the crown was airtight, and so was the verdict.

On the morning of June 25, 1942, as German warplanes flew overhead, the Blackout Jack the Ripper met his fate at the end of a hangman's rope. It was noted in the press that the event was heralded by prostitutes throughout London, who had given up the work so long as this killer was on the streets. With Mr. Cummins now safely dispatched, the ladies could once again return to the blackened-out streets of London.

John Christie — 1953

When the new tenant moved into number 10 Rillington Place, Notting Hill, London, the old terrace house was already in ill repair. It would need much work, which had not been done by the previous resident — John Christie. Christie had lived in the house for ten years with his wife Ethel. And for some of that time John Christie had invited young women over to rape and murder them. With no place else to put the bodies, he naturally kept them in his house. His wife, before she became one of his victims, was blissfully unaware that she was living with a serial killer. She did, however, know there was a problem.

On March 21, 1953, Christie left his home and the "new people" moved in. Three days later the new tenant, Mr. Beresford Brown, decided he needed to put up some brackets for his new radio set he was putting on the wall. As he tapped for a solid stud he located a hidden cupboard. He found "a woman's body inside." Christie had covered it up with wallpaper and little else. When the police looked inside they saw a woman's body seated in a chair. A second corpse was propped up against a sidewall and was covered with a blanket. A third victim had been wrapped in a blanket, and was standing in a corner. All three had been gassed and then strangled. Medical evidence showed the very good possibility that Christie had had sex with the corpses.

These were not the first victims of John Christie, however. Christie, who was born in 1898 in Yorkshire, had been killing for quite a while, but it is unclear when he began. Serial killers often begin killing in their early twenties or late teens, but there are no known victims attributed to Christie during that early period of his life. He was, however, having a great deal of trouble sexually, which began at an early age. He found it nearly impossible to have normal sexual relations with a conscious woman.

During World War II he became a reserve constable, and he used that authority to bring women to his home. In 1943 Ruth Fuerst accepted his offer of company, and Christie took full advantage. He gassed Miss Fuerst and raped her in his bedroom before strangling her. The next year he had his wife's friend over when his wife was out of town and also killed her in the same manner.

It seems that Christie took some time off from murder at this point, although it is far from certain, and waited until 1949 to kill again. This time his victims were the wife and baby daughter of his friend Tim Evans. Christie had convinced Evans that he could perform a safe abortion on Evans' wife. While Evans was at work, his wife Beryl came to Christie's home. During the "procedure," however, Christie became excited and beat Mrs.

Evans unconscious. He then raped and strangled her and killed the baby. For some reason Christie was able to talk Mr. Evans into accepting the blame. Evans confessed and was later executed for the two murders. Christie was not even a suspect.

The next "known" victim of this serial killer was his wife, whom he killed in December of 1952. He simply strangled her and placed her under the floor. He then went on to kill the three young women later found in the concealed cupboard. Two of them had been prostitutes, but the third had been the girlfriend of a man Christie knew who had stayed over at his home for one night. He lured the woman back the next day and killed her.

For his "cupboard crimes" Christie was sentenced to death. He was hung on July 15, 1953, after he confessed to all the murders he had committed at number 10 Rillington Place, London.

Jack the Stripper — 1964/5

The name "Jack" would once again make headlines in London when another serial killer began his work in 1964. He would be known as Jack the Stripper or the Nudes Killer, and his targets were the same as Jack the Ripper; they were all prostitutes. He would also begin his work by dumping his first victim in the river Thames; but unlike with the Thames Torso Killer, these victims were not cut into easy-to-transport pieces.

Hannah Tailford was last seen on January 24, 1964. The former waitress and then full-time prostitute had been working around Bayswater Road in London when she disappeared. It is possible that she had spent some time with her killer, as her body was not found until February 2. She had been strangled and knocked unconscious before she had been stripped and thrown into the river near Duke's Meadow. She was found one-half mile away from where she had been dumped into the Thames near Hammersmith Bridge. The only clothes remaining on the body were her stockings and her panties, which were stuffed into her mouth.

On April 8 the next victim was found naked on the foreshore of the Thames at Duke's Meadow. This victim had also been strangled. The body had been in the water for about twenty-four hours and had been found around 300 yards from where the first body had been located. She was identified as Irene Lockwood, a well-known local prostitute. By now the police knew that once again a serial killer was roaming the London area near the Thames.

A little over two weeks later, on April 24, the third victim of Jack the Stripper was found in an alley in Brentford. The naked body of a striptease dancer and occasional prostitute, Helen Barthelemy, was found with marks on her body, but she had not been strangled. In this case the victim had been asphyxiated. The killer had also become more violent, as four teeth of the victim were missing and one had been pushed into her throat. It was also the first time in the series that a victim had been found away from the river. There was also a clue to be found — her body had small flakes of paint on it, indicating that she had been kept in or very near a paint or body shop.

With police now on increased alert in the area, the killer laid low for a while, but the police were sure that he would kill again. On July 11 the fourth victim was found, out in the open, at around 5:30 A.M. The body was in a sitting position outside a garage in Chiswick, London. The first person to see the body of Mary Fleming thought he was looking at a clothes dummy, but before long the police were on hand to investigate the murder. Once again the victim had been stripped, strangled and teeth were missing.

There was another pause until the decomposed body of Margaret Mc-Govan was found on November 25 in a car park in Kensington. Her corpse had been covered with trash and other debris. She had gone missing on October 23, and had probably been killed very near that date. McGovan was described as a street girl and occasional prostitute.

The final victim in the series would be found on February 16, 1965. Bridie O'Hara's nude body was located behind a work shed on the Heron Trading Estate in North West London. She had last been seen on January 11 outside a local hotel and pub at around 11 P.M. Once again, some of this victim's teeth were missing and she had been strangled and asphyxiated. The killer was now, however, leaving the police more clues. The partly mummified corpse had been held in storage, and small paint particles were once again found on a victim. Motor oil was also present. The spray pattern on the bodies showed conclusively that at least two of the victims had been held in a small room next to a car repair and paint shop. Every shop and garage in the area was closely searched as extra detectives were brought onto the case. The authorities were closing in.

The break came when the room where O'Hara's body had been held was located. It was a small transformer building located at the back of a factory on the Heron Trading Estate, next to the paint shop. The police could not believe that the killer could be so bold as to dump a body this close, within yards of where she had been kept and possibly killed. The only problem came when the police learned that nearly 7000 people worked on the estate, with many having access to the transformer building.

It was at that point the murders stopped. The police were never able to charge anyone with the crimes, but were able to focus attention on a security guard at the estate who had been on duty each night a murder had occurred. The man committed suicide, however, before he was identified by the police and thus could not be interviewed. Upon further investigation the police were unable to link any of the murders to this one man, but Jack the Stripper never killed again. All that was left was a note by this prime suspect stating that he was "unable to stand the strain any longer." He never confessed to the murders in that cryptic note. Perhaps, just perhaps, Jack the Stripper took his own life. If he did, he would have been a very rare serial killer indeed.

Mary Ann Cotton — 1872

Not to be outdone by the men, women have also been found to be serial killers, albeit of a much smaller percentage than the men. They, of course, have their own methods of dispatch. Top of the list in Britain is Mary Ann Cotton. Mary had been a nurse before she moved to West Auckland in 1871. By then she had been married three times and was well past her 40th birthday. The "widow" Cotton looked every bit her age, and then some, as she made her new start in life looking for a new husband.

She moved in with her new husband Frederick, who had somehow forgotten to inform his new wife that he was already married. The family was completed with Frederick's two stepsons and Mary's six-month-old baby. It would not to be a long-lasting relationship, however, as the formally healthy 39-year-old Fred soon succumbed to gastric fever. His untimely death left the door open for one of Mary's many gentlemen friends, a Mr. Joseph Natrass, to move in as a lodger.

The very fickle Mary soon tired of Joseph, however, and became pregnant by a man named Quick-Manning. This, of course, meant that Mr. Natrasses services were, as they say, no longer required. It was time for Mary Cotton to once again clean house. In quick succession, from March 10 to April 1, 1872, Natrass, Frederick's oldest son and Mary's newborn all died. Then, after a short time, the other son of Frederick also died on July 12.

This became a bit more than one of her neighbors could stand, and the police were called into the matter. Before long a postmortem on the latest victim showed considerable amounts of arsenic in the stomach of the boy. When two others were exhumed it was discovered that the cause of their deaths had also been arsenic poisoning. Mary was then taken into custody and charged with willful murder. It could easily be shown that she had purchased the poison, so there was no doubt in this case who was to blame.

She was soon found guilty and sentenced to death. It was found, during an investigation of her past, that she could very well have murdered as many as 15 other individuals within a period of 20 years. It was the method she used to remove an extra husband or two or to acquire their insurance. In fact, she may have murdered a total of 21 people, all of whom had close ties to the merry widow of County Durham. And, despite a growing call for her sentence to be commuted to life in prison, she would see the gallows on March 24, 1873. It was reported that the hangman had done his job rather badly — or quite well, depending on one's perspective on the matter. The man had not allowed enough of a drop to snap the neck cleanly, and Mary twisted and convulsed at the end of the rope for a full three minutes, her body fluids draining, before the darkness came. Her corpse was allowed to hang for a full hour longer, however, just to make sure that the job had finally been done. The hangman, bad job or not, wanted to be assured of his fee.

H. H. Holmes — the Torture Doctor — 1896

On the other side of "the pond," America (or the Colonies, as some in England still call the United States) could boast its own share of serial killers. In fact, it can now be argued that the United States is number one in that deadly field. Fully 80 percent of the world's serial killers are now thought to be found in North America. The first recognized in the U.S. was Herman Webster Mudgett, but he is better known to history as H. H. Holmes— the Torture Doctor. He was born on May 16, 1860, in Gilmanton, New Hampshire, where for a short period of time he was a schoolteacher. He later attended the University of Michigan, where he received a medical degree in 1884. Mudgett began his working life as a chemist at a local drugstore in Chicago in 1888 (the same year "Jack" began his work). Before that time he involved himself with fraud and a second bigamous marriage to one Myrta Belknap, from a very wealthy family. He seemed to have forgotten that he had already been married on July 4, 1878, to Clara Lovering. He had also forgotten to get a divorce. By 1890 the business at the drugstore had increased, and due to a very good business in the sale of patent medicine it had thrived. Naturally, the woman who owned the business, the widow Mrs. Holden, "disappeared" at about this time, which left Mr. Mudgett in charge of the operation and the money. He had been acquiring extra money at the time, and when Mrs. Holden began to suspect, she "decided to take a long vacation in California."

By that time the handsome ladies' man was living in an apartment above the store. He was, however, not alone. Mudgett managed to convince a jeweler named Icilius Conner to move in and share the expenses. He did not really need the monetary help, but he did need the company of a willing female. As would be expected, Conner's wife, Julia, also moved in, along with their young daughter. Mr. Conner's beautiful 18-year-old sister Gertie also moved in, much to the delight of "Doctor Holmes." Before long Julia was working as Mudgett's secretary, with a few extra late night personal duties added on.

With business doing so well, Mudgett had found the needed money to purchase a large vacant lot across the street from "his" drugstore. His plan was to build a huge Gothic-style hotel, which would include battlements, defensive positions, trap doors and over 100 rooms. To complete the project, Mudgett hired a not so honest contractor named Benjamin Fuller Pitzel, who finished the work in 1891. Before long the guests began to pour into "Holmes Castle," but many of them seemed to just disappear, being last seen at or near the hotel. When contractor Benjamin Pitzel died during an insurance fraud scheme, the police naturally investigated his involvement in the castle. Mudgett ran at once — because he knew what they would find — but was soon caught and put out of the "hotel" business.

When the police did a detailed search of the hotel they were stunned. Pitzel, under orders from Mudgett, had built a modern day chamber of horrors. The entire hotel had been built to hold, isolate and murder people. Rooms had trap doors on the beds which were connected to greased chutes, as well as peep holes so that "the Doctor" could enjoy the view. The unknowing guests would be slid down the chutes into large vats of acid or onto spikes and impaled. Other rooms could be sealed airtight and gas could be introduced from hidden inlets. The police also found the skeletons of several females in the torture room hidden in the basement. That room was next to Mudgett's bedroom.

This was, of course, an open and shut case, and Mudgett, who was captured and tried in Philadelphia, was found guilty of multiple murder. The Torture Doctor would eventually confess to "only" 27 murders before he went to the gallows, but many more must have died, including Julia Conner and her daughter, who were never found. The police would estimate that over 200 died at his hand. He was hanged on May 7, 1896, at Moyamensing Prison, Philadelphia, and his torture hotel was soon torn down. Before his sentence was carried out he told the large crowd, in a very calm voice, which had gathered to view the event that he had "only killed two." "Gentlemen, I have very few words to say. In fact, I would make no remarks at all this time were it not for my feeling that by not speaking I would acquiesce in my execution by hanging. I wish to say at this instant that the extent of misdoings in taking human life consists in the killing of two women. They died by my hand as a result of criminal operations. I only state this so that there shall be no misunderstanding of my words hereafter." He then took a drop of six feet, his body bouncing in the air as his neck loudly snapped, causing his legs to move as if the corpse was walking in thin air at the end of the rope. It would be a short walk, however, as the crowd roared its approval.

All of these cases had endings in which the killer or killers were known or suspected, and most were brought to the bar of justice. It would not be such an easy case to solve, however, when another torso was found in 1887 in one of the great cities of the Old World — London. These murders were, however, only the latest in a series of murder cases familiar to the British people, which continue to this day. They may have even seemed almost commonplace. And if not for the spectacular coverage by the press, these crimes would surely have been forgotten long ago.

The East End of London was certainly a place where a serial killer would have felt well at home. It was a target-rich environment, and this madman was ready to begin his work fully one year before the Ripper began his. This first death in the London Torso series would be called the Rainham Mystery of 1887, and despite its long history of catastrophic events, neither the people of London nor the authorities would be prepared for what was to come.

Chapter 3

The Rainham Mystery of 1887

"I will cut off your head!"
— serial killer Severin Antonovich Klosowski, quoted in
Trial of George Chapman (Hargrave L. Adam, ed.)

IT BEGAN IN A VILLAGE BY THE THAMES

The river Thames had flowed along its meandering banks for many centuries before it began serving the people of London. It would become the central life-blood of that great city, bringing with its now cleaner waters commerce and prosperity to an ever-increasing population. The river has also demanded payment in kind for its many gifts. The Thames has always brought with its life giving flow a demand for death. The river, like many waterways of the world which interact with man, is at times called upon to wash away the crimes we humans seem compelled to inflict upon ourselves. May 1887 would be one of those times, and no one seemed to be very much alarmed at the prospect. Despite the amount of crime in the city at the time, there had not been many murders that year. One, however, would prove to be more than enough for that quiet riverside village.

Her name has been lost to history. In fact, she may not have even been missed by those who must have known her in the far eastern end of London in the small village of Rainham. Perhaps she was only passing through, just like her killer. And if it had not been for events soon to capture the imagination of a press just feeling the power of their words we might not even have a simple description of the woman who was to become the first known victim of the Thames Torso Killer.

From medical and inquest reports we find that she was probably from 27 to 29 years of age, but perhaps as old as 35. The doctors reported that she "…would probably have dark hair" and was a full 5 ft. 3 to 5 ft. 4 inches in life (about average for that time). She was also said to have been "…a stout, well-nourished woman." There is no other information from which to form a history, and indeed much of her own body was never recovered—most notably her head. Could this be a clue to her killer? Could he not allow the police the opportunity to identify her for fear her name would lead directly to her killer? In the Ripper series the killer appears to strike time and time again at seeming strangers, thus relieving the need to hide their identities. In fact, that serial killer seemed more than willing to display his work for all to see. In fact, that may have been the plan. The Torso Killer, on the other hand, seems to have had no such luxury in his demented quest for serial death. And he was at the time on the move from Rainham to central London. He needed to cover up the identity of his victims, but for what reason no one knows.

Was this murder showing the two demented sides of a single serial killer? Or were two such killers working nearly the same dark back streets and alleys of Victorian London? The police would say two or more, but were they correct? After all, they did not solve this case, so a final answer to that question was not within their purview to fully know. The question must also be asked if this was truly a murder case or something completely different?

THE FIRST BUNDLE

Work on or around the river was never easy. This was hard, demanding work, calling for long hours and strong men. And even though it was a tough living, the work did indeed put bread on the table and provide enough money for the occasional drink at the local pub for the men who called the Thames their home. It was indeed more than many could claim at the time. For the workmen who were standing near the ferry dock on that early Wednesday morning of May 11 at Rainham, Essex, it was going to be just one more hard day's work. They could not have known that the river was about to give up its first bundle of body parts to them as they looked out over its cool morning waters, waiting for work. They were near "the river wall at Falls Point, near Mr. Hempleman's factory."

River workers are quite used to seeing various debris of all shapes and sizes floating down the river. And none that day could say why this particular bundle, confined to an old piece of sacking, demanded any more than the briefest of attention — but somehow it did. First to spot the remains was lighterman Edward Henry Hughes. It seemed somehow well out of place, even in the polluted late Victorian period of the river. So it was that with poles and sticks the curious men hooked onto the large, water soaked sack and pulled it to shore. It was heavier than the men would have expected because it had floated. They knew they had something of interest, and perhaps it was of value? Perhaps that was the real reason they investigated in the first place.

Mr. Hughes, who worked out of the Victoria Docks, would later testify, "On Wednesday morning, the 11th, I was on my barge, which was lying alongside the jetty at Mr. Hempleman's factory. The tide was flowing at the time, and I noticed what I thought to be a bag in the water and being washed up on the shore by the tide. I picked it up and brought it ashore."

It was not long before the men's curiosity and expectations were replaced by the horror that they had uncovered the remains of what had once been a human being. "Co' blymy mate, it's a body." The Thames Torso Killer had begun his work, and this was the first solid evidence of his "craft." In 15 short months Jack the Ripper would begin his series and thus remove most of the public's memories of the Rainham Mystery. For now, however, this murder would make some of the newspapers, but it was certainly not front-page news. There was, after all, an election coming up, and the racing season was about to begin.

The old sacking was made of a common coarse canvas, which had been used to transport the cut-up remains to the river, which was then thrown away like yesterday's trash. The remains were meant to be taken downstream by the tides and away from the murder site. Inside was the partial torso of a young woman, sans arms, legs and head. It could also be easily seen that the killer had removed the upper part of her breasts as he butchered his victim's corpse. It was an extremely violent, and certainly an unusual, crime, even for the most crowded and crime-ridden areas that portions of the East End of London had become in the late 1800s. It would take a few moments for the hardened workmen to fully come to grips with what they had found. The mind does not want to accept such things as this with an easy grace. It was a mental body blow to their confined and regular existence, which had to be shaken off with effort.

Before long, however, the men had recovered their abilities sufficient enough to react, and one of them was sent to locate the nearest constable on beat duty. On duty was Constable Stock, who quickly moved to the Rainham Ferry to inspect the sacking, which had been "tied up with cord, which was twisted round it several times; it was partially undone, and I noticed that it contained a part of the body of a woman." Soon the area was swarming with police as Inspector Allen ordered an immediate search of the river by patrol boats of the Thames River Division. The riverbanks and canals were also closely searched in the hopes that other body parts of this mysterious woman would be located and reunited. It would be important to discover who this victim had been. That would need to be step one in the long investigation sure to follow. A search for her killer would have to wait until more clues could be established. The remains were then taken to a holding shed located next to the Phoenix Hotel to await further examination.

The detailed search of the river by the Thames Police, to include bridges, ships and out buildings, soon proved to be fruitless. No one had seen anything out of the ordinary — out of the ordinary, that was, for those who lived and worked on the river. At least no one was reporting anything useful to the investigators. Trust in the local police forces did not come with great ease even before serial killers made London their home. The authorities were therefore compelled to suspend their searches until other evidence could be uncovered or other remains floated down the river. There was simply nothing to base any further investigations upon. The killer had even taken her clothes, which could possibly aid the police in any identification.

The police did, however, make a published announcement requesting help from the general public in the hopes of identifying the woman in the Rainham Mystery. Although several people did come forward, none were able to positively identify the partial torso. There was very little evidence to work on, which was exactly what the killer had intended. So far his plans were working quite well, and for this serial killer that was a blanket invitation to continue.

The *Times* of London — May 16, 1887

> On Saturday the coroner for South Essex, Mr. C. C. Lewis,
> opened an inquiry at the Phoenix Hotel, Rainham, into the circumstances attending the death of a woman, a portion of whose
> body was discovered in the Thames off Rainham on Wednesday
> last, wrapped in a piece of coarse sacking.

A Coroner's Inquest

It had rained the evening before as Dr. Edward Galloway, who lived in nearby Barking, completed his examination of the torso, which had been brought to his surgery by the local police. The good doctor had never before been called upon to bring forth a medical opinion on such a brutal murder in all the years he had done medical work for the police. Certainly he had been consulted on many murders, but the doctor knew that this was something very different. He would need to carefully check his notes in order to testify at the inquiry soon to be brought to order in a small room at the Phoenix Hotel. He wanted to be as detailed and as accurate as he could. He was very much in mind to help the police as best he could.

Rainham did not really have a proper inquiry hall, so the hotel would do just fine. Besides, for the jurymen there was food and drink to be had when the work of inquiry had been completed. There was, however, a surprising lack of information in this case, and the session was not expected to last very long.

"Oyez, oyez, oyez."

The elected coroner for South Essex, Mr. C. C. Lewis, opened the inquiry with a brief description detailing the finding of the bundle. On hand for the police were Superintendent Dobson of Brentwood and Inspector Allen. After swearing in the jurymen the coroner informed them that this case would be an unusual one — to say the least. He then went on to Doctor Galloway who detailed what the workmen had found.

"The remains consisted of the last two bones and half of the lumbar vertebrae above the trunk, and practically the lower half of the body, but without legs or thighs. The trunk had been sawn through perfectly straight by a very sharp saw, the integuments surrounding the vertebrae being cut by a keen-edged knife, which had also passed through and separated the abdominal wall. The upper half of the bust, the head, arms, legs, and thighs were missing, the latter having been taken clean out of the sockets of the pelvis, the muscles of the thighs being cut obliquely from the inside to the outside. These were also quite clean cut, and must have been done with a very fine sharp-edged instrument. There was no jaggedness about any of the incisions, showing that they had been done by an expert. There were no marks of external violence. The deceased had probably been dead about a fortnight" [two weeks].

The doctor also judged the victim to have been from 27 to 29 years of age at her death. As to whether or not this was some sort of medical student's version of a practical joke he was quite sure it was not. "The general appearances led me to believe that the body had never been used as a hospital subject, and it would be quite contrary to the Anatomical Act for a body to be parted with without the knowledge of the hospital authorities. I am of opinion that the case is one of murder and that the guilty parties had pursued this method of getting rid of the body piecemeal." The possibility of a woman's body freshly dug up who may have died of natural causes never came up at the inquest, and the police never looked into that possibility. There was no doubt in anyone's mind that this was a case of murder, and a very strange one at that.

And to the all-important question of medical skills and training, Doctor Galloway was very sure of his answer. "I am certain that whoever cut up this body had a *thorough knowledge of surgery*, for not only had the cutting-up been performed in an exceedingly skillful manner, but the operation had been carried out on that part of the spine offering the least resistance to separating, and that would only be done by a person having a very intimate knowledge of anatomy." Through this testimony Dr. Galloway had ruled out a very large segment of the population of the East End of London. In fact, he had ruled out most of the population in all of London. The police were now looking for an educated and highly skilled surgeon — who would soon become a serial killer! It was the first major clue to the identity of the murderer, yet the number of men in London with those skills was still quite large.

Coroner Lewis then took the testimony of several workmen who described the finding of the torso along the riverbank. With this evidence taken, the coroner adjourned the day's inquiry. The case would be held open for the next three weeks (until June 3) in order to give the authorities time to uncover any new evidence which could throw light upon this latest death discovered along the river Thames. For the most part all the police could do was wait for more body parts to surface. They did, however, begin looking at hospitals and medical schools for possible suspects. It should be noted that this was a pre–Ripper murder, so there was very little excitement caused by this death.

When the inquest was reconvened on Friday, June 3, at the Phoenix, the question of cause of death was addressed. However, when Dr. Galloway was called he could not give an explanation which would be useful to the police.

> Juryman: "Could you tell from the appearance of the body whether it was a violent or a natural death?"
> Dr. Galloway: "There were no external marks to go by of any description."
> Juryman: "I thought, perhaps, the blood vessels might show that."
> Dr. Galloway: "No, there was nothing."
> Juryman: "Did it comprise the whole of the trunk?"
> Supt. Dobson: "Only about 18 inches of it."

During the past days several women had been identified as possibly being the woman in the case. Mrs. Cross of 11 Albany Terrace had reported that her "daughter of weak intelligence and fond of going on the barges on the river" was missing. Also missing was Mrs. Carter of Vauxhall Street, Lambeth, and a woman from north of London who was reported missing by her husband. All of whom would eventually be shown to have not been the Rainham Murder victim.

At that point the jury rendered an open inquiry verdict of "Found dead." The investigation would continue as another inquest session was scheduled in a few weeks.

MORE DISCOVERIES UP RIVER

On June 5 the authorities found their next clue in the form of a second bundle containing limbs. The newest discovery had been floating on the river near Temple Stairs and had not been in the water for a very long time. Because this latest set of body parts was found upstream from Rainham it gave a vital clue as to the movements of the killer. It was also a look into the killer's mind. He was moving to central London along the river, and he was bringing his body parts with him. The fact that he would keep body parts around was at once disturbing and a bit confusing to the authorities. This was primary evidence of his guilt, and it was a very risky venture to keep these samples with him as he moved about. And why not just bury the remaining evidence and be done with it? This skilled killer was a collector, and he was moving to an area just southwest of Whitechapel — near the heart of the Ripper's future killing ground! He had found his most comfortable working area, and when he was ready he would "work" again.

Essex Times (South Essex, London) — June 8, 1887

RAINHAM.
THE RAINHAM MYSTERY.
On Sunday morning great excitement was caused on the Victoria Embankment on its being made known that a portion of the mutilated remains of a female had been picked up near the Temple Pier. The Thames Police were immediately communicated with, and on their rowing out to the pier a portion of a human leg was handed over into their possession. It appears that at ten o'clock on Sunday morning the attention of J. Morris, pierman at the Temple, was drawn to a large parcel that was floating near the lower side of the pier. On opening it Morris discovered the thigh of a human person wrapped in a piece of coarse canvas and secured with a piece of cord....

As with the first find, this bundle was contained within a course sacking of the same common type. Dr. Hammerton, the assistant divisional surgeon, was called first, and he reported that "the thigh has been taken clean out of the socket of the pelvis." He could not say whether or not this was a new murder until he could consult with Dr. Galloway. The limbs were soon transported to Dr. Galloway, who was able to show that this was not a new crime, as first thought by the police due to the freshness of the parts, but it was a continuation of the Rainham Mystery. The search area, however, had by now greatly expanded. The police were no longer able to confine their searches to a small area around Rainham Village. They now had a large section of the Thames River to contend with. It would not be an easy job — the killer would see to that. The killer had also delivered a second clue. He knew how to preserve body parts to keep them from decaying, and he had some type of transportation. At least he had the funds to use the available local transportation, but that would have been very risky. He was not a poor man, which again brought the possible suspects list to an even smaller number.

Once again Dr. Galloway commented that the killer had genuine surgical skills and would have been trained in that demanding field. "These body parts have been removed with skill, not simply torn off to hide a murder." Doctors and hospital staff naturally came under investigation once again, but no one from any hospital would ever be charged with this brutal crime.

The next discovery came on the same day as the last. This time it was the "upper portion of a human body which was discovered, wrapped in a piece of sacking, on the foreshore of the Thames near the Battersea Park pier." The bundle had probably been deposited off of one of the bridges which span the river, and could not have traveled far downstream, as the meandering channel sweeps left then right. It is these very sweeps which deny unpowered bundles of any kind the opportunity for lengthy travel upon the water's surface. It also gave the police a general idea of just where the bundle began its journey. Short trips make for smaller search areas.

With more and more body parts being located, the authorities decided to hold a consultation on June 11, near the river at Battersea. That Saturday afternoon Doctor Galloway traveled west to meet with Mr. A. Braxton Hicks, the district coroner for the Battersea area, and Dr. Kempster, the divisional surgeon. Also on hand for Scotland Yard were Inspectors A. Eyre and John Shore of the Criminal Investigation Department (CID). They were hoping the doctors could give them another solid clue to work on.

The gathering soon confirmed, beyond any doubt, that only one murder had occurred; yet the singular method of disposal concerned the authorities. Bodies had been found before — murder was not new to old London.

Yet, the method of disposal, over a large area and over a long time period, was an unusual aspect to the case. This was not a "normal murder." It was something much different than the usual murder for profit or an act of personal rage on a person well known to the killer. This killer was a type as yet unknown to the men of Scotland Yard. The term "serial killer" had not yet been invented, but the method and type of killer in this series was one and the same nevertheless. It was also generally agreed upon that the killer was "a man well versed in medical sciences."

The *Times* of London — June 13, 1887

The Rainham Mystery
...careful examination of the remains [those of a woman], and was satisfied beyond doubt that they formed part of the body to which the pelvis, recently found on the Essex shore, belonged. His [Dr. Galloway] theory that the dissection was performed by a man well versed in medical science was more than strengthened. The sacking in which the trunk was enclosed was exactly similar to that found at Rainham and off the Thames Embankment.

Despite these new discoveries there was still no great concern shown by the public — or, for that matter, the general London press. One dead body, no matter how abused it had been before or after death, did not make for continued copy in London's press. However, it was to be expected that the authorities would generally do whatever they could to solve this crime. That does not seem to have been a universal feeling in the halls of justice, however, as evidenced by the actions taken when the Temple Stairs' discovery came to the attention of a local coroner, one Mr. Langham. It was later reported in the London *Times* that in preparation for the June 11 conference, Scotland Yard had dispatched an inspector to the office of Mr. Langham to acquire the Temple Stairs body part. The attendant on duty at the time in the city mortuary was asked, "What is going to be done with the thigh?" The attending coroner's officer informed the police officer that he did not know and that he was unable to show the thigh to the inspector. It would take further questions from a now very determined inspector before the attendant would admit that "...the limb has been put into a pauper's coffin and sent to the City of London Cemetery at Ilford for burial...." This was not proper procedure at any level of authority, and it would need to be investigated. That would come later; for now it was critical for the inspector to get his hands on that very important "piece" of evidence.

The shocked inspector did not quite know what to think about this lack of regard for a possible murder victim and pressed the man for more details. The only additional information the attendant could provide was that he could not confirm whether or not the limb had yet been buried. "Perhaps Mr. Langham would know." Mr. Langham, it was soon discovered, had indeed caused the limb to be buried and had declined to hold an inquest on the matter or even discuss the case with police authorities. Mr. Langham, it would seem, felt that nothing would be gained by holding an inquest because there was so little to go on and all that was known was that a body part had been found! No effort had been made to investigate the circumstances of the finding of the limb. At this point it would be easy to state that Mr. Langham was covering up something, but the facts would show that he was simply not very interested in this discovery. He had other pressing cases to attend to, and he had a very small staff, with an even smaller budget.

The *Times* would later report, "It is not improbable that the Home Secretary will be asked to grant an order of exhumation." It was than reported by the *Essex Times*, "Yesterday [Tuesday] evening the remains of the body of a woman which were found in the Thames off Rainham, and interred at Rainham Churchyard, were exhumed. At the City of London Cemetery, another portion of the body was exhumed." Having acquired the now well-traveled parts, Mr. A. Braxton Hicks instructed the inspectors "...to procure a glass jar and place the remains in spirits of wine. [This is not unlike the kidney section of a Ripper victim, placed in red wine, which would be sent to the head of a vigilance committee formed to locate the Ripper in the following year.] This was done in the course of the afternoon, and the vessel hermetically sealed, so that in the event of the head or other missing portions of the body being found the parts can be compared."

On Thursday, June 23, another "parcel containing a portion of the remains of a human body was picked up near the spot where part of a woman's body was discovered some time since." It would soon be identified as coming from the mystery woman.

On Thursday, June 30, the final remains would be found, and again they would be located near the water. A local laborer named William Gate had the dubious honor of being the last to locate a body part. Mr. Gate had been walking along the Thames at Regent's Canal, Chalk Farm, near St. Pancras Lock, when he spotted something unusual in the water. He had located the final bundle floating in the canal and was more than a little shocked at what he had found. "Inside were two human legs." Once again the remains had been held in a rough sack, which had been simply tossed into the water. It was a type of sacking which was so common in the London area as to be untraceable, and thus of no use to the police in their investigations.

Mr. Gate soon recovered his composure and brought his discovery to the local police station. He had heard of the Torso Murder and was certain he had discovered pieces of the body. He was quite correct. However, due to the extended period of time the upper portion of the torso had spent in the water, this latest discovery appeared to have come from a much older woman. It was first thought that this was evidence of a new crime, but that would soon prove to be an error. When this latest discovery was rejoined with the other now-preserved body parts it could be shown that it was indeed from the same Rainham victim. There was no second murder — not yet at least!

On Tuesday, July 19, Dr. Galloway was interviewed by the press. "The thigh found in the Thames corresponded with the trunk. The chest also corresponded exactly with the trunk, and had been sawn through. The collarbone and the breasts had been taken off. I have formed the opinion that the trunk had been in the water about a fortnight [two weeks], and that the death of the woman took place in May. I have seen the remains found at St. Pancras, and I am of opinion that they belonged to the same body. The canvas in which they were found was similar to that in which the other parts, except that of the thigh, were found."

The *Times* of London — July 21, 1887

The Rainham Mystery
The various human remains, which have been found from time to time at Rainham, Essex, in the Thames off Waterloo Pier, on the foreshore of the river off Battersea pier, and in the Regent's canal, Kentish Town, the remains comprising the arms (divided), the lower part of the thorax, the pelvis, both thighs, and the legs and feet, in fact the entire body excepting the head and upper part of the chest, are now in the possession of the police authorities.

Once again the police posted a request for information on the identity of the Rainham victim. There was still very little in the hands of the police to go on, other than pieces of the body, and a positive identification would be a very good starting point from which to continue the investigation. And again a few individuals came forward in an attempt to identify the torso, but none could say for sure that the remains were someone they had known.

The police authorities will be glad to receive information regarding women missing about this time who may in any way correspond with the particulars ascertained.

THE INQUEST'S VERDICT

The final inquest hearing into the Rainham Mystery was held in Crowndale Hall in Camden Town. Dr. G. Danford Thomas, coroner for Central Middlesex, was now in charge of the case on August 13, 1887.

Present, and representing the Home Office, was Dr. Thomas Bond, F.R.C.S., Divisional Police Surgeon for A Division, who was on staff at the Westminster Hospital. Dr. Bond would soon find himself deeply involved with the investigation into the Ripper murders, but that series, and his involvement, was a full year away. For this case, Dr. Bond had examined the now assembled remains (at least they were mostly in one place) and would conclude that she had been a "…young woman in her twenties about five feet two to five feet four inches in height, and that she had never given birth." Doctor Bond was brought into the case by Assistant Police Commissioner Monro. Monro felt that a second opinion in this murder was needed to acquire as many facts as could be gained in an examination of the torso and other parts. Dr. Bond further testified that "the different parts had been divided by some persons having a knowledge of anatomy. The head has not been found, and I believe that the weight of the bones would be sufficient to keep it from rising."

For the most part Dr. Galloway agreed with Dr. Bond, adding, "The time of death would probably be about [four] months ago. The body had been divided by someone who knew the structure of the human frame, but not necessarily a skilled anatomist. [A slight change of opinion from earlier statements can be found here.] There are no marks on the portions of the body recovered to show the cause of death or to afford means of identification." The doctor gave the hope that the victim would in time be identified. And if enough parts could be located, a cause of death could be ascertained. In the witness box Inspector Arthur Hare stated, "Since the adjournment every inquiry with respect to the case has been made, but up to the present no clue to the identity of the woman has been obtained."

In fact, the woman in the Rainham Mystery was never identified. Dr. Bond would later write, "…the removal [of the head] was not for the study of anatomy, but was done for the purpose of covering up a murder." It had been a completely successful operation, as the inquest jury rendered a verdict of "Found dead."

It was further stated, "that the remains found were those of a woman between twenty-five and thirty-five years of age, and, after hearing the medical evidence, they were of opinion that there was not sufficient evidence to show as to how or by what means the said woman came by her death." The science of the day could not even tell if a murder had occurred.

Despite the singularly brutal nature of the crime and the eventual full newspaper coverage, the public still did not seem overly concerned. After all, came the cry, this was a crime committed on an unknown individual and was merely one more background event pressed into the miserable lives of those who lived in the abyss of London's ghettos. And even though Rainham is not technically in the East End, it was very close to it. It was just one more, albeit bizarre, reminder of the criminal brutality that existed in 1887 in the East End of London. Even the press had yet to grasp the possible effects the event would have on a terrified population. That would come later, as London — and the world — was introduced to the crimes of a killer soon to be known as Jack the Ripper.

Later, as the police increased their investigations into the Torso series, a follow-up report was filed with reference to the medical report completed by Mr. Bond in the Rainham file. It was the final report on the Rainham murder. It had been written by Inspector Arthur Hare, who had worked on the case from its beginnings. It had been written during the intense investigation into the Ripper and second Torso Murders. Many of the same men were working on both cases, but few involved would express any kind of a linkage between the two.

METROPOLITAN POLICE
CRIMINAL INVESTIGATION DEPARTMENT
SCOTLAND YARD,
18th day of January, 1889.

SUBJECT Rainham
Mystery
REFERENCE To PAPERS.
45492

I beg to report that in the case of the Rainham Mystery Mr. Bond was requested to make an examination of the portions of the body found, by Assistant Commissioner, Mr. Monro. He did so and submitted his report. After that some other portions were found in the Regents Canal and Dr. Thomas, the Coroner, decided to hold an inquest. Mr. Bond gave evidence but it was at the instigation of Police and the Coroner was not consulted. I believe the Coroner paid Mr. Bond his fee for attending the inquest but his bill for everything else was sent to Assistant Commissioner who referred it to Receiver for payment.:

A. Hare. Inspr.
John Shore
Supt.

It would seem that even in a murder case the work is never done unless the paperwork is complete and the fees are paid. In the end the Rainham murder investigation would be an open one, as murder files are never truly closed until a suspect is caught and found guilty. Even today, if evidence could be brought forward of a significant nature, Scotland Yard would be more than a bit interested in looking into the matter.

As for the killer, he would relocate from Rainham to near central London and wait a few months to kill again so as to learn all he could about his new home. Plans needed to be made if he was to continue to be successful at his "craft." In that East End ghetto he would find a background of crime and poverty — all he would need as cover for his series of murders, which had just begun. It would be a rich environment for a serial killer.

Chapter 4

A Rich Environment
for a Serial Killer
(Crime and Poverty in the
Late Victorian East End)

"Schwer und bitter ist das Leben"
Old Yiddish Saying

LIPSKI!

One year before the Ripper took the murder headlines from all but the worst, and before the Torso Killer had a chance to build on his body count, Londoners would learn of a man named Lipski. In the mostly Jewish area of Whitechapel, a small Jewish petty criminal named Isreal Lipski had entered the room of a young woman named Miriam Angell. He had planned to rob her while she slept, but the clumsy Mr. Lipski was not very good at this type of "work" and the girl awoke to find an intruder in her room. In fact, this was the first time Isreal had committed this type of crime. It would also be his last.

"Mirian Angell awoke before I could search about for money and cried out, but very softly. Thereupon I struck her on the head and seized her by the neck and closed her mouth with my hand, so that she should not arouse the attention of those who were about the house. I had long been tired of my life and had bought a penny worth of aqua fortis that morning for the purpose of putting an end to myself. Suddenly I thought of the bottle I had in my pocket and drew it out and poured some of the contents down her throat. She fainted, and recognizing my desperate condition, I took the rest. The bottle was an old one which I had formerly used, and was the same as that which I had taken with me to the oil shop. The quantity of aqua fortis I took had no effect on me. Hearing the voices of people coming upstairs I crawled under the bed." It would not be a very long trial, and the verdict from the jury of twelve came with great ease.

As Mr. Lipski was awaiting his fate in the condemned cell at Newgate Prison, a conference, lasting several hours, was held at the Home Office between Mr. Lipski's attorneys, Home Secretary Mr. Matthews and Mr. Justice Stephen, the prosecutor. Late in the day a messenger would deliver the results to Lipski's solicitor (attorney) on the fate of the condemned killer.

Whitehall, August 20

Sir, — With reference to the case of Isreal Lipski, I am directed to acquaint you that after full consideration of the circumstances and of all the representations made by yourself and others on behalf of the prisoner, the Secretary of State sees no reason for advising any interference with the due course of the law.

I am, Sir, your obedient servant,
Godfrey Lushington

The Times of London — August 23, 1887

Execution of Lipski

At 8 o'clock yesterday morning Isreal Lipski, 21, a walking stick maker, who was convicted at the last Sessions of the Central Criminal Court of the willful murder of Miriam Angel [sic], a young married woman, was executed within the walls of Newgate Prison, where he had been confined since his conviction. The case, perhaps, will be memorable for the strong exertions made on the convict's part in Parliament and elsewhere to obtain a reprieve. Death was instantaneous, a drop of 6 feet being allowed. A large crowd had meanwhile assembled within the precincts of the gaol in the Old Bailey, and upon the black flag being hoisted indicating that the last sentence of the law had been carried into effect it was received with cheers.

The Lipski murder case and trial, for the most part, were not unusual events as far as the people of the East End were concerned. It was just one more execution of one more murderer in the Victorian London of the late 1800s. In fact, a second execution had also occurred with the hanging of

Henry Hobson, who was also given a drop of 6 feet, for the murder of Ada Stodhart on that very same day.

What made the Lipski affair so different was that it crossed the moral lines of the East End. Moral, that is, in the minds of the mostly non–Jewish Londoners. A proper English gentleman, it was said, would not think of entering the bedchamber of another man's pregnant wife, but Lipski, a foreigner and a Jew, did! And even though his victim was also Jewish, the line had been crossed by the luckless Mr. Lipski. It would also be stated, in the months to come, that a proper Englishman would never have committed the Torso or Ripper murders either, but that remained to be seen. It should be remembered, however, that Mr. Lipski was not executed because he was Jewish; he was executed because he was a murderer.

For many years hence, whenever a non–Jew in London wished to throw a racial epithet at a Jew he would simply yell "Lipski." In fact, on the night of the infamous "double event" in the Ripper series on October 30, 1888, a man seen very close to the first murder victim on that cold and wet night did yell out "Lipski" at a Jewish witness, who may very well have been the last to see that Ripper victim alive. It would be that epithet which would quickly cause the nervous witness to go on his way, leaving Elizabeth Stride to her deadly fate, within a few minutes, at the hands of Jack the Ripper!

A BACKDROP OF CRIME

The East End of London had once been an area of prosperity and good business; however, by 1887 the area had become a pressure cooker of crime and poverty. The East End had become a dumping ground for Europe's displaced masses, creating an immigrant ghetto in the very heart of London, just east of the city's center. Along with the rest of the English born population, 40,000 Jewish immigrants called the overcrowded area home. It was not a good or easy mix. Even some of the press fanned the racial fires, as seen in February 1886 when one local paper reported that "...the foreign Jews of no nationality whatever are becoming a pest and a menace to the poor native born East Ender." These types of reports were well noted by the British government who attempted to tread very lightly around the subject. It would color and slow down the investigation into the Ripper and Torso murders. These reports were also noted by the Jewish community. The situation would even cause the removal and destruction of vital clues to the identity of Jack the Ripper. To be sure, the Ripper was not of the Jewish faith, but he would take full advantage of the situation caused by the mistrust and fear which had been generated. And that was a very smart thing to do for a man on the run as he killed. By pointing to a Jew he may very well have postponed his final fate for at least a decade or more.

Few in England, outside of London, knew, or cared to know, of the depravity and criminal activities which had become commonplace in the East End. And even fewer outside of England had ever heard of the daily struggle to survive in one of the world's most crowded and dangerous ghettos. If it had not been for the brutal murders committed by Jack the Ripper and the Thames Torso Killer it is debatable whether or not there would be much written about the problems of the Victorian East End today. One, or possibly two, serial killers changed all of that, forever linking crime, poverty and prostitution to a single square mile of London. Even today there are many areas in the East End which are simply not safe to travel through at night, even for a local. It is still — to this day — a target rich environment for a serial killer, as prostitutes still stand on the same corners where "Jack" and the Torso Killer claimed their victims. Some of them are still drinking at the same pubs where Jack and his "women" drew a pint or two. The question is: When will a serial killer strike again and how many will be taken this time? And will he be Ripper or Torso in his deadly method?

There is no one single cause which creates a serial killer. And, indeed, there is much debate on the nature vs. nurture aspects of the crime. One general aspect is clear; if the killer is to be successful in his craft, prostitution is many times needed within his working area. Prostitutes seem, statistically at least, to have become the most likely targets of the serial killer. And they must be readily available in an area, most likely near where the killer lives or works, or at least nearby at the start of his crimes. An area of high crime and death is also a good backdrop in which to begin, as it affords a certain amount of cover because few individuals are likely to step forward and inform the authorities. The East End was all of that — and a great deal more.

Strangely, the East End seems to have held a morbid attraction for those who viewed the ghetto as a sort of plaything. It was at times viewed as fashionable to go slumming in and around the dark cobblestone alleys of Whitechapel and Mile End. One could become lost for a time where no one knew your name and one did not have to behave like a proper British gentleman. It has even been widely reported that Prince Albert Victor, an heir to the British throne, was often about the pubs and dark places of the East End wearing a disguise. Much later, well after his death by venereal disease, he became a very unlikely candidate for the mantle of Jack the Ripper. However, it can be shown, by witnesses and documentation, that he was away from London during most of those murders. When Queen Elizabeth II was asked about his possible involvement in the case her response was "Rubbish!" In any case, the prince was not one to chase women around of any class. He was not a lady-killer, as young men and boys were more to his liking.

One of the first problems a new arrival would notice in the East End was the most common situation of drunken men and women creating problems for all around them. Drink was one of the few escapes these people had — and the inhabitants of the ghetto did a lot of escaping. More often than not drink would bring on disorderly conduct. From the excellent research of *East End 1888* we read: "Sundays the labouring poor found solace in their one place of freedom — the pub — offering nightly the vulgar camaraderie of the bar. But comradeship, often short-lived, soon turned to drunken violence. It was within the precincts of the pub that vicious assaults on men and women became part of a continuing street show. It resulted in a daily parade of offenders and victims before the Thames Police Court."

It would seem, however, that even a drunken rage which ended in the death of a pubgoer would not effect a long sentence. One such violent assault in 1887, which ended with the death of a man, yielded only 18 months in prison for one William Whitwell of Poplar, East End. It was not an unusual sentence handed down by London courts at the time. Crimes against property were held in greater disdain and would often end with much longer sentences at hard labor for the convicted individual.

Each day the constables on duty would go around picking up those who were "drunk and incapable." At least they would pick up the men and women who fell to the usually wet ground on most main thoroughfares. It would have been impossible for the police to have taken all of the drunks into custody on any given night. There were far too many drunken people, especially on the weekends. Those who were taken to local police stations were usually held only as long as it would take for them to become somewhat sober. They were then given a court date for the offense and released. And the local civilians were not the only ones to make it to court. Even the police were not above becoming part of the drunken backdrop which was the East End of London.

East London Observer— April 21, 1888

> It seems that the Poplar Police would do well to remember the
> reputation they once had. Such scenes as those which occurred
> after the Garden Party in the recreation ground on Thursday
> week when intoxicated guardians of the peace lent themselves to

assault and uproar are begetting feelings in the neighborhood so
different from the esteem in which the local police were at one
time held, that it is perhaps fortunate for the police themselves,
as well as the public, that the Chief Commissioner has inter-
posed, and that the whole matter is to be gone into at the
Thames Police Court.

At times, not uncommonly, the police themselves were the victims of
individual and mob violence. "H" Division serving Whitechapel had long
been known for its "no go areas" for patrolling constables. These areas around
the well known "wicked quarter mile" were often double patrolled, not
for the purpose of intercepting crime but for the protection of the beat
constables themselves. Some of the assaults on officers were due to drunken
East End residents, but not always. Many in the immigrant-crowded ghetto
simply did not trust any police authority — and with good reason. Many
had come from mainland European nations whose police and military
forces had been used to round them and their neighbors up, to be taken
from their homes. Trust did not come easy to the population of the East
End, be they native or recent immigrant. Adding to this mistrust on the
other side was the very large influx of non–English speaking people. It was
not just a local problem, as the national government was beginning to
show concern. It was not long before personal attacks became a daily problem for local authorities, and the beat constable was the first to feel the
heat of street battle.

Three examples of the type of attacks played out on the local beat constables may be found in the daily reports of the Thames Court, as reported
in the local papers. The *East London Observer* reported on February 4, 1888,
of a ship's Steward who had gotten drunk and was armed. He "...drew an
unloaded revolver [unknown at the time by the officer] after a Police Constable tried to stop him entering the *Queen's Palace of Varieties* in a drunken
state. The P.C. "requested" him to go away; he drew the revolver and said
"I'll settle you at once." The gun was wrested from him by the aid of another
and the prisoner taken into custody." The man was fined 40s [shillings]
for his behavior, but the court, having found that he was without funds,
sent him to prison for a month of hard labor.

It was later reported, on June 9, that a constable, identified only as 37H
out of Whitechapel, was assaulted by one Daniel Hickey, age 40. "On Saturday night the officer saw the prisoner behaving in a very disorderly manner in Great Alie Street, Whitechapel. He was drunk and using filthy language,
and as he would not go away he was taken into custody. Hickey then
became very violent — kicked the officer several times in a dangerous part,
hurting him at the time, but the pain has now gone. Prisoner, who said he

recollected nothing of the occurrence, was sentenced to 10 days hard labor." It can be questioned as to which the court felt was the most grievous offence — the attack on the officer or the "filthy language."

Later that month the *East London Observer* reported a most troubling and very cowardly attack by a drunken man, aided by a mob, on an officer. "On Sunday night the prisoner, who was drunk, and others were singing an indecent song in Burn Street, Limehouse. On attempting to arrest [John] Canarvan, the latter struck the P.C., wrenched himself free, and he and seventeen others proceeded to stone the constable, who was alone. Another P.C. arrived on the spot, when all the men ran away, but the prisoner was caught. The accused was fined 40s or one month's hard labor."

Gangs were also very prevalent in the East End, many of which were comprised exclusively of children, some as young as 12 or 13. The most popular crime committed by these young gang members was theft. Hit and run attacks on street venders and baker's shops was very common — to the point of being accepted as the price of doing business in the East End. If caught, the young criminal could expect to be whipped by a birch reed or placed in a reformatory school for a period of time. The time spent at the school, however, would do no more good than to advance the criminal abilities of the individual doing the time.

Highwaymen roaming at night were also not uncommon in the East End. It had been a long practiced crime in and around London since the earliest days of this trading town. A swift attack by one or more men on an unaware or intoxicated individual, male or female, was an almost everyday event. With too little police patrolling, badly lit streets and a crowded immigrant population looking the other way, there was very little chance of being caught.

Whole families were also involved in criminal activities, especially when it came to break-ins and burglaries. It was not unknown for a father to train his sons in the "profession," even to the point of going out on the same "job." Later it would be expected that the criminal father would hand down his burglary tools to his son, who would "take over the family business." As the winter winds and cold rains subsided in spring, the season of burglaries would begin. The work was a very risky business, as sentences for property crime, more often than not, far outweighed crimes against individuals. Long sentences at hard labor could be expected for those who were not as good at their craft as they had supposed. It would also be expected that if the burglar was caught in the act his "accidental death at the hands of the resident" would not be looked at with a great deal of effort by the police or the courts.

Crimes against children were also of epidemic proportions. Drunken parents and low incomes taken from boring and dirty jobs were often the root cause of child abuse in the Victorian East End. However, a general lack of interest in child welfare greatly helped create an atmosphere of lawlessness aimed at the most vulnerable in society. Many women with children lived from day-to-day, some turning to prostitution, not knowing where their next meal would come from. A child would have been just one more mouth to feed — one more reminder of a life barely worth living. Some of the worst turned to drink and then turned to attacking their children. The papers were often reporting crimes against children. But they were never able to report that the Torso Killer or the Ripper had attacked a single child. Brutal as they both were, children were not their "cup of tea."

East London Observer— March 24, 1888

> The prisoner forced him [her five year old son] to the ground and then jammed filth into his mouth. She then put the poker in the fire until it was red hot. In the meantime, she put soil in a cloth and tied it round the child's mouth so that it went down its throat. She then took the poker from the fire and, having stripped the child, applied the weapon to the bottom of his back, burning him severely. She kept the poker in one spot for about three minutes. Prisoner then knocked the poor child down, and kicked him about the ribs, and afterwards jumped on him with all her force. She also knocked the child's head across the door... Witness had seen the prisoner assault the child every day since.

It should be noted that this situation (which in this day and age would be considered attempted murder and torture) came to the attention of the authorities days after these continued attacks began. The witness, who lived very nearby, never attempted to rescue the child or interfere with the brutal attacks in any way. It was later reported that a police constable and a local doctor had verified these vicious and cowardly attacks made on the child. As for the mother — she was ordered held for "two consecutive weeks." The five-year-old boy was most likely returned to his "mother." His fate was not reported on by the press. There were many more crimes to report, and other events were much more important to the newspapers.

Crimes upon children of a far more destructive nature were also common in the East End ghettos of Whitechapel, Spitalfields and St. George-in-the-East. Incest and sexual assault on young family members was also a daily occurrence. And these assaults were not just for the perverted pleasure of family members. At times these children were used to acquire additional monies for parents who were more interested in visits to the local pub than in the welfare of their children.

One of the many reported cases to find its way to the Thames Court involved the attack on a seven-year-old girl living at 4 Boarded Entry, St. George-in-the–East. Rose Johnson lived with her parents, who let out rooms to lodgers for extra, and much needed, money. One such lodger was a 48-year-old laborer named John Oakley. Oakley had befriended the child and had offered her two spoonfuls of sugar in his room. As reported in the *East London Observer* of May 19, 1888, after Rose had entered "…he then placed her on his bed and committed the deed with which he was charged, afterwards rewarding her with a half-penny." The child was left alive and reported the attack to her parents.

Earlier that year, 25-year-old Philip Jacobs was arrested for sexual assault on a 2½-year-old while visiting the child's home. Somehow the child was able to convey to her parents that an attack had occurred. When a doctor checked her she was found to have been infected with a venereal disease. It was also reported that a 28-year-old named Charles Clarence, who lived with his family on Canal Road, Mile End, had been arrested for a sexual attack on his own four-year-old daughter. He was held after the little girl was shown to have been infected with a venereal disease.

These cases, although disturbing, were not uncommon by any measure. Nor were the many cases of infanticide, which had also reached epidemic proportions. Young women who became pregnant and were unmarried were often left to make their own way if the fathers did not stay with them. Many found the only escape was to be rid of the "problem" permanently. These cases were often reported in the local papers, but little, if anything, was ever done to stem the flow of death.

> The baby, recently delivered, was found in a box by a Dr. Barton. The child was pinned in a bundle. There was a piece of tape round the child's neck, and it was tied in a knot… Death was due to strangulation.

Jack London was correct when he wrote of the area being simply "a giant killing field." There were many ways to die in the East End, so it would seem that a serial killer would have chosen well to have come to Victorian London to do his bloody work.

If the Ripper had been reading the local papers, as it seems he must have, he would have noted that just before he began his "Autumn of Terror" three women had been murdered that year. The first had been killed by her jealous husband in what would have been just one of the many daily assaults by husbands on their wives— had she not died. The second was a gang rape of a local Whitechapel prostitute, which in two days would lead to her death due to the effects of the brutal attack, which caused internal bleeding. And the third homicide, as yet unsolved, was of a woman whose mutilated remains were found in a tunnel linking Whitechapel with Aldgate East in the City.

These deaths came under the backdrop of a local mentality that looked at rape as an almost acceptable event. At least it was one not to be complained about too much. The Victorian East End would have seemed an open invitation for anyone with a taste for murder — be he a Torso Killer or a Ripper!

Deep within the confines of that East End ghetto was a large section of individuals comprised of mostly Russian Poles. Many had come from the same villages, forced out by Imperial Russian military forces with orders to remove all Jews. It was a distinctive sub-culture which would unknowingly hide a serial killer — Jack the Ripper. Would the Torso Killer also be found among these people?

A HEAVY VEIL OF POVERTY

In the mid–1880s William Preston published a small pamphlet entitled *The Bitter Cry of Outcast London.* Although his work was descriptive and very well researched, it received very little attention until sections were republished in a London paper — the *Pall Mall Gazette.* The *Gazette* would spend days on the work, informing its readership about the abject poverty and depravation to be found less than a mile away from the center of one of the greatest cities on earth.

> What the evil is everyone knows. It is the excessive overcrowding of enormous multitudes of the very poor in pestilential rookeries where it is a matter of physical impossibility to live a human life. Men, women, and children are herded together in filthy sties; there is a family in every room; morality is impossible, and indeed has ceased to exist; and in these reeking tenements are bred the stunted, squalid savages of civilization.
>
> The outcasts are driven to huddle more closely together in the few loathsome places still left to them.
>
> Many are lucky enough to die, others live on, in turn to propagate their kind, and to hand down to another generation the curse which never leaves them from the cradle to the grave. All this seething mass of misery and vice exists at our door.
>
> The evil is a growing one. Not only have existing slums remained almost untouched by past efforts, but our great cities, especially London, are yearly adding new layers of brick and mortar to their already excessive circumference. Many of these,

though not slums now, are bound, seeing the reckless fashion
in which every inch of ground is being built over, and the kind
of buildings there erected, to become slums hereafter.

One way those in other parts of London with a few pounds to invest
could reap a good consistent income was to buy into lodging houses being
built in the poor areas of London. These cheap and plentifully built structures were meant to house the very poor, but they were soon degraded when
landlords became absent and local managers assumed control of daily operations. Unfortunately, these local "doss house" managers were not always
of the best reputations. It must also be said that the residents themselves
were not of the highest standards of humanity. Many had never had a proper
home before and were ill prepared to live in a large city.

For 4d (pence) a night anyone could rent a small bedstead barely covered with a cheap threadbare blanket. Individuals or couples could spend
a night in the dirty sheets, cleaned once a week if they were lucky, and no
questions would be asked. It was not unusual for common criminals and
prostitutes to be housed next to local beggars and whole families. It would
be from these crowded, dirty doss houses that the Ripper would take most
of his victims and the Torso Killer would take the only one identified in
his series. Anyone who lived locally knew that many low-class prostitutes
used these run-down doss houses as their bases of operations. So did the
local serial killers.

For those who could not even acquire the small funds needed for their
"doss," their only rest could be found by sleeping "raw." Thousands each
night would crawl up into a stairwell (where Ripper victim Martha Tabrum
was found), under a railway arch (where the Pinchin Street Torso and Ripper victim Coles were found), or out on one of the grassy fields or in doorways in the back alleys of the East End. This rest was not always for a full
night, however, if a constable came by on beat duty and "moved them along."
Yet, with all of the women who must have been sleeping in these doorways,
not one was ever taken by the Torso Killer or the Ripper and killed where
she slept. Perhaps these killers could not be sure they were prostitutes, and
both killers seem to have wanted to be sure of that fact. And as far as research
can take us, neither killer ever made a mistake on that count.

The murders in the East End did have the effect, however slight, of
focusing public attention on the desperately poor of the area, at least for a
few months. However, even as women were being murdered on the street,
the local doss house managers, many of them women, still continued to
toss out men, women and even children onto the cold and damp streets.
This situation continued, but several groups and individuals attempted to

help by providing shelters. As reported in the *East London Advertiser* of October 27, 1888, the results often became a double-edged sword when outsiders came to inspect. "Since the recent calamity in the east of London, several benevolent persons have come forward to provide night shelters for the outcast men and women."

"Being given to understand that this shelter is occupied nightly by about 150 people, I considered it my duty to visit these premises, which I did on the 20th last at 11 P.M." This visit by Dr. Taylor was not a good one for the locals. He reported the crowded and unsanitary conditions to the Mile End District Sanitary Committee. Subsequently, the private shelter was closed, placing, once again, 150 men, women and children back onto the crowded and filthy streets of Mile End simply because the accommodations were not up to the monetarily well-off Dr. Taylor's standards.

Attempting to address the overcrowded conditions, so-called "model dwellings" were being built in and around Whitechapel. In 1889, by the time the Ripper had murdered seven and the Torso Killer three, Whitechapel could count some 23 of these block-long multistoried developments. In total, these buildings could hold 9,429 individuals, adults and children, in spartan conditions. But at least they represented a real, solid shelter. They were, however, small remedy for an ever-increasing problem, and they were not free. Payment, small as it was, was still required.

One of the most infamous of these buildings could be found on George Yard in central Whitechapel. Known as the George Yard Dwellings, they had been built in 1875 and were already showing the decay brought on by ill use. From this humble building would be found one of the keys to the Ripper murders. Within its dark first floor landing would be discovered the remains of Martha Tabram, the Ripper's first murder victim. Upstairs at the same time one could find the cheap solitary rooms of Severin Antonovich Klosowski, 23-year-old surgical student from Warsaw, local barber/hairdresser, future serial killer who would be condemned to death, and most likely — Jack the Ripper!

As would be expected, these quarters were very crowded. Indeed, many who "lived" there did so only when they could not find a dark dry place to crawl into for the night, or wanted to engage in other activities. They were the shadow residents, familiar to many such buildings in the area. The regular residents were all, for the most part, hard pressed to earn the few shillings needed to stay for any length of time. No job was secure in the East End, and so no lodging was ever secure. So even in the hyper-crowded "wicked quarter mile" rooms were left unrented in the George Yard Dwelling, to the point that they were soon converted into student and artist housing in 1890. By then they were renamed Balliol House, and a few more poor inhabitants of the East End found themselves back on the streets looking for a safe and dry place to stay.

Hunger and starvation was also a way of life, as half the local population struggled to find the few pennies needed each day for bread. It was not uncommon for a beat constable to come across an individual who looked to all the world to have been sleeping in some dark corner, only to discover that the individual had simply laid down to die of starvation. Time and time again readers of the *East London Observer* read of these reports, but very little was being done. In one such article, from May 19, 1888, the newspaper reported on a solution, brought forward by Charles Booth, an individual noted for his plotting out and drawing maps of London's poverty. It was not a popular solution as it focused attention and responsibility for the poor and starving directly on the British Government. "The entire removal of this class [poor] out of the daily struggle for existence, Mr. Booth believes to be the only solution of the problem of poverty ... that they are a constant burden to the State; and suggests that the time has arrived when some means should be found of carrying voluntarily on our shoulders the burdens which otherwise we have to carry involuntarily round our necks."

Sewage and sanitation problems were also a great concern and were a prime factor in breeding diseases. It was a major reason why infant mortality was so high in the ghettos. Again the area was condemned with too many people and too few funds to address the situation. Although the main thoroughfares of Whitechapel High Street, Commercial Road and Wentworth Street were relatively garbage free, mostly due to business being conducted in and around those areas, they were not the norm. For the most part, trash was allowed to pile up well beyond safe levels and was removed — at times — only when the smell became overwhelming. Poor sanitation habits among the poor were rampant.

Sewage in central London was always a problem, especially during the warm and humid summer months. In the East End it was a killer, and sewage repairs were not high on the government's list of priorities. Typhoid was a constant killer in the East End. It was followed closely by tuberculosis, a particular burden on bootmakers and tailors who worked in sweatshops throughout the ghetto. It can only be wondered why another great plague did not break out in the East of London at the time. From the *East London Observer* of December 22, 1888, we read that the medical officers working in the area found houses "in a deplorable and insanitary condition. Three closets [latrines] out of ten ... stopped and the filth and liquid overflowing over the backyard. The houses were very dirty and dilapidated; they form a portion of the Cable Street area reported on to the Metropolitan Board as an area unfit for habitation." Yet to Cable Street would move a young barber/surgeon and his new wife just before that report was published. It can only be wondered why Severin Klosowski would move to such a filthy area. Was he trying to hide something or someone?

And even when disease struck, few who lived in the area wanted anything to do with hospitals. Whitechapel's London Hospital was feared by the local people, who knew it to be a death trap. Better to find one's cure on the streets or in a back alley shop than in the hospital, even if they were with child. Dr. Frederick Treves, who was an intern at London Hospital during 1888, wrote of the horrors felt by the population, relating, "The hospital in the days of which I speak was anathema. The poor people hated it. They dreaded it. They looked upon it primarily as a place where people died. It was a matter of difficulty to induce a patient to enter the wards. They feared an operation and with good cause, for an operation was a dubious matter. There were stories afloat of things that happened in the hospital, and it could not be gainsaid that certain of these stories were true." Medical experiments, perhaps, done on the very poor? Perhaps that is one reason the police authorities first looked to hospitals in their efforts to locate the Ripper and Torso Killer. Were they aware of the situation? One would think they would have been fully aware, as these efforts were reported in the press.

ON THE GAME

They were called the "unfortunates," and there were estimated to have been from 60 to 80,000 of them working the streets of London in the late 1800s. They were the prostitutes of Victorian London who had, for whatever reason, been "on the game." Many saw that work as simply a way of life and had adjusted to the path they had taken. But many more had been forced into prostitution as the only way they could earn enough money to buy one more cheap meal, to pay for one more drink, to pay for one more night's wishful rest in a filthy doss house.

For many they began "work" in the West End, where they could earn more in a day of prostitution than they could in the local sweatshops during a full six-day week. Eventually, however, disease and deprivation would set in, along with the realization that they had indeed become an "unfortunate" and were now in the ghetto of the East End.

It was not always a voluntary job selection for children of women who were themselves prostitutes. Some daughters as young as 12 were put on the streets into child prostitution in order to earn extra money for their alcoholic mothers. It was a dirty little Victorian secret in the upscale West

End that the services of a very young East End girl could be had for very little money. Some of the girls would be "employed" by a West End businessman, only to find that other services, not normally part of a business, were required. Many may have even been promised marriage at some point, but that was soon found to have been a ploy. And if the girl became pregnant she was usually tossed out, only to be followed by the next "employee."

Prostitution for many of the poorest women of the East End became the only way they could find to survive, and it was a sure way to become a target of a serial killer. But the odds were with the "unfortunates" of Victorian London. Many more would choose the river long before they could become victims of the Thames Torso Killer. He and the Ripper were just getting started, however, and they were both very much on their game. It was time for the Torso Killer to double his count, as the people of London began to read about the Whitehall Torso Mystery of 1888.

> *The most successful serial killer is not the one who has the largest known body count. He is the man who is still out there doing his "job" unknown to all, even those closest to him.*
> — Unknown serial killer

Chapter 5

The Whitehall Torso
Mystery of 1888

"A perfect carnival of blood in the World's Metropolis"
New York Times—Oct. 3, 1888

By September 1888 the Ripper had taken five from the dark streets and back alleys of the East End, simply killing some while cutting others to pieces. These crimes seemed to have been committed by a madman with an ever-increasing lust for blood, and no one could begin to understand why he killed or when he would kill again. To add to this terror pressing down on Londoners came a second victim of the Thames Torso Killer. This time, however, the killer had tried to hide as much of the evidence as he could.

Frederick Moore was a common laborer working in Pimlico near the Thames River Embankment adjacent to Cannon Row Police Station on September 11, 1888. He was just outside the gates of the Deal Wharf, his job site for the day near Grosvenor Road, when he noticed a group of men beginning to discuss seeing something that had washed up on the shore. He looked over the embankment towards the river off of Ebury Bridge near a sluice and at once spotted the item the men had been talking about. "I went over and picked it up. I found it was a woman's arm, with a string attached to the part nearest the shoulder. I looked about the shore to see if there was anything else, but as there was not I gave this to the police. I did not see the arm until my attention was directed to it by others. The tide was low at the time, and the arm was on the mud."

The constable who received this most unwanted item was William James, 127 B Division. James would later testify that he took possession of

63

the arm and escorted Mr. Moore to his local station. Later the arm would be transferred to the mortuary by Constable T. Ralph, 634A, for the attention and examination of Dr. Nevill. Dr. Nevill could only state that the right arm had belonged to a woman and that it had been in the Thames for a period of time. He also stated that he did not feel that the arm had been taken with great skill. "It having been cut with some care from the flesh above the shoulder, and with the arm pit attached." The good doctor did not have a body from which to compare wounds and surgical skills with that of the Ripper series. He did report that the arm had been freshly amputated. The torso discovery would come later; for the time being all the authorities had was one extra arm, found near the Thames River during that "Autumn of Terror." It was enough, however, to know that another murder had probably been committed in London.

With all of the excitement going on about "old Jack," the extra arm barely raised an eyebrow in the East End. As far as the population of the Whitechapel ghetto was concerned, if the corpse was not found in their neck of the woods it was not their problem. They had enough to worry about with tales of the Ripper flowing over the population on a daily basis. Indeed, many had hoped that the Ripper had moved on. Only later would the Torso Killer visit Whitechapel and invade the Ripper's own prime hunting ground. As for the Ripper himself, he was still very much in residence—and working with increasing speed.

THE SECOND TORSO

It has always been a long work day on the site, thought Frederick Windborn as he walked past and nodded to police constable Barnes, a reserve officer on the job from A Division. The new officer had been called to duty in support of search operations then ongoing in Whitechapel. Constable Barnes did not really believe he would see anything of value at the work site, but an assignment was an assignment. Who knows, he had told his wife, "I may even push this temporary assignment into a full-time position." For Windborn it was just one more day of work on October 2, 1888, on the grounds of what had been the old Tudor Palace of Whitehall. But at least he had steady work when many did not.

Mr. Windborn had been a carpenter for many years, unlike many of the new men at the work site. In fact, Windborn did not trust any of the new men and had taken to hiding his very valuable tools in dark places. The New Scotland Yard building site (Metropolitan Police Headquarters from 1889 to 1967), which had originally been chosen for the National

Opera House, had a great many hiding places, but none were as deep, or as hidden, as the vault. This was where Windborn was headed at 1 P.M., deeper and deeper into the dark recesses of the latest construction project of his employers, Messrs. J. Grove & Sons, Ltd.

As he worked his way deeper into the dark basement the constant din of the men above slowly abated until he could barely hear their work. As he moved from one sub-level to the next he passed through progressively darker arches and stairways until the bright sunshine from above became a cool gray darkness. It felt like a cool damp tomb as he made his way along the final steps to the vault area. Finally he came to the nook in which he had hidden his tools behind a small plank of board. They were next to a parcel he had seen earlier on Monday but had not bothered to investigate.

"On Tuesday afternoon last I was at work at the buildings. My work took me during the day to all parts of them. On Monday morning at 6 o'clock, I had occasion to go to the vaults to fetch my tools, which had been taken there on Saturday by a laborer. I was not there on Saturday. When I went to the recess on Monday morning my mate was with me, and I felt something there. It is a dark place, and I struck a light and looked at it. I could not form any idea of what the parcel was, and we both came away. Neither of us touched it in the least. I saw it again next morning [the 2nd], and came away again. I did not notice any smell. At 1 o'clock that day [Tuesday] Mr. Brown, the assistant foreman, came down to where I was at work, and I told him of the parcel in the vault, and he ordered it to be opened. The parcel was brought out by the laborer [George Bodden] and opened."

The parcel was about 2½ feet long and two feet wide, and had been tied with a cheap twine and wrapped in paper. The discovery was laid out in an area with better lighting and was soon opened. To their great shock the men stared down on the partially decomposing remains of a woman. The torso, which lacked arms, legs and a head, had been dumped in the heart of New Scotland Yard headquarters, and it was full of maggots.

It took a while for the men to catch their breath, but soon one of them was on his way to alert the local constable. "Constable, another one! In the vault."

The *New York Times*—Wednesday, October 3, 1888

LONDON'S RECORD OF CRIME
ANOTHER MYSTERIOUS MURDER
BROUGHT TO LIGHT
A PERFECT CARNIVAL OF BLOOD IN THE WORLD'S
METROPOLIS—THE POLICE APPARENTLY PARALYZED
LONDON, Oct. 2.—The carnival of blood continues. It is an extremely strange state of affairs altogether, because before the

The Whitehall Torso Mystery (from the *Illustrated Police News*, October 1888).

Whitechapel murders began several papers called attention to the fact that these have been more sanguinary crimes committed in London and its vicinity this summer than ever before known in this city in the same space of time. The Whitechapel assassin has now murdered six victims and crimes occur daily, but pass unnoticed in view of the master murderer's work in the East End.

When Mr. Windborn was questioned by the coroner during a later inquest, he was asked to further explain the condition of his find and what the vault area looked like. "The parcel was in the same condition when Mr. Brown saw it as when we first saw it. It was not touched in the interval—by anyone, and when it was sent for by Mr. Brown it was just as we had first seen it. This vault had been used for some three weeks, and for that time I have placed my tools there from each Saturday to Monday—not on other days. I have never seen anyone carrying such a parcel on the works. The way I went to the vault was not difficult to me, but it would be rather puzzling to anyone to find the place if they were not acquainted with the way and the spot. I could not see in the recess or vault without striking a match, it was so dark even in daytime, and people who did not know the place could not have found their way there."

Earlier, the week before, on Saturday the 29th of September, laborer Ernest Hodge had reason to enter the same area of the vault, also looking for tools. He had struck a match to look around and had seen no tools. When he looked at the area where the torso would be found he did not see any bundle. It simply was not there on the 29th, according to Mr. Hodge. With his testimony the police would have a time frame to work on for the dumping of the torso, but it may not have been a correct one. The honest Mr. Hodge may simply have missed the package in the almost overwhelming darkness of the vault.

The discovery event was also described by bricklayer's laborer George Bodden, who had gone with Fred Windborn to fetch the mysterious parcel held deeply within the newly constructed police vault. "I was in the vault where the body was found at about 2:55 on Tuesday last. I had been told to go and see what a parcel down there contained. I struck a light and saw the top bare, and the rest wrapped up in some old cloth. I thought it was old bacon, or something like that, and I could not make anything of it, so I took hold of the string around it—it being tied up—and dragged it across a trench into a part of the vault where there was light. I cut the string there and opened the wrapper. The strings—a lot of old strings of different sorts— were tied up all round it several times across each way. There was only the wrapping I saw, no paper, and when the parcel was opened I saw the body of a woman. I was not alone when the parcel was opened; there were present the Forman bricklayer, Mr. Brown, and Windborn. I cannot say how long it was before that I was there—a long time. It is a very dark place, always as dark as the darkest night in the day. The police were sent for at once when the body was found, and they took charge of the body and wrapper. I was only told before I went to the vault to go and see what a parcel contained that was there."

At 3:30 P.M. C. William Brown arrived at the King Street police station to inform the police of yet another murder in the East End. On duty was Detective Hawkins of A Division. It did not take him long to grab "a couple of men" and follow Brown back to the work site. What he saw, according to what he understood of the case, did not appear to be the work of the Ripper, but it was no doubt in his mind a bloody murder. "I saw lying in the vaults of the new police buildings an open parcel in dress material, which had been tied round, and a body of a woman in it. I looked further along the recess where it had been and saw a piece more dress material. I saw the place where it had stood. The wall was very black, and the place full of maggots. I left the body in charge of a constable, and sent for the medical officer, Mr. Bond."

Police Surgeon Doctor Thomas Bond from A Division (Westminster) arrived on site a little after 4 P.M. He viewed the body as it was lying in the basement. "The strings which had tied it had been cut, and it was partially unwrapped. I visited the place where it was found, and I saw the stained black at the place where the parcel had rested against it. I thought the body must have been there several days from the state of the wall; but I could form no definite opinion as to how long it had been there. The lower part of the large bowel, and all the contents of the pelvis, were absent. The decomposition was very far advanced, and the body was absolutely full of maggots. I directed the detectives to take charge of the trunk and of the wrapper, and to remove them to the mortuary."

Dr. Bond had served in the Prussian military in 1866 and had been a police surgeon since 1867. He was deeply involved with the Ripper investigation at the time and would not only complete a detailed report on the Mary Kelly (Ripper) murder, but would send a general report on all of the murders, then to date, to Assistant Commissioner Sir Robert Anderson. In that report he would conclude that "All five murders [to date] were no doubt committed by the same hand. In the first four the throats appear to have been cut from left to right. The murderer must have been a man of physical strength and of great coolness and daring." Dr. Bond would later commit suicide after a long illness, which caused depression and an extended period of insomnia. The good doctor threw himself out of a window to end his life only a few years after his service on these serial murder cases.

At Westminster mortuary the torso was cleaned, disinfected and placed in alcohol. There would be no immediate examination that evening. It would not be necessary to find a time of death, owing to the obviously long time the torso had been buried. The criminal had long gone and the men needed to be well rested to do a good job. The post-mortem would be conducted the next morning.

With the news of this death, at least one London paper could claim an interesting readership. Wrapped around the torso was a section of the *Echo* dated 24 August, 1888. It was not reported whether or not this news increased or decreased readership for the paper. Later the doctors would also discover pieces of the *Daily Chronicle,* but the issue was not from 1888. What would cause the killer to keep this old paper? Did it show a record of his other crimes?

It did not take long for the hard-pressed police authorities to issue reports that the latest murder was not the work of Jack the Ripper. In fact, before the medical men had any chance to investigate the torso, Scotland Yard had already placed this murder in another column, any column but Jack's. There were no available resources to expend on an ever-increasing killing ground if this were to be viewed as a Ripper murder. The police, however, could not be sure. Ripper or not, the police knew the public must be made to believe that the Ripper had not expanded his turf!

Internal Memo

2 Octr. 88. Clerk of the Board of Works Whitechapel District Fds Resolution passed at a meeting of the Board — asking that the Police Force in the neighbourhood of Whitechapel may be strengthened.

In the meantime, the torso investigation team, under the command of Chief Superintendent Dunlap, and directed by Chief Inspector Wren of A Division, used what resources they had, including reserve police officers, to comb the grounds between the Victoria Embankment and Cannon Row, the area of the worksite discovery. They also included bloodhounds in their work. As they were looking for buried body parts and not a suspect, it was felt that the dogs should be able to find any other pieces deposited along the Thames from the site to the bank. The police also drained an ancient well in the area, but no more remains were discovered. It would be days before another body part was discovered, at least one which matched this latest torso victim.

Daily Telegraph — October 4, 1888

THE WHITEHALL MURDER
Very little additional information has been allotted by the authorities regarding the identity of the victim of the atrocious crime whose dismembered remains were found on Tuesday afternoon in the new Police buildings, on the Embankment at Westminster.

The next day, as Doctors Bond and Charles Hibberd were examining the torso, the London police were going over every inch of the worksite to discover how the woman's trunk could have been deposited. As reported in the London *Times*:

Towards the Thames front of the site there are some underground steps. These steps lead to a door at a lower depth. An inclined plane leads to a lower level. This lower level is a place of arches, from which the light is partially excluded by the walls for the floors above, and is in constant shade. The ground is very rough; building material being plentifully scattered about. In one place there is a deep recess, in which, even when the sun is shining brightly outside, there is complete darkness. This leads by a dangerous way to another recess. In one corner of this farthest dark recess stands a piece of boarding, two pieces of board held together by a cross piece, as if it had formed once part of a builder's boarding round the building. This stands crossways against the wall, leaving a triangular space. It was within this space that the parcel containing the body was found. The devious ways which have to be taken to reach this secret spot, and the fact that this is the most secret spot on site, lead to the conclusion that the person who placed the remains there must have been well acquainted with the place, and the deposit must have been made in the day.

The people in charge of the workmen's entrances in Cannon Row, where time is booked, do not think that a man could pass in with a bundle such as this must have been. Moreover, he could not have got over the gates, unbolted the gate, admitted the parcel, and then, after depositing the parcel in the dark recess, have escaped out of the door, for the doors have never been found unbolted. There was no watchman on the site, and there were no policemen stationed in Cannon Row. The question therefore arises whether entrance was obtained from the Thames Embankment. It is possible that the bundle was conveyed by the carts that enter at the side of the building and deliver materials. It is remarkable that the severed arm was found near a wharf whence wood for building is carted to places where building is being carried on.

Evidence concerning a possible conveyance of the torso, and the number of men who may have been involved in the murder, came during the inquest into the case. As reported in *The Illustrated Police News* of October 20, 1888, there came a report of "Fresh Evidence:"

> The police are in possession of what is likely to prove a most important piece of evidence in connection with the discovery of the mutilated body in a cell of the new police buildings at Westminster. It has been supplied by an inhabitant of Llanelly, of South Wales. He happened to be in Cannon Row on the Saturday before the body was found, and at an hour when the place was practically deserted. His attention was at that moment directed to a man who climbed over a boarding into the ground where the police office is being erected, and where afterwards the body was discovered. Two other men were with him, who had a barrow on which was a bundle. The whole proceeding seemed curious, and afterwards, when the remains were found, the South Walian "put two and two together," handed in his information, and also a description of the man. The result is that a workman has since been interviewed in the vicinity, who admits having been on the spot the day in question, though his business there is not very clear. Beyond this the police, it is said, succeed in obtaining no clue.

A TORSO EXAMINATION

It would be an early start for Dr. Bond and Dr. Hibberd as they made their ways to the mortuary on Millbank Street in Westminster. Both men arrived between 7 and 8 o'clock in the morning. Doctor Bond had gone to the headquarters of A Division to consult with detectives before going to the mortuary. Dr. Hibberd had first checked in at Westminster Hospital, where he was a staff member, before he could proceed to the mortuary. It did not take long for Dr. Bond to arrive at his first conclusion.

"I have an arm that will fit it."

The examination was conducted behind closed and guarded doors, lasting nearly two full hours. The condition of the examination areas were not the best, as the room was quite full of bodies and not fully refreshed by an ample supply of good air. In fact, the term "mortuary" was a bit of a stretch. The so-called Milbank Street Mortuary was reported as being "in the yard attached to a dwelling house and shop, and it is almost devoid of proper modern appliances. A few wooden partitions have been run-up, but there is neither antecedent room to conduct post-mortem examinations, nor means for ensuring the most ordinary sanitation and assisting in the ready and safe identification of the dead."

Along with the torso could be found the body of a woman who had been killed in a boiler room explosion, another woman's body who had been murdered by her husband, and a man who had committed suicide by hanging himself. Even without the Ripper and Thames Torso Murderer at work, the East End of London was not a very safe place to live. It was, however, a very convenient place to die!

The first problem to confront the medical men was the fact that even with the care taken the night before to preserve the remains with alcohol, the torso had advanced considerably in decomposition. The decomposition was so great that it was impossible for the doctors to decide whether she had dark or fair skin. They did agree, however, that she had been "a very fine woman." It is fair to read into that statement that they believed that this latest victim was not a prostitute, at least not a low-class one. It was not the condition of her clothes or her identification which pointed to this conclusion, but her eating habits. It was thought that a prostitute would not be eating regularly, and this woman had been "exceedingly well nourished."

The doctors would also find that her internal organs were healthy, and her heart, lungs and liver were still intact. She had not had an extremely hard life up until she met her death. She did, however, show signs of pleurisy, an inflammation of the membrane that envelopes the lungs. It was not an uncommon condition to find in an individual who had lived in London in the late 1880s. She had been, by all accounts, a "very fine woman, between 25 to 30 years of age who had stood 5 feet 8 to 9 inches tall."

It was discovered that the killer had chosen to cut up the lower portion of the torso in a most complicated manor. He did not cut off the legs as one might expect, just short of the main torso. Instead, the killer cut the lower portion of the body itself, 1½ inches below the navel, effectively opening up the lower body cavity. This cut separated the lower intestine and allowed the cavity to be emptied. Several sections of this cavity would never be found. Just as in the Ripper series, this killer was a collector who was saving body parts. At least, that could be inferred by the strangely cut area and the missing body parts.

The medical men were most interested in establishing a date of death in order to aid the police in their investigations. Both men agreed that the murder must have occurred about six weeks earlier, around August 20. This placed the murder between two Ripper deaths. This was at least a starting point from which to work. Death probably occurred before the 24th, as it is remembered that it was partially wrapped in a newspaper with that date.

After a lunch break and some other duties the doctors returned to the mortuary at 2 P.M. The coroner had signed an order allowing the right arm, found earlier at Pimlico, to be conveyed to the Westminster mortuary for examination. Under the observation of Detective Inspector Marshall, the post-mortem continued. The arm was "placed on one of the tables," and it was not long before the men could easily establish that it was a perfect match. Each cut on the arm matched the jagged (or ripped) flesh where it had been connected to the torso. It was no longer an extra arm which had been found in the Thames. Nor was it a joke played on the police by a medical student. The arm belonged to the Torso Murder victim of Whitehall.

When the work was completed the arm and torso were placed, interestingly enough, in wine. A future examination, if needed, would require the remains to be in as good of shape as possible, and the doctors felt that wine would keep the remains as fresh as possible. As for Doctor Bond, he went immediately to the Home Office in order to file his medical report, with a copy forwarded to the district coroner, Mr. John Troutbeck.

The next day the police would receive a letter sent to the *Central News Service* through the mails signed "Jack the Ripper." Although it was clearly not from the killer — none of the Ripper letters were — it does show the general feeling going around London at the time that this murder was not "Jack's" work. The writer of the letter was never identified, so it could have come from any source in London—including someone in government! Propaganda directed at local target audiences to achieve a governmental goal is not new to leaders of nations. Even the United States Army has several propaganda teams (called Psyop units), well trained in the craft of state deception. And they are, by all accounts, very active and very good at their jobs.

5 Oct. 1888

Dear Friend
    In the name of God hear me I swear I did not kill the female whose body was found at Whitehall. If she was an honest woman I will hunt down and destroy her murderer. If she was a whore God will bless the hand that slew her, for the women of Moab and Midian shall die and their blood shall mingle with the dust. I never harm any others or the Divine power that protects and helps me in my grand work would quit for ever. Do as I do and light of glory shall shine upon you. I must get to work tomorrow treble event this time yes yes three must be ripped. Will send you a bit of face by post I promise this dear old Boss. The police now reckon my work a practical joke well well Jacky's a very practical joker ha ha ha keep this back till three are wiped out and you can show the cold meat.

yours truly
Jack the Ripper

By this time nearly 700 such "Ripper" letters had arrived at police stations and news agencies around London. Each letter caused great problems for the authorities, who had to investigate each and every one. Adding to the letter investigations were the general problems of strangers moving in and out of the East End at all times. As reported in the *Illustrated Police News* of October 20, the problem was more than just a mild suspicion of strangers in the East End. All of London was in fear. "The difficulties the police have to contend with have been enhanced by so many men wandering about the East End who, by their strange behaviour, unaccountable movements, and apparent resemblance to the vague description of the man who is wanted, have given rise to suspicions which have necessarily terminated in police investigation. The murder scare has spread to other parts of the Metropolis...."

THE WHITEHALL INQUEST

For the next few days investigators followed up the few clues they had in this second Torso Murder. It would not be long, however, before there were simply no more leads to follow. The police were not able to arrest any suspects and were looking forward to the upcoming inquest in the hope that witness testimony would point them in the correct direction. The police were not even sure how the suspect had entered the vault area. The *Police Chronicle* of October 6 reported that "The prevailing opinion is that to place the body where it was found the person conveying it must have scaled the 8 foot boarding which encloses the works, and carefully avoiding the watchman who does duty by night, must have dropped it where it was found."

Adding to the general confusion at the time was a most unusual find in Guildford, north of London. On August 24 a set of bones, a right foot and a portion of a left leg, were found on the railway tracks near the village of Guildford Station. The local doctor who examined the remains had reported that the bones had been cooked or boiled, which prevented him from stating whether they had come from a man or a woman. On October 5 the remains were brought to London by Inspector Marshall, who had traveled to Guildford to expedite the transfer. The bones were then taken to the Millbank Street Mortuary and examined by both Dr. Hibberd and Dr. Bond. Before long this latest mystery had been solved.

The *Times* of London — October 8, 1888

> On careful examination of them [bones] on Saturday [October 6],
> Dr. Bond and Mr. Hibberd discovered conclusively that they are
> those of a bear, and therefore have no relation to the human
> remains found at Westminster. The inquest will be held today.

October 8, 1888, dawned cold and miserable in London. It had rained that night, as it had for most of the past week, and this new morning would bring little in the way of good weather — or good news. By mid–October thick, smoke-filled fog dominated much of London, fed by the many coal-burning fires. For the men of the inquest jury it was just one more misery to bear as they first viewed the torso remains at Millbank Street Mortuary, and then made their way to the Sessions House on Broad-Sanctuary Street in Westminster. The inquest into the headless torso of Whitehall began as the room was called to order by Coroner John Troutbeck, elected Coroner for Westminster. Keeping an eye on things for Scotland Yard was Detective Inspector Marshall.

The first witness called was the man who had found the torso, Mr. Frederick Wildborn. After explaining how he had come across the body he was asked to look at a map of the work site which had been prepared by the police. Walking over to the plan he pointed to the vault area on the western end of the work site. He was then asked to show on the map the difficult path he had to walk in order to find his way to that darkened area. It soon became clear that only those who knew the work site would be able to take that path to his secret hiding place. (An educated man who knew the worksite, who had perhaps fallen on hard times.)

Windborn was followed by George Bodden, who had gone with Mr. Windborn to help remove the parcel. He made sure that the jury understood that he was never alone with the torso as he described how he had helped to move it to a better-lighted area for unwrapping. Mr. Bodden did not wish to be accused of anything improper.

After Detective Hawkins of A Division described being called to the location, it was Frederick Moore who was next called. Moore had discovered the right arm along the Embankment, and once again he related the story of its discovery. By this time the police had gained very little in the way of new material on which to continue their inquiries. That situation would change as the coroner called Mr. William Brown to the stand. Brown's testimony would show that any individual capable of placing the torso into the vault would have either personal knowledge of the site or have gotten such information from someone who had worked there. It was clearly possible to enter the work site unseen, but, once inside, finding the vault area was a very difficult task. The area was simply not easy to see nor easy to find in the dark. And it was always in the dark.

The assistant foreman for Messrs. Grover Builders then gave a detailed description of the area. "The works on the embankment are shut off by a boarding 8 ft. or 9 ft. high, [the boarding had not been damaged] and there are three entrances with gates, two in Cannon Row and one on the Embankment. It is three months since the vaults have been completed. No one, except the workmen and Carmen, are or have been admitted to the works, except those who had business with the clerk of the work. There are notices to that effect on boards. The gates, however, have not been attended and persons could get in. All the gates, with one exception are locked at night, and the exception is one which has a latch with a string above to admit those who know how to pull it. There was no watchman at night. [A different view on this point.] The approach to the vault from Cannon Row was first by planks and steps, and planks again. There was work being done in the vaults a week before the discovery. There was no one there on Sunday or Saturday night. The locks of the gates were not found forced at any time, nor was any gate open on Monday last or at any-time. I do not think it possible that anyone could have lowered the parcel from Richmond Mews (at the side of Whitehall Gardens) and then have carried it across the grounds of the vaults."

With the discovery of the arm near the Thames River, and the torso discovery, a theory was forming in the minds of the police that the killer had wanted to dump the torso in the river but was prevented from doing so. Perhaps the arm's discovery, or the added patrols in the area due to the ongoing Ripper murders, made it necessary for the killer to look for other ways to dispose of a body or two! If it were beginning to smell, then time would have been short. Someone may have become suspicious.

During the inquest into this Torso Mystery, Londoners became aware of yet one more body found in that cold river. She was an unknown found floating, but she did not seem to have any connection to the latest string of crimes. The woman's death was a wholly common occurrence in Victorian London, and the Torso Killer would not have the opportunity to take this one.

The *Times* of London—October 9, 1888

DROWNED IN THE THAMES.—Yesterday the body of a woman was found floating in the Thames near Waterloo Bridge. About noon attention was drawn to a dark object floating on the ebb tide near the Surrey shore. A Thames police galley rowed to the spot, and the object proved to be the body of a woman, apparently about 29 years of age. She was floating face upwards, and her long hair was disheveled by the action of the tide. The body was secured by a tow rope and taken to the Lambeth pier, where it was placed in a shell. It was subsequently conveyed to the Lambeth mortuary, High Street, there to await identification and an inquest.

After a brief recess the jury returned to hear testimony from the medical men who had been called into the case. The first to give evidence was Doctor Thomas Bond—Police Surgeon. "I am a surgeon and reside at the Sanctuary, Westminster Abbey. On October 2nd, shortly before 4 o'clock, I was called to the new police buildings, where I was shown the decomposed trunk of a body. It was then lying in the basement, partially unwrapped. I visited the place where it had been discovered, and found that the wall against which it had lain was stained black. The parcel seemed to have been there for several days, and it was taken to the mortuary that evening and the remains placed in spirits. On the following morning, I made a post-mortem examination assisted by Mr. Hibbert. The trunk was that of a woman of considerable stature, and well nourished. The head had been separated from the trunk at the sixth cervical vertebra, which had been sawn through. The lower part of the body and the pelvis had been removed, and the fourth lumbar vertebra had been sawn through in the same way as in the removal of the head, by long, sweeping cuts. The length of the trunk was 17 in., the circumference of the chest was 35½ in., and the circumference of the waist was 28½ in. It was all very much decomposed, but the skin was not so much decomposed as the cut parts, and I examined it for wounds. I found none on the body. The skin was light. The breasts were large and prominent. The arms had been removed at the shoulder joints by several incisions, which had been made apparently obliquely, and then downwards around the arms. The joints had been removed straight through the joint—that is, disarticulated through the joint. Over the body were clearly defined marks, where string had been tightly tied. The body appeared to have been wrapped up in a very skillful manner.

"On close examination we could not find the linea alba which would indicate that the woman had borne children. It was impossible to ascertain owing to the decomposed condition of the remains, whether there had been any wound inflicted on the neck in life. The neck had been divided by several incisions and sawn through below the larynx. On opening the chest, we found that the rib cartilages were not ossified; that one lung was healthy, but the other lung was adherent, showing that for some time the woman had suffered from severe pleurisy. This was of long standing. The heart was healthy, but there was no blood in it, and no staining of the organ with blood. That, to my mind, is an indication that the woman did not die from suffocation or by drowning. The liver was in a normal condition, and the stomach contained about one ounce of partly digested food. There was no appearance of inflammation. The kidneys were normal, and the spleen also. The small intestines and the part, which attaches the intestines to the body, were in place, and were healthy. The lower part of the large bowel, and all the contents of the pelvis, were absent. The uterus was absent. We found that the woman was of mature age and over 24 or 25 years of age.

"She was, to every appearance, a well-nourished woman, and was, in fact, a large, well-nourished person, with fair skin and dark hair. There were no indications that she had borne a child, but it was possible that she might have done so. The date of death, as far as we could judge, would have been six weeks or two months before the discovery, and the decomposition occurred in the air, and not in the water. I subsequently examined the arm, which had been brought to the mortuary from Pimlico, and this was fully examined and will be described by my colleague, Mr. Hibbert. I found that the arm accurately fitted to the trunk. The cuts corresponded, and the general contour of the arm corresponded with the body. It was a fleshy, rounded arm. The hand was long, the fingers tapering, and the nails very well shaped. It was the hand of a person who had not been used to manual labour. Mr. Hibbert has compared the hairs, and he will tell you the results."

CORONER: "About the cuts? Were they made after death?"

DR. BOND: "Undoubtedly? It is impossible, owing to the state of decomposition in which the body was, to say whether there had been a cut round the neck during life, which would have caused death. The decomposition was far advanced, and the body was absolutely full of maggots. I could not have ascertained from the condition of the trunk whether any wound on the neck was made in life."

CORONER: "Then there was nothing to indicate the cause of death?"

DR. BOND: "Nothing whatever. There was nothing to show that it was sudden, but I am satisfied that it was not a death by suffocation. It was more likely death from hemorrhage, for the heart was pale, and free from clots, whereas in the great number of post-mortem examinations, which I have made after a very long period, where death has been from drowning, the interior parts of the heart have been very much stained with blood. In this case the interior part of the heart was quite pale, proving, to my mind, that the woman died from hemorrhage or fainting. I did not anatomically examine the arm, but merely fitted it to the trunk."

There would be no testimony as to why the killer had removed the head. However, the only logical possibility was one of identification removal. Possibly the killer could have been identified if the victim herself could also be identified. Without the head it would be a most difficult case to solve. The next report came from Doctor Charles Alfred Hibbert, M.R.C.S.

"I saw this arm first on the 16th of September, and then made an examination of it. It was the right arm, which had been separated from the trunk at the shoulder joint by a cut, which passed obliquely round. The arm measured 32 in. in length, and its circumference at the point where it was separated was 13 in. The hand measured 7½ in. The arm was surrounded in the upper part by a piece of string, and this made an impression upon the skin of the arm. When the string was loosened it was found that there was a great deal of blood in the arm. The skin of the arm was in a fair condition, and was not very much decomposed, but the skin of the hand was very thin, white, and corrugated through immersion in the water. The hand itself was long, well shaped, and carefully kept, and the nails were small and well shaped. There were no scars or marks of any kind, and there were no bruises. There were a few dark brown hairs left under the arm. The woman must have been over 20. The arm had apparently been separated from the body after death. The calculation as to the height of the woman, founded upon the measurement of the arm, made her about 5 ft. 8½ in. high. I thought the arm was cut off by a person who, while he was not necessarily an anatomist, certainly knew what he was doing—who knew where the joints were and cut them pretty regularly. There were not many cuts—about six or seven. They had evidently been done with a very sharp knife. I was enabled to examine the arm at the same time as the trunk, and found they exactly fitted. The skin cuts corresponded, and the bones and the hair corresponded. The hair was precisely the same, and when the two lots were mixed together they could not be separated."

> CORONER: "Is a division like that one which you have done for any pur-
> pose of anatomy?"
> DR. HIBBERT: "No. For a surgical motive, the cut would have been so
> made as to leave the skin outside. In this case the skin was cut
> through by several long cuts, and then the bone was sawn through.
> The pieces of paper produced, which were found near the body,
> are stained by some animal blood. It is certainly not the blood of a
> bird or reptile. There was no mark of a ring on the finger of the
> hand."

With the doctors' reports finished, Coroner Troutbeck recalled Detective Inspector Marshall to explain to the jury how he felt the killer had entered the area and how long he felt the torso had been in its hidden vaulted position.

"It is easy, I think, to get over the boarding in Cannon Row, but there are no indications of anyone having done so. It is quite easy for anyone to open the latch referred to. I should think the body had been where it was found for days, from the stain on the wall, but the witness who has been examined declares most positively that it was not there on Saturday, as he was on the very spot."

When pressed for more details, the inspector stated that he had no other evidence at that time. The coroner was not satisfied and again pressed the officer for details.

> CORONER: "Is it possible that any other evidence would be forthcom-
> ing?"
> MARSHALL: "One or two more of the work people might be examined.
> Of course, the all-important task is to find the head."
> CORONER: "As there are other witnesses, and there seems to be this
> doubt as to whether the parcel was in the vault before Saturday, I
> think we must adjourn, and I therefore adjourn the inquiry until
> this day fortnight [two weeks]."

MORE DISCOVERIES ON SITE

For the next few days the police continued to search the general area of the worksite, and approaches to the site from the Thames, with no luck. The killer had left no trace as to how he had entered the site or why he had hidden the torso so deeply. The police needed help, and it came in the form of a London reporter named Mr. Waring and a mixed breed Russian Terrier.

Just after noon on Wednesday, October 17, Mr. Waring and his dog were escorted by police through the construction site and into the recesses of the vault area. The area was still very badly lit as the dog was placed on the exact spot where the body had been found. It did not take long for the terrier to find something and was soon digging in an area close to the parcel's former location. With a bit more than six inches of dirt removed, the excited animal grabbed onto something and began to pull. His discovery was soon identified as a human leg.

Before long, Doctor Bond was once again called to the scene, and he confirmed that the animal had indeed found a human left leg with a foot attached. It had been cut off with skill above the knee. He was able to tell that the general shape and form corresponded quite well with the torso and arm which had already been found, but he was unable to, as yet, state that it matched the other remains exactly.

This new discovery was taken at once to the mortuary and placed alongside the other remains. Now able to make direct comparisons, Doctor Bond was soon able to show that his original suspicions had proved correct. This latest body part matched perfectly the torso at the mortuary. Once again, the cut marks were used to match each piece. There was no doubt that the killer had buried the leg at the same time he dropped off the rest of the torso. Yet why did he not bury the torso as well? Was he disturbed in the middle of his work? Was he standing in the deep shadows as workmen went about their jobs in the vault area of the new police headquarters? Was he one of the workmen? After all, most serial killers have jobs like everyone else!

The police were still having trouble with just how long the torso had been hidden in the vault. Several men by then had given statements or testified to their beliefs that the parcel containing the torso had only been in the vault for a few days before it was discovered. But clearly the remains had been in place much longer. The wall where the parcel had set against was greatly stained by the fluids of decomposition. And this staining could not have been so widespread nor as deeply made unless the torso had been in contact with the wall, and for many days. The ground beneath the parcel was also deeply stained and had settled down due to the load. The doctors who had examined the parcel in-situ and in the mortuary were quite clear on the type of decomposition they had discovered. Fresh air and light were not involved. The torso had been buried or covered for some time, most likely since the arm was deposited in the Thames River weeks before. The police now had a major investigative problem to solve. Had the torso been buried in the vault and covered up for a while before it was exposed to the workers looking for their tools? And if so, who had discovered it originally and possibly said nothing about it? Was it the killer?

That evening the police returned to the work site with the same dog. The operation was kept secret from news reporters and other interested parties in order to minimize the number of people involved. It was also conducted at night, and in the fog, so that none of the workmen would know about the several hours long search. From the *Times* of London readers would later learn, "The scene is described as a very weird one, for the only illumination of the dismal place was by candles, and the dog did not seem in the best of form, this possibly arising from the strange surroundings." The police were then working under the theory that at least one workman on that site had personal knowledge of the crime, even if he were not the actual killer. But if that were true then that workman would have also been responsible for the Rainham murder as well. It was a possibility not lost on the men of Scotland Yard, even though it was official policy to view these two cases as separate murder investigations.

The nighttime search did indeed bring new evidence to light in the form of the missing left arm. Six inches deeper than where the left leg and foot had been discovered, the dog, despite not being in top form, found the missing limb. The ground had become packed in, and it was clear that the arm had been in the ground for some weeks.

The police were still trying to track down who the victim was, based on local and London-wide missing persons reports. They were looking for a woman with darkish hair, over 25 years of age and from 5 ft. 8 to 8½ in. tall, who had pleurisy. As reported in the *Times,* "Unfortunately there are numerous women reported to be missing, and the investigation of all such cases takes up much time, especially where minute points which promise much have to be followed up." In the end, despite all police efforts, including London-wide newspaper descriptions of the Whitehall Torso victim, the authorities would never identify "the woman in the vault."

On October 18 the London police completed a massive house-to-house search in and around the Whitechapel area in search of the Ripper. Familiar East End streets, such as Hanbury, Commercial, Dorset, Brick Lane, Buck's Row and many others, were gone through from room to room. Adding to this effort, the police handed out thousands of handbills to every house-hold and lodging house in the district. And, although the normally recal-citrant residents were most open to this intrusion into their lives, no real evidence would be found linking either the Ripper or Torso murder cases. The Torso Killer may not have lived there and the Ripper had moved out of the area, just ahead of the search.

Part of the force on those cold October mornings could be found, once again, going over the ground between the Whitehall worksite and the Thames Embankment. This search would also prove to be in vain, as the police began to wonder if they were ever going to find the missing body parts, most importantly—the head!

The public was more than willing to do whatever they could to help the police track down the killer or killers of these women. This included sending literally thousands of cards and letters to the police headquarters and the Home Office with suggestions on how to nab the suspect. So many had written, that Charles Warren, Metropolitan Police Commissioner, sent a letter to the London papers with an acknowledgement of those letters and a thank you to the people of the East End for their understanding and help during the massive and unprecedented search.

THE EAST-END MURDERS

————o————

We are requested to publish the following: -

Sir Charles Warren wishes to say that the marked desire evinced by the inhabitants of the Whitechapel district to aid the police in the pursuit of the author of the recent crimes has enabled him to direct that, subject to the consent of occupiers, a through house-to-house search should be made within a defined area. With few exceptions the inhabitants of all classes and creeds have freely fallen in with the proposal, and have materially assisted the officers engaged in carrying it out.

Sir Charles Warren feels that some acknowledgement is due on all sides for the cordial cooperation of the inhabitants, and he is much gratified that the police officers have carried out so delicate a duty with the marked good will of all those with whom they have come in contact.

Sir Charles Warren takes this opportunity of acknowledge-ment the receipt of an immense volume of correspondence of a semi-private character on the subject of the Whitechapel mur-ders, which he has been quite unable to respond to in a great number of instances; and he trusts that the writers will accept this acknowledgement in lieu of individual replies. They may be assured that their letters have received every consideration.

THE INQUEST ENDS WITH A VERDICT

As the fire crews were putting out the final hot spots on a large tenement fire begun the night before on Bow Lane in the East End, the Whitehall Torso jury was being seated for the final day's testimony into the murder mystery. On October 22, 1888, Westminster Sessions House once again played host to the inquest into the mutilated body found at the New Scotland Yard worksite. Mr. Troutbeck was again presiding as Detective Inspector Marshall looked on for the "Yard." The first called was Mr. William Brown, who lived in Hornsey and was at the time one of the assistant formen for the project. He was recalled by the coroner in an attempt to pinpoint the time the body had been placed in the vault.

> CORONER: "Did you go into the vault on Friday, 28 September?"
> MR. BROWN: "I had on Friday the 28th to go into the place where the body was found on the 2nd. I was down there measuring up for the surveyors on Friday the 28th of September, and had a light there. If the parcel had been there on that Friday I think I must have trodden on it. The premises were left after work was finished each day without any watchman. I did not examine the recess. The body might have been in the corner without my seeing it."

The clerk of the works at the discovery site, Mr. George Erant, was then called to testify about the comings and goings of the work crews. He testified to being on the site on Saturday the 29th and felt that no one could have come into the area with such a large bundle without him noticing the man who carried it. In fact, he had seen no packages at all. Mr. Erant also backed up Mr. Brown's testimony about how the site was situated after the day's work was completed. There was no watchman on duty at night.

The coroner then called carpenter's laboror Richard Lawrence of 40 Sterndale Road, Battersea, to the stand. He had been in the vault area on the 29th of September.

> CORONER: "Did you have need to enter the vault area on 29 September?"
> MR. LAWRENCE: "I left my tools in the vault on Saturday, the 29th of September, shortly after midday. I went there again at 6:10 A.M. on Monday morning, the 1st of October. They had not been disturbed, and I did not notice anything. If the parcel had been there when I went for the tools I could not have seen it, the place was so completely dark."

Jasper Waring, newspaper reporter, was next called to go over the discovery of the leg and arm found buried on the opposite side of the vault from the torso area. It was becoming clear that the torso and the appendages were all in place for weeks, despite the inability of the work crews to stumble across the parcel or see it in the dark. "The place where the leg was found is in the opposite side of the same recess where the body was found. The arm was found some 12 inches down. The dog refused to work when many police came, as they did soon after. There was no appearance in the earth there of its having been disturbed for some time."

Mr. Angle, also a reporter, had accompanied Waring on the search for remains in the vault; he repeated Waring's remarks and added, "I had an impression that the earth where the leg was concealed was a little higher than the other ground. I thought the leg was found at only a depth of four or five inches when the stones were removed. The ground where the leg was discovered was very hard, as if it had been trodden upon."

Finally, Doctor Thomas Bond was recalled for a scientific review of the length of time the remains had lain in the vault. "I examined the earth which had covered it, and I found that this gave unmistakable evidence of having covered the leg for several weeks—that the leg had been there for several weeks. Decomposition had taken place there, and it was not decomposed when placed there. [Evidence that the body parts had been disposed of soon after the murder.] The upper part of the leg was in a good state of preservation; but the foot had decomposed, and the skin and nails had peeled off."

And as to the skills of the killer, Doctor Bond stated, "We found that the leg had been divided at the knee joint by free incisions, and very cleverly disarticulated without injury to the cartilages."

The doctor then addressed the seeming discrepancies in testimony concerning how long the body had been in place in the vault. "I took the opportunity, I may say, while in the vault to examine the spot where the body was found, and I am quite sure that the last witness is wrong as to the body not having been there a few days before. The body must have been lain there for weeks, and it had decomposed there."

After a final word from Inspector Marshall insuring the members of the jury that the police had no other evidence to offer at that time, Coroner Troutbeck summed up the case. He informed the jury that not only did the woman still remain unknown, but that a cause of death had not been established. He did state that the medical men were able to deduce that the "body had been cut up after death, and that no mortal wounds had been discovered.... It is now up to the jury to say whether you will return a verdict of "Found Dead" or of "Wilful Murder" against some person or persons unknown." It would not take long for the jury to decide for a verdict of: "Found Dead!"

The body count for the Thames Torso Killer would now stand at two, and even though the jury did not agree, it was very possibly a murder, with no suspects and no victims as yet identified. So far it was a perfect set of crimes by a serial killer who had left no real clues for the authorities to track. In fact, some members of Scotland Yard did not believe the same man had been involved with this latest killing and the Rainham Mystery. Perhaps it was even "Jack." For most at the "Yard," however, that feeling would change.

For now, the London police had their hands full working on the Ripper investigation, and it would not take long for their attentions to be drawn completely away from the Whitehall Mystery. Soon enough the killer known as Jack the Ripper would strike again, with his most bloody mutilation murder to date of a well known East End prostitute. The Whitehall Torso Murder would soon become lost in the shadow of Jack the Ripper.

Chapter 6

In the Shadow of the Ripper

I send you half the Kidne I took from one woman...
"Letter From hell" received October 16, 1888

The Autumn of Terror

Between the Torso Murder of August 1888 and the murder of Elizabeth Jackson in June of 1889, the Ripper would kill six women. Perhaps it was the speed in which he worked, killing more in those nine months than the Torso Killer dispatched in 15 years. Perhaps it was the fancy name he was given by a ravenous press, or maybe it was because his victims all had names, which made his victims more memorable. Whatever the reason, no one — not the government, the public, the newspapers or even the police investigators themselves— had anywhere near the emotional connection to the Torso Murders as they did with the Ripper murders. Yet the Torso Murders were at least as brutal, with body parts and torsos spread over a much larger area of London. The outcry and sheer panic over the Ripper's terror would become a force of its own, one that could have brought down a government. For the Torso Murders there would barely register any concern. Why?

It did not take long for the good, but poor, men of Whitechapel to understand that a monster was living among them — after the death of Martha Tabram on August 7, 1888. Murder was one thing, but the brutality of her death was a singularly vicious crime they knew had to be solved, and they were going to help solve it. The day after her murder the Whitechapel Vigilance Committee was formed to hunt down the killer of

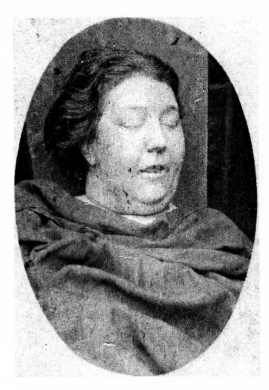

Martha Tabram

this 39-year-old prostitute. A few days later, 70 local men, bolstered by students from Toynbee Hall, formed the St. Jude's Vigilance Committee. Men were then selected from that group to patrol selected streets in search of the Whitechapel Killer.

Despite the strangeness of this crime, the press were not yet ready to devote full-page coverage to the murder. There was no fancy name for the killer, as yet, and no description to pass around. However, the papers were quick to point out the dangers. On August 11 the *East London Advertiser* would report, "...there is also a feeling of insecurity to think that in a great city like London, the streets of which are continually patrolled by police, a woman can be locally and horribly killed almost next to the citizens peacefully sleeping in their beds without a trace or clue being left of the villain who did the deed."

As the vigilance committees organized their patrols, centered around the streets and back alleys of Whitechapel and Spitalfields, the Torso Killer was silently and deadly working off the streets at an undiscovered location. In fact, the distribution of the victims dumped by that killer seems to indicate that he was on the move from place to place as he sought out his victims. He would find his next around August 20, but she would not be discovered for many days to come. The next East End murder victim to come to the attention of the authorities—and an ever more concerned London population—was Mary Ann (Polly) Nichols. It would be her death, the ability of the killer to escape detection, and the first mutilation in the Ripper series, which would send shock waves throughout the East End. It would also place the killing of this Whitechapel prostitute on the front pages of newspapers around the world. It would be an immortality in death that poor Polly could never have achieved in life.

Martha Tabram's body was found in the George Yard dwelling.

Polly Nichols had been killed on Buck's Row, a dark and mostly deserted cobblestone road, at night. It was badly lit, as were many of the streets in London's less affluent areas, and it was known to have been used by many of the hundreds of full- or part-time prostitutes in the area. It was also not on the list of streets then being patrolled by any of the newly formed vigilance committees. That oversight would soon be corrected, too late, of course, to save Polly, but perhaps soon enough to save another lost soul in the abyss of London's East End. As for the lighting, that problem was well expressed by the *Illustrated Police News* of September 8, 1888. "Buck's Row, like many other miser thoroughfares in this and similar neighborhoods, is not overburdened with gas lamps...." Many years down the road that flaw would be corrected by the bombs of World War II!

The *Times* of London— September 1, 1888:

Another murder of the foulest kind was committed in the neighborhood of Whitechapel in the early hours of yesterday morning...

As the news of this most recent murder began to flow over London's population, L. P. Walter wrote

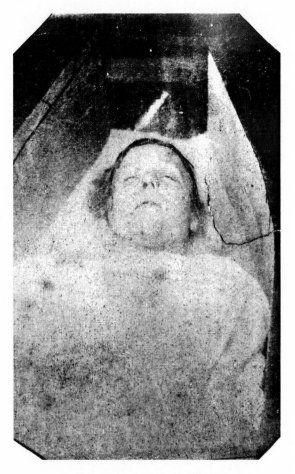

Mary Ann (Polly) Nichols, Ripper victim.

a letter to the Home Office recommending the government offer a reward for information on the killer. The wheels of government would turn slowly on the matter, however, as Leigh Pemberton, replying for the Home Office, informed Mr. Walter that the practice of giving rewards for criminal information had been discontinued.

When Polly Nichols was buried in the City of London Cemetery, Manor Park, on September 6, 1888, there would be no large crowd to see her off. The large crowds and public outrage had yet to surface as her polished elm coffin was lowered into the ground on that cloud covered day.

Mary Ann Nichols, aged 42; died August 31, 1888
— Brass plate on her coffin

Buck's Row, East End, London — the site of Polly Nichols' murder by Jack the Ripper. Looking west/southwest.

The police, at least a large percentage of them, believed that they were not only dealing with a single killer in this series but that a new type of crime was being committed. They did not, as yet, have a name for these criminals, but today they would be called "serial killers." There were, however, no lists of proposed suspects on which to focus, as it became clear that these were cases of murder against strangers. And although it had not become a generally accepted fact on the force, many believed that the murders would continue until the killer was apprehended or killed. The police were starting to believe that a madman was walking the streets of the East End of London, and they did not have a clear idea on how to catch him. They did, however, know which man should be assigned to the case. Inspector George Frederick Abberline from Scotland Yard would be given responsibility for hunting down the killer at the street level. He had spent many years in Whitechapel and would return to lead the largest manhunt in police history.

> Sir, I would suggest that the police should at once find out the whereabouts of all cases of "homicidal mania" which may have

been discharged as "cured" from metropolitan asylums during the last two years.
— A country doctor to the London *Times* editor

The upper levels of official London did not, however, see these murders in the same light as the beat cops and inspectors assigned to the case. A typical response may be viewed by a memo written by the newly appointed Assistant Commissioner for Crime, Robert Anderson. The future "Sir Robert" would write, "I am convinced that the Whitechapel murder case is one which can be successfully grappled with if it is systematically taken in hand. I go so far as to say that I could myself, in a few days, unravel the mystery provided I could spare the time to give individual attention to it." After writing that memo, Commissioner Anderson promptly went on vacation to the mainland of Europe!

The police would have little time to ponder the two murders already placed on their doorsteps, as the Ripper increased his pace. It would be little more than a week before a new and even more frightful murder would capture the attention of the world. And, contrary to popular belief, the killer did not always kill on the streets of the East End. Indeed, Martha Tabrum had been killed inside on a first floor landing, and his next victim would be found in the small backyard of 29 Hanbury Street. The killer wanted (or needed) his work displayed, but was also doing everything he could to avoid being captured. He had also added a new and frightening twist to his series of deaths— he was removing and carrying off freshly butchered body parts!

With this next murder of prostitute Annie Chapman came a wave of panic throughout the East End. The streets were at once alive with resi-

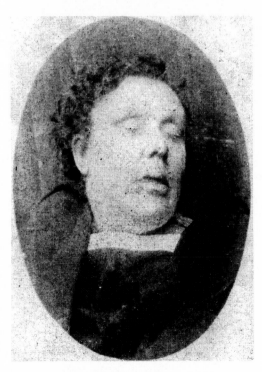

Annie Chapman, the Ripper's third murder victim.

dents demanding an end to the killings and blaming an inactive police force, and an uncaring government, for a perceived lack of progress in the case. In point of fact, the police were stepping up their investigations and organizing as many men as they could to hunt down this killer. The government, however, seated a mile and a half to the west, was still slow to understand what was happening in the ghettos of the east side. The press, however, ever eager to sell their papers, exploded with massive coverage of this latest killing, publishing edition after edition, at times several in one day. The presses could not keep up with demand as individuals who could get a copy of any paper would read the latest reports to all who would stand and listen. The world press was also starting to put an excited twist to their stories of the bloody crime spree going on in London.

The *New York Times* — September 9, 1888

> Not during the riots and fog of February, 1886, have I seen London so thoroughly excited, as it is to-night. The Whitechapel fiend murdered his fourth victim this morning and continues undetected, unseen, and unknown. There is a panic in Whitechapel which will instantly extend to other districts should he change his locality, as the four murders are in everybody's mouth.

This *New York Times* report was not too far off the mark. The panic would have indeed extended had the authorities admitted that the killer was expanding his territory. The government would soon find that the costs of this investigation were going to be the greatest they had yet encountered. They simply could not afford to let the public believe that this killer was moving far away from his "home" in Whitechapel.

Not to be outdone by the foreign press, the London papers were understandably hot on the story. One of the most descriptive and inflammatory newspapers of the day was the radical *Star* who reported in its September 8 edition: "London lies today under the spell of a great terror. A nameless reprobate — half beast, half man — is at large, who is daily gratifying his murderous instincts on the most miserable and defenseless classes of the community."

What the paper failed to convey to its readers were the facts that this killer "only" killed the lowest class of prostitutes and "only" killed in the East End of London. And he did not kill daily. In fact, the murders were occurring in a very small area of the East End centered on the ghetto of Whitechapel. Most of the population of London need not have feared this madman — if he continued to target these women alone. But with a madman in their midst there were no guarantees, which, as would be expected, was no comfort to the over 1200 low-class prostitutes working "Jack's" home ground. They had every right to be on "edge," as Jack increased his count.

Men were now being brought in by the police, but mostly for acting

Opposite: 29 Hanbury Street — Chapman and the Ripper entered the building by the door on the left, at no. 29.

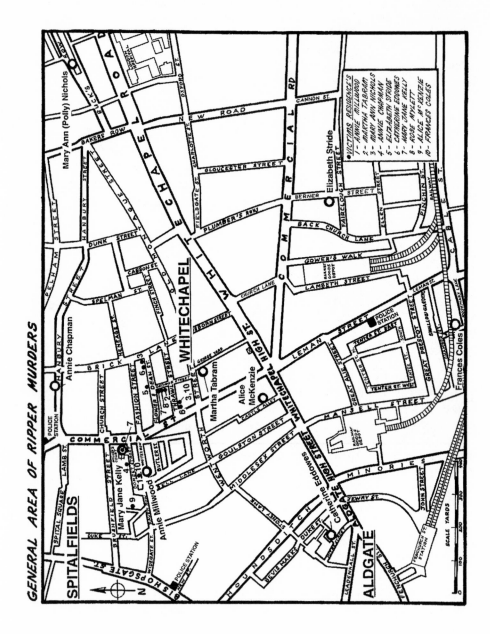

GENERAL AREA OF RIPPER MURDERS

strange or "talking too much" about the murders. Men who did not "seem to belong in the area" were also being approached wholesale by groups of men and women who lived in the area. The police, for their part, were on the lookout for a man known as "Leather Apron" because of a garment of the same type found at the scene of this latest murder. The apron was soon discovered to have belonged to one of the residents, who had nothing to do with the murders, but the press continued the coverage of "Leather Apron" nevertheless. It would not be long before John Pizer, i.e. Leather Apron, was captured, investigated and soon cleared of all suspicions. In the meantime, the authorities had their first real piece of evidence — a description of the killer!

Official Police Notice

Description of a man who entered a passage of the house at which the murder was committed of a prostitute at 2 A.M. on the 8th.— Age 37; height, 5 ft. 7 in.; rather dark beard and moustache. Dress-shirt, dark vest and trousers, black scarf, and black felt hat. Spoke with a foreign accent.

It was not much of a description, granted, but at least the investigators could focus the search on a general type of individual. At this point it would be possible to narrow the search and concentrate the efforts— if the description was correct.

On September 14 Annie Chapman was buried in the same cemetery as Polly Nichols. Her family, rightfully fearing large crowds, kept the arrangements secret. She was laid to rest with her family in attendance as a cold damp wind brushed through the East End. It was a chill felt by all as the coffin was lowered into the ground marked with a brass plate which read:

Annie Chapman — died Sept. 8, 1888, aged 48 years

Within the first twenty-four hours after Annie's death, and armed with a description, the police swarmed into over 200 local common lodging houses looking for the killer. The police interviewed and investigated all of the male occupants, as well as taking statements from many of the women. It is a very good possibility that the police came face-to-face with "Jack the Ripper" during the search. The Ripper, however, was a stone cold killer and would not have given himself away in any interview. In fact, he would have enjoyed the talk. It would have meant that he had beaten them.

It was at this point in the investigation that James Monro's "Secret Department" went into action. Through this department, Monro had direct

Opposite: **A single square mile of Victorian London would be all the Ripper would need to complete his deadly series. And he would take all of his victims from an area no larger than 350 sq. yards.**

access to the Home Secretary. This group of investigators was not part of the Criminal Investigation Department (CID). It was known as "Section D," and was paid for by "Imperial" funding. Normally they would be on the lookout for subversives and anarchists, but for the present they would train their practiced eyes on finding a single killer from Whitechapel. At the same time, Assistant Police Commissioner Henry Smith placed almost one third of his force into plain clothes, with the hope that one of them would spot the killer before the killer could spot them.

With at least three murders in the Ripper's column, business began to dramatically slow down in the area. Businessmen were complaining that if this killer was not found very soon, outside people would stop coming to the East End for the many markets and services found there. With this in mind, among other reasons to be sure, 16 local businessmen met and formed the Mile End Vigilance Committee. They would meet at the local Crown public house at 74 Mile End Road. Their stated purpose was to "...strengthen the hands of the police." They hired men to patrol a number of streets and gathered funds for a reward. Handbills were printed and posted on many of the local store windows throughout Whitechapel, Mile End and Houndsditch.

IMPORTANT NOTICE

> To the tradesmen, Ratepayers, and Inhabitants Generally of
> Whitechapel and District.— Finding that in spite of Murders being
> committed in our midst, and that the Murderer or Murderers are
> still at large, we the undersigned have formed ourselves into a
> Committee, and intend offering a substantial **REWARD** to anyone,
> Citizen, or otherwise, who shall give such information that will
> bring the Murderer or Murderers to Justice. A Committee of Gen-
> tlemen has already been formed to carry out the above object, and
> will meet every evening at nine o'clock, at Mr. J. Aaron's the
> "Crown", 74 Mile End Road, corner of Jubilee Street, and will be
> pleased to receive the assistance of the residents of the District...

The formation of these businessmen was covered in the London *Times,* which reported on September 11: "The movement has been warmly taken up by the inhabitants, and it is thought certain that a large sum will be subscribed within the next few days."

Although the committee fully intended to follow up on its commitment to bring forward a large reward, they would soon find that even with the East End firmly under the shadow of a mad killer, reward money would be very hard to come by. It was, after all, a poor ghetto. In the meantime, the secretary of the committee wrote to Henry Matthews, the Home Secretary, requesting government funds be set aside for a reward. This request, as would all subsequent ones, was set aside with a polite but firm response that rewards were no longer considered a valuable tool in the detection of crime. The question is asked: How large a reward would have been forthcoming if the victims were from the rich ruling classes of the West End? For the time being the police would continue to work the situation in the usual manner. That would be until a letter arrived signed "Jack the Ripper."

Dear Boss,   25. Sept. 1888

I keep on hearing the police have caught me but they won't fix me just yet. I have laughed when they look so clever and talk about being on the right track. That joke about Leather Apron gave me real fits. I am down on whores and I shan't quit ripping them till I do get buckled. Grand work the last job was. I gave the lady no time to squeal. How can they catch me now. I love my work and want to start again. You will soon hear of me with my funny little games. I saved some of the proper red stuff in a ginger beer bottle over the last job to write down with but it went thick like glue and I can't use it. Red ink is fit enough I hope ha ha. The next job I do I shall clip the ladys ears off and send them to the police officers just for jolly wouldn't you. Keep this letter back till I do a bit more work, then give it out straight. My knife's so nice and sharp I want to get to work right away if I get a chance. Good luck.

                                        Yours Truly
                                        Jack the Ripper

Dont mind me giving the trade name

In the postscript, written with great speed on a 90 degree angle from the letter, and in red crayon, the letter writer wrote:

Wasn't good enough to post this before I got all the red ink off my hands curse it. No luck yet. They say I'm a doctor now ha ha

On October 1 a second communication, a locally available post card also written in red crayon, arrived at the Central News Agency. It was penned by the same hand and postmarked "London, E., Oct. 1."

It read:

I was not codding
dear old Boss when
I gave you the tip.
you'll hear about
Saucy Jackey's work
tomorrow double
event this time
number one squealed
a bit couldn't
finish straight off.

had not time
to get ears for
police. thanks for
keeping last letter
back till I got
to work again.
Jack the Ripper

The police took both the letter and card very seriously. They printed a facsimile of both on posters and placed copies at every police station in the area. It was not, however, the work of the Whitechapel Killer (Jack's original nickname). Most likely it was written by a news reporter hoping to keep the story alive and on the front pages. It not only helped keep the story going but also helped continue the terror throughout the East End. More than 110 years after the murders had ended, that name still brings the terror of a serial killer to mind around the world.

The response to the letter was electric. The name of "Jack the Ripper" was flashed around the world. There was little interest in other crimes at this point, and the two Torso Murders were all but forgotten by the people of London. From this point on the talk would be of "Jack" and when he could be expected to strike again. In point of fact, by the time the post card arrived, the Ripper had already been back at work — twice!

Before 1 A.M. in the early morning of September 30, 1888, Elizabeth Stride was murdered in a passageway leading into Dutfield's Yard, just off of Berner Street. Less than ¾ of a mile away and forty-five minutes later, Catharine Eddowes would become the second victim that night to have her throat cut by the madman who walked the East End at night hunting prostitutes. For Stride it would be a simple

Elizabeth Stride

Site of Elizabeth Stride's murder: Corner of Fairclough and Berner Street; the Working Men's Educational Club is second building from the right; Dutfield's Yard entrance is seen to the left of the club down a short passage.

matter, if such things can be called simple, for her killer cut her throat with a two-inch wide gash; for Eddowes it would be something entirely different. Not only would Eddowes be ripped open at the throat and abdomen, but also parts of her body would be removed, including one of her kidneys, and taken by her killer. She would also become the first in the series to have her face mutilated for no apparent reason other than to give pleasure to her sadistic killer. No reason was ever discovered.

Even though she had been seen with a man, by no less than three witnesses, only minutes before her death just outside Mitre Square, the killer would still take the extravagant chance of taking Catharine into the darkened corner of the square and end her life. She must have realized that help was very nearby, but they could do nothing to save her from her fate. The killer would do more damage to her corpse than he had ever done before in the series.

It was 1:45 A.M. as Constable Edward Watkins, 881 City, rounded the corner and moved into the square to see the most frightful sight he would

Mitre Square, looking toward Church Passage. Kearley & Tonge is seen on the left. Site of Catharine Eddowes' murder is just to the right of this view.

ever see while on duty with the police force. "The clothes were pushed up to her breast, and the stomach was laid bare, with a dreadful gash from the pit of the stomach to the breast. On examining the body I found the entrails cut and laid round the throat, which had an awful gash in it, extending from ear-to-ear. In fact, *the head was nearly severed from the body*. The murderer had inserted the knife just under the left eye, and, drawing it under the nose, cut the nose completely from the face...."

The Ripper had enjoyed that kill, but his work was not yet complete for the night. He would leave a cryptic clue, which has never been fully explained, other than to mislead the authorities. The killer had wiped his blade on a section of Eddowes' apron and thrown it on the ground. Above the bloody apron on a wall was the message, freshly written in white chalk:

> The Juwes are
> The men That
> Will not

be Blamed
for nothing

The message was found on Goulston Street, only a few blocks from the George Yard buildings, and it was towards George Yard that the killer had traveled after the Mitre Square event. This was a major clue to his location, and the authorities were quick to react to that clue. But before they could deploy, the Thames Torso Killer would get in on the act and drop off a torso right under the noses of the police. He would leave it in the deep cellar of the then under construction Police Headquarters at Whitehall. The torso was found on October 2, and the authorities had had enough. It was time to do something dramatic — and soon!

Catharine Eddowes, Ripper victim.

The *New York Times* — October 3, 1888

The Whitechapel assassin has now murdered six victims and crimes occur daily, but pass unnoticed in view of the master murderer's work in the East End

Waves of shock flowed over the East End of London as news of the double murders hit the now fully terrified population. Mobs began to gather at both murder sites, protesting the inability of London's finest to catch the Ripper. The press, as would be expected, flooded the city with as many copies of their papers as possible, with reports of murder and homicidal monomania. These crowds would last for days, as street venders

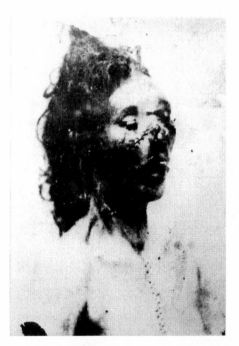
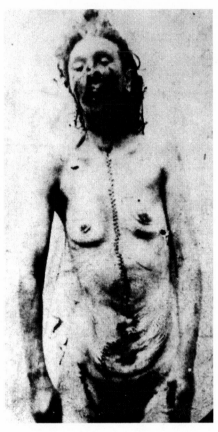

Catharine Eddowes autopsy photos.

were set up near the murder sites selling food and drink to the assembled crowds. The police, for their part, redoubled their efforts and questioned over 2000 lodgers in the general area of both murder sites. Added to this effort were 80,000 handbills handed out to nearly every household in the area.

POLICE NOTICE.
TO THE OCCUPIER

On the mornings of Friday, 31st August, Saturday 8th, and Sunday, 30th September, 1888, Women were murdered in or near Whitechapel, supposed by some one residing in the immediate neighborhood. Should you know of any person to whom suspicion is attached, you are earnestly requested to communicate at once with the nearest Police Station.

Metropolitan Police Office, 30th September, 1888

On October 16 the head of the Mile End Vigilance Committee, builder George Lusk, received a package in the mail. It would contain the only authentic communication from the serial killer known as Jack the Ripper. Along with a poorly worded note, the killer had sent something that no imposter could ever send. The small brown package contained half of a human kidney, which had been preserved in spirits of wine. The note appeared to have been penned by an individual who was just a bit too busy at the time to spend any time hunting humans, but that would soon change.

> From hell
>
> Mr Lusk
> Sor
> I send you half the
> Kidne I took from one woman
> prasarved it for you t other piece I
> fried and ate it was very nise I
> may send you the bloody knif that
> took it out if you only wate a whil
> longer
> Signed Catch me when
> you can
> Mishter Lusk

The Ripper now had one less piece of flesh to be concerned with, but he still had several others and he would need to be very careful when he transported them. If he were going to move, now would be a good time, as time was running out in the "wicked quarter mile." The authorities had devised a plan to conduct a detailed search of the prime area. They were not so much expecting to locate a killer (through that would have been just the ticket), but they were trying to show the public that something grand and dramatic was being done for the protection of the population. As it turned out, Junior Surgeon Severin Klosowski both lived and worked in the center of the search area, but not for long!

Personal memo—Sir Robert Anderson

> One did not need to be a Sherlock Holmes to discover that the criminal was a sexual maniac of a virulent type; that he was living in the immediate vicinity of the scenes of the murders.

The great Ripper search would begin on October 13, but no one was prevented from moving about or leaving the area, so the police were not really looking for an individual; they were looking for physical evidence in the form of a weapon or body parts. It was an unprecedented operation which was bounded by Albert Street, Dunk Street, Chicksand Street and Great Garden Street on the east; by Lamb, Commercial and Buxton Streets and the Great Eastern Railway to the north; by the central City of London on the west; and by Whitechapel Road on the south. And, although no evidence was recovered, the massive search did serve to calm the East End population. This was something they could understand and, for the most part, fully cooperate with. The Ripper, however, was no longer in the area, but he was still very close, very close indeed.

London's Finest Hunt for a Madman

> I am quite prepared to take the responsibility of adopting the most drastic or arbitrary measures that the Secretary of State can name which would further the securing of the murderer, however illegal they may be...— Sir Charles Warren

Londoners had never seen anything quite like it, but if the Whitechapel Killer was going to be found it had to be done. It would involve a great many men, and the inhabitants of the East End might put up a fight. However, Sir Charles, Metropolitan Police Commissioner, was willing to go as far as he could in order to find the killer's hiding place. With only minimal backing from Her Majesty's government, Warren ordered a house-to-house search of a large section of the East End. It would become the largest, most detailed search in London's long history, and it would uncover nothing. But, just perhaps, that was not the point.

> The Rt. Hon. Henry Matthews　　　　　　Buccleuch House,
> 　　　　　Q.C.M.P.　　　　　　　　　　　Richmond
> 　　　　　　　　　　　　　　　　　　　　Oct. 3. 1888
>
> My dear Matthews
>
> There is no doubt but that the Whitechapel murderer remains in the neighbourhood.—Draw a cordon of half a mile round the centre & search every house.—This would surely unearth him.
> It is a strong thing to do, but I should think such occasion never before arose.—
> I should say he is an American Slaughterman, an occupation largely followed in South America.
>
> 　　　　　　　　　　　　　Truly Yours
> 　　　　　　　　　　　　　J. Whittaker Ellis

Within governmental halls, those in or near power debated the best ways to approach the problem. All knew there were no laws covering such actions. And even though illegal searches had been conducted in the past, never had such a wide scale operation been conducted or even planned.

Smaller illegal searches had been conducted on a case-by-case basis, but only when a suspect was known and the authorities had a good idea where to locate the individual.

Memo Whitechapel Vestry Clerk

Oct 4 1888 Whitechapel Murders
Resolution of the Vestry expressing sorrow at the murders, and urging the government to use their utmost endeavour to discover the criminals

The Home Office at Whitehall received the resolution from the Parish of St. Mary Whitechapel. Secretary of State Henry Matthews replied that all would be done that could be done to catch the killer or killers committing these two sets of crimes. A letter was then sent to the Parish, with copies published in the *Pall Mall Gazette* and the *Daily News*.

The Clerk to the Vestry of the Parish of   Whitehall
St. Mary, Whitechapel   6 October 1888
5 Great Prescot St, Whitechapel E
Sir,

I am directed by the Secretary of State to acknowledge the receipt of your letter of the 4th instant forwarding a copy of a Resolution of the Vestry of the Parish of St. Mary Whitechapel, expressing sorrow at the recent murders in the east of London and urging the Government to use their utmost endeavour to discover the criminals, and I am to state that Mr. Matthews shares the feelings of the Vestry with regard to these murders that the Police have instructions to exercise every power they possess in their efforts to discover the murderer, and that the Secretary of State after personal conference with the Commissioner in which all the difficulties of the case have been fully discussed, is satisfied that no means will be spared in tracing the offender and bringing him to justice.

I am,
Sir,
Your obedient Servant,
(sd) E. Leigh Pemberton.

By October 4 Sir Charles Warren had reviewed the letter sent to the Secretary of State by Sir John W. Ellis, the former Lord Mayor of London, as well as the resolution by the members of the Whitechapel Vestry. And although Warren was more than willing to take whatever legal or illegal means he could to capture the killers in the East End, he was not sure the government would back him or his officers. In fact, Warren went so far as to bring up the possibility that one or more of his own police officers could be held accountable — and hung — if any lives were lost during any illegal search efforts. His letter to the private secretary of Home Secretary Matthews, Evelyn Ruggles-Brise, brings home the problems and concerns of the Police Commissioner whose back was most decidedly up against the wall.

4 Oct 1888

Dear Mr. Ruggles Brise,
I return Sir W Ellis letter

　　I am quite prepared to take the responsibility of adopting the most drastic or arbitrary measures that the Sec of State can name which would further the securing of the murderer however illegal they may be, provided H.M. Gov. will support me. But I must observe that the Sec of State cannot authorize me to do an illegal action and that the full responsibility will always rest with me over the Police Constables for anything done.
　　All I want to ensure is that the Government will indemnify us for our actions which must necessarily be adapted to the circumstances of the case — the exact course of which cannot be always forseen.
　　I have been accustomed to work under such circumstances in what were nearly Civil wars at the [*illegible*] & then the Government passed acts of Indemnity for those who have gone beyond the law.
　　Three weeks ago I do not think the public would have acquiesced in any illegal action but now I think they would welcome any thing, which shows activity & enterprise.
　　Of course the danger of taking such a course, as that proposed by Sir W. Ellis is that if we did not find the murderer our actions would be condemned — and there is the danger that an illegal act of such a character might bond the Social Democrats together to resist the Police & might be then said to have caused a serious riot. — I think I may say without hesitation that those houses could not be searched illegally without violent resistance & blood shed and the certainty of one or more Police Officers being killed & the question is whether it is worth while losing the lives of several of the community & risking serious riot in order to search for one murderer whose whereabouts is not known.
　　I have ascertained from Mr. Williamson that he thinks that though under certain circumstances such action might be adopted or should not be justified at present in doing so such an illegal act. We have in times past done such a thing on a very much smaller scale but then we had certain information that person was concealed in the house [*illegible*] In this matter I have not only myself to think of but the lives & protection of 12,000 men, any one of whom might be hanged if a death occurred in entering a house illegally.

Truly Yours
Charles Warren

The highest levels of British government had thus been informed.

The Home Secretary wasted little time answering Warren's letter by the next post. He suggested that Warren instruct the police under his command to enter and search only those houses "which appear suspicious upon the best inquiry your detectives can make." The problem with that suggestion was clear. Warren had implied in his letter that he had no such information to work from, only a general idea of where the killer could be found. No single house or business was under suspicion. And with no specific location to search, a warrant would be unlikely to have been issued for any search. Beyond that, the Home Secretary could only write that Warren should "keep the houses under observation." Clearly the highest levels of government were not about to place their own political fortunes on the line to catch a murderer or two in ghettos of the East End. The question is asked whether or not the British Government would have acted in the same way if the murders had occurred in the rich and powerful West End of London. Warren was on his own, and he knew it.

For more than a week Warren tried to find governmental support for the massive search, but only general acceptance would be offered. By that time the ever-searching newspapers had gotten wind of a search to be conducted in and around Whitechapel. One paper even reported that the killer could be "found between Brick Lane and Middlesex Street." It was a very good guess, as there was at least one serial killer living and working between those two streets— Severin Klosowski on George Yard! By October 13 Warren, with little government support, began his search operation. By then the Whitechapel Killer had been fully warned by an overactive press and was likely, if he was smart, moving out of the area as fast as he could carry his hard won body parts with him.

On October 13, 1888, the grand search began with officers entering as many homes and businesses as they could. The area, however, was not cordoned off, as people were allowed to come and go as they pleased. The area was bounded on the west by the City of London; on the east by Albert Street, Dunk Street, Great Garden Street and Chicksand Street; on the south by Whitechapel Road; and on the north by Buxton Street and the Great Eastern Railway. George Yard and the George Yard Dwellings were in the center of the search area!

For five days Commissioner Warren's plainclothes officers moved from street to street and house to house looking into each room, checking each cabinet and storage area and even looking under beds. As would be expected, they also interviewed all of the men found in the area and inspected each and every knife they could find.

The officers soon found that the population, whom they had expected would be difficult to deal with, were for the most part more than cooperative in the effort. And although only those places where the occupants gave permission to search were examined, very few people caused any problems and most buildings were searched. A surprised and quite pleased Warren would report that "with few exceptions the inhabitants of all classes and creeds have fallen in with the proposal and have materially assisted the officers engaged in carrying it out." The cooperation and indeed "material help" of the East End residents was remarkable considering the long-lived mistrust on both sides. This unexpected cooperation would long be noted as an example of what could be done when the government and its people worked together for a common goal.

By October 18 the job was done, and although no solid evidence of the killer or killers was found, the East End residents at least had something to point to to show that official and grand efforts had been made on their behalf. The radical newspaper the *Star* was quick to point out that the effort had been great; and for the *Star*, whose editorial comments and news reports were anything but complementary to the police, that was a major turnaround in its reporting. "The failure of the police to discover the Whitechapel murderer is certainly not due to inactivity. No one who has occasion to visit the police officers whence the investigations are being conducted can escape the impression that everybody is on the move, and it is probably a fact that very few of the chief officials and detectives have had their regular rest since last Sunday morning. One hears no complaint against the demand for extra duty, except in instances where the pressure is unevenly applied, for the police are individually more interested in the capture of the murderer than anyone else."

Confidential memo—Sir Robert Anderson

> Oct 24, 1888. The public generally and especially the inhabitants of the East End have shown a marked desire to assist in everyway, even at some sacrifice to themselves, as for example in permitting their houses to be searched.

Did the police interview the killer? Very probably. And if they did, this serial killer would have seemed quite at home in the East End. He was part of all that seemed normal in the Victorian ghetto of Whitechapel. Did the police search his home? Yes! There is very little argument on where the killer must have lived in order to kill as many people as he did in such a small area of London. Yet he had so much time to simply move his collected body parts that even a general search of his rooms or workplace would have found nothing out of the ordinary in the East End of 1888.

The search had indeed been grand, but the effort had failed because it had been conducted fully and completely out in the open and by the most legal means available. The police did not get their man but the people kept their rights, and in the end it would be the people themselves who would force these killers out of the area.

The search did have the effect of slowing down the attacks, but the Ripper was not about to be stopped as long as he felt the need to kill. Even though, for the most part, the streets were no longer a safe hunting ground, there were all those prostitutes who "worked" alone in small rented rooms throughout the district. He would find his next target in the form of 25-year-old prostitute Mary Jane Kelly. Kelly, most interestingly, had lived for a short period of time, only a few months earlier, in either George Street or George Yard in the George Yard Dwellings, depending on the source.

On that early rainy morning of November 9, 1888, Mary Jane walked the cold streets of Whitechapel looking for a customer. It was a wet and miserable night as she located a man whom she seemed to have known from an earlier time. She invited him into her tiny room at 13 Miller's Court, just off of Dorset Street, and closed the door. The Ripper had thus

13 Millers Court: site of Mary Kelly's murder.

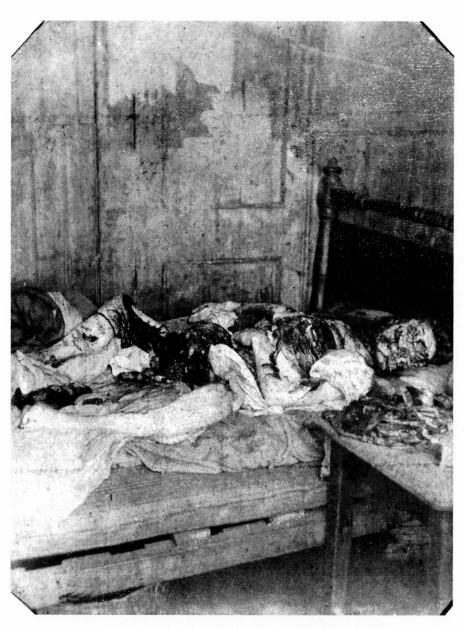

Mary Jane Kelly, only victim photographed in situ.

been given the opportunity to do whatever he wanted for as long as he wished with Mary Jane. He took full advantage of the situation as he tore into her body while her corpse lay on the bed. From Doctor Thomas Bond, who would be called upon to examine the body, came a report that "The whole of the surface of the abdomen and thighs was removed and the abdominal cavity emptied of its viscera. The breasts were cut off, the arms mutilated by several jagged wounds and the face hacked beyond recognition of the features ... the uterus and kidneys with one breast [were found] under the head, the other breast by the right foot, the liver between the feet, the intestines by the side...."

It would be the most destructive attack ever to occur in the Ripper series. And it would be this brutal attack which would fully destroy the people's confidence in the police's ability to catch this killer. No longer was the killer satisfied to work the streets, he was now invading the very homes of the women of the East End.

In a letter, now to be found in the Public Record Office, to Robert Anderson, then head of the CID, Dr. Thomas Bond reported on his thoughts concerning the ongoing Whitechapel murders on November 10, 1888. He had just finished his post-mortem on Mary Jane Kelly when he put down his thoughts on the murder series.

7 The Sanctuary,
Westminster Abbey
November 10th '88

Dear Sir,

Whitechapel Murders
I beg to report that I have read the notes of the four Whitechapel Murders viz-:

1. Buck's Row
2. Hanbury Street
3. Berners Street
4. Mitre Square

I have also made a Post Mortem Examination of the mutilated remains of a woman found yesterday in a small room in Dorset Street-:

1. All five murders were no doubt committed by the same hand. In the first four the throats appear to have been cut from left to right, in the last case owing to the extensive mutilation it is impossible to say in what direction the fatal cut was made, but arterial blood was found on the wall in splashes close to where the woman's head must have been lying.

2. All the circumstances surrounding the murders lead me to form the opinion that the women must have been lying down when murdered and in every case the throat was first cut.

3. In the four murders of which I have seen the notes only, I cannot form a very definite opinion as to the time that had elapsed between the murder and the discovery of the body. In one case, that of Berners Street the discovery appears to have been immediately after the deed. In Buck's Row, Hanbury St., and Mitre Square three or four hours only could have

elapsed. In the Dorset Street case the body was lying on the bed at the time of my visit two o'clock quite naked and mutilated as in the annexed report. Rigor Mortis had set in but increased during the progress of the examination. From this it is difficult to say with any degree of certainty the exact time that had elapsed since death as the period varies from six to twelve hours before rigidity sets in. The body was comparatively cold at two o'clock and the remains of a recently taken meal were found in the stomach and scattered about over the intestines. It is therefore, pretty certain that the woman must have been dead about twelve hours and the partly digested food would indicate that death took place about three or four hours after food was taken, so one or two o'clock in the morning would be the probable time of the murder.

4. In all the cases there appears to be no evidence of struggling and the attacks were probably so sudden and made in such a position that the women could neither resist nor cry out. In the Dorset St. case the corner of the sheet to the right of the woman's head was much cut and saturated with blood, indicating that the face may have been covered with the sheet at the time of the attack.

5. In the first four cases the murderer must have attacked from the right side of the victim. In the Dorset Street case, he must have attacked from the left, as there would be no room for him between the wall and the part of the bed on which the woman was lying. Again the blood had flowed down on the right side of the woman and spurted on to the wall.

6. The murderer would not necessarily be splashed or deluged with blood, but his hands and arms must have been covered and parts of his clothing must certainly have been smeared with blood.

7. The mutilations in each case excepting the Berners Street one were all of the same character and showed clearly that in all the murders the object was mutilation.

8. In each case the mutilation was inflicted by a person who had no scientific nor anatomical knowledge. In my opinion he does not even possess the technical knowledge of a butcher or horse slaughterer or any person accustomed to cut up dead animals.

9. The instrument must have had been a strong knife at least six inches long, very sharp, pointed at the top and about an inch in width. It may have been a clasp knife, a butcher's knife or a surgeon's knife, I think it was no doubt a straight knife.

10. The murderer must have been a man of physical strength and of great coolness and daring. There is no evidence that he had an accomplice. He must in my opinion be a man subject to periodical attacks of Homicidal and erotic mania. The character of the mutilations, indicate that the man may be in a condition sexually, that may be called Satyriasis. It is of course possible that the Homicidal impulse may have developed from a revengeful or brooding condition of the mind, or that religious mania may have been the original disease but I do not think either hypothesis is likely. The murderer in external appearance is quite likely to be a quiet inoffensive looking man probably middle-aged and neatly and

respectably dressed. I think he must be in the habit of wearing a cloak or overcoat or he could hardly have escaped notice in the streets if the blood on his hands or clothes were visible.

11. Assuming the murderer to be such a person as I have just described, he would be solitary and eccentric in his habits, also he is most likely to be a man without regular occupation, but with some small income or pension. He is possibly living among respectable persons who have some knowledge of his character and habits and who may have grounds for suspicion that he isn't quite right in his mind at times. Such persons would probably be unwilling to communicate suspicions to the Police for fear of trouble or notoriety, whereas if there were prospect of reward it might overcome their scruples.

Dr. Thomas Bond

The London *Times* reported that "The excitement in the neighborhood of Dorset Street is intense, and some of the low women with whom the street abounds appear more like fiends than human beings. The police have great trouble to preserve order, and one constable, who is alleged to have struck an onlooker, was so mobbed and hooted that he had to beat a retreat to Commercial Street Police Station, whither he was followed by a huge crowd, which was only kept at bay by the presence of about half a dozen constables, who stood at the door and prevented anyone from entering."

It would be the murder and butchering of Mary Jane Kelly that would cause the authorities to issue an extraordinary document. Commissioner of Police Sir Charles Warren wrote out a "Queen's Pardon."

> MURDER — PARDON — Whereas on November 8 or 9, in Miller's Court, Dorset Street, Spitalfields, Mary Janet [sic] Kelly was murdered by some person or persons unknown: the Secretary of State will advise the grant of Her Majesty's gracious pardon to any accomplice, not being a person who contrived or actually committed the murder, who shall give such information and evidence as shall lead to the discovery and conviction of the person or persons who committed the murder.
>
> CHARLES WARREN, the Commissioner of Police
of the Metropolis
Metropolitan Police Office, 4 Whitehall Place,
S. W., Nov. 10, 1888

Men were now being dragged from the streets and some were not being brought to local police stations in the best of shape. One man was nearly clubbed to death by an angry mob when he stupidly claimed to be the killer. The police arrived just in time to drag him, bloody but alive, away from an angry mob to a local station and then to the hospital. Despite all of this agitation, Severin Klosowski, local friendly barber, continued his late night "walks" around the East End.

From Queen Victoria came a letter to the Home Secretary, Henry Matthews; official London was starting to worry.

> The Queen fears that the detective department is not so efficient as it might be.
> No doubt the recent murders in Whitechapel were committed in circumstances which made detection very difficult; still, the Queen thinks that, in the small area where these horrible crimes have been perpetrated, a great number of detectives might be employed and that every possible suggestion might be carefully examined, and, if practicable, followed.
> Have the cattle boats and passenger boats been examined?
> Has any investigation been made as to the number of single men occupying rooms to themselves?
> The murderer's clothes must be saturated with blood and kept somewhere.
> Is there sufficient surveillance at night?
> These are some of the questions that occur to the Queen on reading the accounts of these horrible crimes.

As 1888 was coming to a close, the East End would see the death of one more local prostitute, but this one would be away from the central Ripper area. Her body would be found in a dirt lot used to store building materials located between 184 and 186 Poplar High Street. Rose Mylett had been strangled, but not ripped, with her body then dumped on the lot. She had been murdered fully two miles away from Whitechapel to the east, and yet she had lived in central Whitechapel. It is interesting to note that she had been killed only a few blocks away from where barber Klosowski had lived and worked when he first came to London, at Abraham Radin's Hair Dressing Shop. It was an area Klosowski knew very well. Even though the police attempted to report that this was not a murder, the coroner would have none of it. As Coroner Wynne Baxter would later put it, "...this nonsense of death by natural causes" would not stand.

"Wilful murder by person or persons unknown."

The bloody year of 1888 was over; the Ripper was firmly at his new location, taking a murder break for seven months. In fact, the New Year would see "only" one Ripper murder, while the Thames Torso Killer would send two to their deaths, and this time one of his victims would be identified. The papers of June 4, 1889, would be busy detailing the Torso

Murder of Elizabeth Jackson. Once again the name of Jack the Ripper came to the forefront, but the public response was much less than only ten months earlier when Jack was, as they say, "doing his thing." Was Jack or the Torso Killer behind bars on some unrelated charge for a time period, or had the "work"simply become too great a burden to bear? Since neither man was ever officially captured, that question may never be answered. As for most of the people of London, the events of 1888 were best kept in the past. Both Jack and the Torso Killer had other ideas however, as official London strained to keep the hunt funded. Police protection in many other areas was starting to fall through the cracks.

> *In the present state of the force, increase of protection in the East End means diminished numbers of police in other quarters ... any additional drain on its resources leads to diminished protection elsewhere, and consequent increase of crime...*
> Mr. Howard Vincent — House of Commons

The police forces were stretched to the limits of their abilities to protect the population from themselves, and with that in mind the public, and members of the many vigilance committees, were told that the Ripper was either dead or locked away in an insane asylum. These lies would last only as long as the Ripper suspended his crime spree. They would also hold firm as long as any new murders were not placed firmly into Jack's column, whether he did them or not.

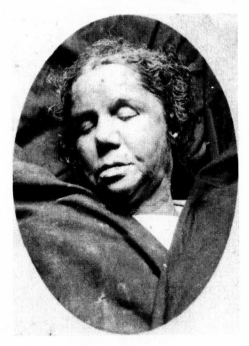

The respite ended in the early morning of July 17, 1889. At 12:45 A.M., Constable Joseph Allen was walking his regular beat along Old Castle Street. He had last been through the alley 27 minutes earlier and had seen nothing unusual. This time, however, as he turned into Castle Alley, only a few steps from a street lamp, he found the still warm body of Alice McKenzie. Blood was still flowing from two four-inch jagged gashes on the left side of her throat. It was the same

Alice McKenzie

New-York, Thursday, July 18, 1889.

THE WHITECHAPEL CRIME.

NO CLUE TO THE PERPETRATOR OF THE LATEST MURDER.

LONDON, July 17.—The woman whose body was found in Castle-alley, in the Whitechapel district, last night was a middle-aged female of the disreputable class. Her throat had been cut to the spine. When the body was found it was lying on its back. The abdomen had been slashed in a horrible manner in several places. No part of the body was missing. Warm blood was flowing from the wounds when the body was discovered.

A policeman, who with the watchman of an adjacent warehouse must have been within a few yards of the spot when the crime was committed, heard no noise. Policemen have been placed at fixed points in Whitechapel since the murders of this character began there, and since the one preceding that of last night officers have been stationed at a point within a hundred yards of the scene of the last tragedy. An old clay pipe smeared with blood was found alongside the body. It is supposed by the

New York Times, July 18, 1889, report on the latest murder by Jack the Ripper.

type of wound which had been inflicted on Ada Wilson almost 16 months earlier. This time, however, the attack had been fully successful, to include a gash on her abdomen. The killer must have been close by as the officer turned into the area. It must have been a very narrow escape.

Even before the body could be investigated by police doctors, official London was well into its propaganda campaign to undermine any attempt to credit this killing to the Ripper. There were no funds to expand the massive investigation, which had continued but had been greatly reduced since the start of 1889. Yet this was a murder, and she was killed in the central Ripper killing zone with a knife. If this was not the work of the Ripper then the East End of London had a new problem to deal with—a new serial killer was in town!

The final murder in the Ripper series would not occur until 18 months had passed, and to this day no one knows why it took so long to happen. Perhaps the killer was busy with family matters or other "works" in other places, such as America, or perhaps he had been jailed on other charges. He was, after all is said and done, a criminal.

The New York Times—February 13, 1891

Jack the Ripper Again
Another Woman Murdered and her Body Mangled

London, Feb. 13.—A renewal of the "Jack the Ripper" scare terrorizes that quarter of the city where the performances of the mysterious murderer have heretofore been the cause of so much alarm. At an early hour this morning the body of a young woman was discovered in a secluded locality in Chambers Street. She had been horribly gashed with a sharp instrument. Nothing is yet known as to who she is or who her murderer was. The woman's head had been severed almost entirely from the body, and it was a ghastly spectacle that met those who viewed the remains. Detectives quickly began a search for the murderer.

On February 13, 1891, almost three years to the day when the attacks began, they suddenly ended with the murder of Frances Coles. Coles was found under a railway arch at Swallow Gardens with her throat deeply and skillfully cut twice. The officer who found her was on the scene so quickly that he not only heard the killer slowly walk away into a deeply foggy night only yards away, he saw Frances open then close one of her eyes before she died. Much as he wanted to run after the attacker, the officer's first duty was to stay with Frances and protect her as best he could.

In a little less than three years the Ripper had killed nine women and unsuccessfully attacked two others. He began with Annie Millwood, who

Frances Coles

lived in a common lodging house in Spitalfields. His last victim would also live in that very same building. And, no matter how hard the police had tried, no one would ever be brought before a judge and jury for any of the Ripper murders. The circle had been completed, as the Ripper slowly walked out of the East End of London and passed into criminal history. And along with him went the terror which he had brought to that desperate ghetto of the late 19th century, in a time long to be remembered as the "Autumn of Terror."

Years later, as a postscript to the events of the Ripper and other murder cases, Inspector Abberline would answer questions of a possible cover-up from official London in a scrapbook he had put together for a friend, Mr. Walter Green.

> Why I did not write my Reminiscences when I retired from the Metro-
> politan Police. I think it is just as well to record here the reason why as
> from the various cuttings from the newspapers as well as the many other
> matters that I was called upon to investigate — that never became public
> property. It must be apparent that I could write many things that would
> be very interesting to read. At the time I retired from the service the
> authorities were very much opposed to retired officers writing anything
> for the press as previously some retired officers had from time to time
> been very indiscreet in what they had caused to be published and to my
> knowledge had been called upon to explain their conduct and in fact they
> had been threatened with actions for libel.
>
> Apart from that there is no doubt the fact that in describing what you
> did in detecting certain crimes you are putting the criminal classes on
> their guard and in some cases you may be absolutely telling them how to
> commit crime.
>
> As an example in the finger print detection you find now the expert
> thief wears gloves.
>
> F. G. Abberline

Descriptions of Jack the Ripper

Witness	Description
Annie Millwood	"The man was a stranger."
Ada Wilson	"He was a man of around 30 years of age with a sunburnt face, fair mustache, standing 5'-6" in height."
Elizabeth Long	"Dark complexion, and was wearing a brown deerstalker hat. He was a man over forty, [from behind] as far as I can tell. He seemed a little taller than the deceased. He looked to me like a foreigner as well as I could make out. He looked what I should call shabby genteel."
Joseph Lawende	30 years old, 5'-7" in height, fair complexion and mustache, medium build, wearing a salt and pepper colored jacket fitting loosely, gray cloth cap with a peak of the same color. Reddish handkerchief knotted around his neck.
Matthew Parker	Age 25 to 30 years old, 5'-7" tall. Long black coat buttoned up, soft felt hawker hat, broad shoulders.
P.C. William Smith	5'-7" tall, hard dark felt deerstalker hat, dark clothes. Carried newspaper package 18"×7", 28 years old, dark complexion, small dark mustache.
James Brown	5'-5" tall, age 30, dark complexion, small mustache, black diagonal coat, hard felt hat, collar and tie.

Israel Shwartz   Age 30, 5'-5" tall, dark haired, fair complexion, small brown mustache, full face, broad shoulders, dark jacket and trousers, black cap with peak.

George Hutchinson Age 34 to 35, 5'-6". Pale complexion, dark hair, slight mustached curled at each end, long dark coat, collar cuffs of astrakhan, dark jacket underneath. Light waistcoat, thick gold chain with a red stone seal, dark trousers and button boots, gaiters, white buttons. White shirt, black tie fastened with a horseshoe pin. Dark hat, turned down in the middle. Red kerchief. Jewish and respectable in appearance.

Martha Tabram

Mary Ann (Polly) Nichols

Frances Coles

THE VICTIMS

OF

Jack

the

Ripper

Annie Chapman

Alice McKenzie

Elizabeth Stride

Mary Jane Kelly

Catharine Eddowes

Photographs from the Public Records Office Image Library.

The Ripper's Victims

February 25, 1888	Annie Millwood (1850–1888)	Stab wounds on legs and lower torso with a clasp knife (survived the attack)
March 28, 1888	Ada Wilson (1849–)	At home when attacked by an unknown man. Stabbed twice in the throat (survived the attack)
August 7, 1888	Martha Tabram (1849–1888)	39 stab wounds; five in left lung, two in right lung, one in heart, five in liver, two in spleen, six in stomach
August 31, 1888	Mary Ann Nichols (1845–1888)	Throat cut down to the vertebrae, cut abdomen several times
September 8, 1888	Annie Chapman (1841–1888)	Strangled? Throat cut deeply, abdomen laid open; uterus, upper vagina and posterior two-thirds of bladder taken
September 30, 1888	Elizabeth Stride (1843–1888)	Throat cut deeply, not mutilated
September 30, 1888	Catharine Eddowes (1842–1888)	Throat cut deeply, face mutilated, body opened from breast bone to pubes, liver stabbed, kidney and womb taken
November 9, 1888	Mary Jane Kelly (1863–1888)	Attacked inside. Throat cut deeply, body and face greatly mutilated, parts removed, heart taken, most mutilated victim
December 20, 1888	Rose Mylett (1863–1888)	Strangled by a cord
July 17, 1889	Alice McKenzie (1849–1889)	Stabbed twice in throat, cut on chest from left breast to navel
Feb 13, 1891	Francis Coles (1866–1891)	Throat cut twice, found still alive

Chapter 7

The Torso Murder of Elizabeth Jackson — 1889

It was opened and thought to contain a human thigh.
— Sergeant William Briggs, quoted in the *Times* of London,
June 5, 1889

THE TORSO PACE QUICKENS!

Jack the Ripper was dead! At least that was how London authorities were playing the propaganda game. As for the Ripper himself—"Not bloody likely!" Nevertheless, the new year of 1889 had been a whole lot less violent in the East End of London as far as murders were concerned. Other types of crime were, however, continuing to increase, and the Torso Killer was about to fill the murder void. This time, however, the victim would have a name, and once again Londoners would react to a vicious murder as body part after body part was found along the river Thames. All of London would soon know that a new victim had met the Thames Torso Killer.

Elizabeth Jackson was, at the time of her death, a homeless prostitute. She was described by her mother, Catherine Jackson, as being "24-years-old, well formed, plump and around 5 feet 5 inches in height." She was further described as being "of fair complexion and reddish gold hair with a beautiful set of teeth and nicely shaped hands." Elizabeth was the youngest of three daughters born to Mr. and Mrs. Jackson, along with sisters Annie and May.

She did not start out to become a prostitute walking the streets of the East End, but things must have just gotten away from her. Elizabeth began work as a domestic servant in her hometown of Chelsea at the age of sixteen. It was 1881, and the work seemed to be well suited to her. She continued as a domestic, with reports of her "excellent character," until she suddenly left her home and her work in November 1888. She would never explain why, but it was clear that a man was somehow involved.

Not long after she had left her position she could be found walking the streets on Turk's Row in Chelsea. It was here that her sister Annie would meet her. Elizabeth had been speaking to a man, unknown to Annie, as Annie called to her. Elizabeth excused herself and went over to speak with her older sister. It was at that point that Annie accused Elizabeth of "picking up men for immoral purposes." This observation led to an argument, as would be expected, as an angry Elizabeth simply walked away. Annie would never see her younger sister alive again.

Not long after that November meeting, Elizabeth, still working the streets and pubs of Turk's Row, would meet a man named John Faircloth. After a few drinks, Elizabeth explained that she had been living with "a man named Charlie," possibly her "protector." This loose connection would not stop her from going off with Faircloth, who must at that point have realized that Elizabeth was, as they say, "easy." Nevertheless, they both went off to Ipswich together for at least the next four months, as her family lost complete track of her.

Faircloth was not the best of people to have gone off with, but at least he was no serial killer. He was later described in press accounts as being "a miller by trade and a native of Cambridgeshire." He was, at the time of their meeting, 37 years of age and had served in the 3rd Battalion of the Grenadier Guards. Described further as being of "fair complexion, 5 feet 9 inches in height, with a twisted nose," he would not have stood out in a crowd in the East End. He also had a temper, which was egged on by drink.

Together this unlikely pair found their way to Colchester on March 30, 1889, in a vain attempt to locate any type of work. Neither one was successful, so a lack of money forced them to walk all the way back to London where they ended up in Jack's Whitechapel. They soon found themselves living in one of the many dirty and crowded lodging houses which infected the East End slum. On April 18, John and Elizabeth moved into a small room at Mrs. Paine's Rooming House on Manila Street, Millwall, having "somehow located a bit of cash." According to Mrs. Paine, "the man called himself John Faircloth," and he was noted as being violent towards Elizabeth.

Once again the pair were without work, and Faircloth decided to try his luck in Croydon. By then Elizabeth had had quite enough of the abusive Mr. Faircloth and told him that she would not be going with him. She told him that she would go live with her mother, but this was a lie. Her mother was staying at a workhouse and was as homeless as Elizabeth. Nonetheless, Faircloth left Manila Street on April 28, never to see Elizabeth again. The next day, after a good night's sleep, and without her "friend" John, Elizabeth left her room at Mrs. Paines owing a week's rent. It was time to go back to her hometown of Chelsea.

Before long Elizabeth was spotted "walking the streets" of Chelsea by an old family friend, Mrs. Minter of Cheyne Road. Elizabeth told Mrs. Minter that she had been living with a man who did not treat her very well for the past few months, and he had left her penniless. In fact, she had been sleeping "out in the raw" for a few days on the river Thames Embankment. Mrs. Minter noted that she was dressed very shabbily and gave her threepence for a meal. She advised Elizabeth to go to the workhouse where she would at least be cared for. It was at this point that Elizabeth broke down crying and explained, "I don't like to do that because for one thing, my mother is there, and she would be angry with me, and, for another thing, I am expecting."

Mrs. Minter tried her best to comfort Elizabeth and gave her a long overcoat called an ulster. Giving her the coat, Mrs. Minter said, "At any rate, it will keep you warm." The next day Mrs. Minter once again ran into Elizabeth along the same street, and she was still wearing the long coat. This coat, soon to be cut to pieces, along with a small piece of linen marked with the name L. E. Fisher, would eventually lead to her identification as the third victim of the Thames Torso Killer. The second hand linen, which would be featured by the press, was purchased by John Faircloth for Elizabeth at an Ipswich lodging house.

Not long after Mrs. Minter's final encounter with Elizabeth, the young girl was seen by a woman named Annie Dwyer. Mrs. Dwyer saw her still wearing the ulster on the Monday before Whit Sunday. This must have been no more than one or two days before her murder. Annie, who lived on Turk's Row in Chelsea, would later report that Elizabeth was with a man who looked like he was in the Navy, wearing a dark cloth coat, light moleskin trousers and a rough cap. He may have been her killer, but he was more likely just one more customer of a Victorian prostitute named Elizabeth Jackson.

Catherine Jackson, quite by accident, saw her daughter on May 31,

1889. Mrs. Jackson was walking down Queen's Road in Chelsea when she spotted her youngest daughter. Calling to her, Elizabeth quickly turned around to walk away, but her mother pleaded for her to stop. After a long discussion, Elizabeth, still wearing her warm coat, agreed to spend the afternoon with her mother.

Elizabeth told her mother that she was expecting, which at the time would have been no real secret. The father was John Faircloth, who, she relayed to her mother, was unable to find any work and had abandoned her in Poplar, East End. It was then that her mother noticed a brass ring she was wearing to indicate that she was married. She, of course, was not. For both mother and daughter that long day was well spent, as they parted with kind words. It would be their last time together.

The *Times* of London—June 5, 1889

> Early yesterday morning, almost simultaneously, two packages containing portions of a woman's body were discovered on the foreshore of the Thames.

THE BLOODY THAMES

For John Regan it was going to be just one more day waiting for work as a waterside laborer along the river Thames. On June 4, however, as he was standing along the bank of the river at around 10:30 in the morning, near St. George's Stairs in Horselydown he spotted a couple of young boys "throwing stones at an object in the water." It was floating about three yards offshore and appeared to be wrapped in an apron. It had not been in the water very long. One of the boys pulled the package to the shore and it became immediately evident that it contained a portion of a woman's body. It was the first discovery to be made of the dissected corpse of Elizabeth Jackson.

It happened that one of the many Thames River Police boats was just then passing St. George's Stairs at the same time as the discovery. The police were called over and shown what had been discovered — to the officer's great astonishment. Constable Freshwater (his real name), No. 63 of the Thames Police, stationed at Wapping, would later testify that he was one of the officers on scene. "[At] about 11 o'clock [I] was called to the foreshore at Horselydown, and was handed a parcel containing what I thought were human remains. I took it to Wapping Station and sent for Doctor McCoy, who examined it." McCoy was the Assistant Divisional Surgeon for the Wapping area. At that point the authorities had no clue as to who had been murdered, or why. For that matter, they were not even sure a murder had been committed. All they really had were some body parts.

At about the same time, a young 15-year-old woodchopper named Isaac Brett, who lived at 7 Lawrence Street in Chelsea, was taking a walk along the Thames near the Albert Bridge. On the foreshore at Battersea, just under the bridge, he had decided to bathe himself. It was not long before he spotted a small parcel tied with a bootlace. At first he did not know what he was looking at and showed his find to a passing gentleman. The stranger advised the boy to bring his find to the police at once, which he did.

The package was taken to the local police station and given to Sergeant William Briggs of V Division. As reported in the *Times* of London on June 17, 1889, "It was opened and found to contain a thigh, wrapped in the right hand corner of a lady's ulster and portion of the right leg of a pair of drawers. The name of "L. E. Fisher" was marked on the band in black ink." The killer had somehow missed that clue. Or did he believe that the name would lead the police nowhere? It would be the only named piece of clothing in the series to ever be located. Police surgeon Dr. Kempster was immediately called to examine the remains. Dr. Kempster had been called into the Rainham case in 1887, so his knowledge of that killer's method would be very valuable in determining whether or not the same killer was at work two years later.

Later in the day the leg was taken to Dr. Bond of Westminster Hospital, as the case became the charge of Detective Inspector John Regan out of the Thames Division. Along with Regan came Detective Inspector Tunbridge of Scotland Yard. Dr. Bond left no doubt that both finds came from the same victim.

The *Times* of London—June 5, 1889

> In the opinion of the doctors the woman had been dead only 48 hours, and the body had been dissected somewhat roughly by a person who must have had some knowledge of the joints of the human body.

Once again London police were on the trail of a vicious killer. The Thames River Police began an immediate search of the foreshore on both sides of the river by boat, as city police investigated the shoreline on foot. The police forces also began to drag the waters near Vauxhall Bridge, one of the suspected dumping sites. Teams of police constables and inspectors searched under bridges, between docks and storage areas for any signs the killer had left more remains. They knew that the recovered remains had not been in the water for long and surmised that most of the remains had been dumped from one of the bridges spanning the Thames at about the same time. (This would later be proven incorrect as the killer returned again and again to dispose of his latest victim.) They also knew that the faster they could recover the remains the better chance they had of finding her killer.

In order to slow the decomposition, the recovered body parts had been "carefully preserved in sprits," on orders from Doctor Felix Kempster. Dr. Kempster reported, after his preliminary examination, that the left thigh had a "very fresh appearance" and that "the woman to whom it belonged could not have been dead more than 24 hours when it was deposited in the water. There are four bruises, as if from fingers on the thigh, and these, there is no doubt, were caused during life." It would become clear, after other remains were found, that Elizabeth did not give up her life easily!

As was the case less than a year earlier on the Ripper matter, this death had occurred on Coroner Wynne E. Baxter's "patch." He was the flamboyant coroner for the South-East Division of Middlesex, and once again he found himself in the center of a series of brutal murders, perhaps even more vicious than the case which had made his name world famous. He opened his inquiry at the Vestry Hall in Wapping, even as more remains were being found along the banks of the Thames. It would be a short hearing on the first day, however, because Mr. Baxter felt that he only needed to establish that a possible murder had been committed. "The inquiry would then be adjourned to give the police an opportunity of further inquiring into the case." The inquiry was then adjourned for a month, which was an unusually long period of time. It would not be long, however, before a great deal more "evidence" came floating by!

Early in the afternoon of June 6, Joseph Davis was working as usual as a gardener in Battersea Park. The park overlooked the Thames, and the property came to an end on the river's edge. It was a bit before 2 P.M. as he worked in a generally secluded area of shrubbery at the bank's edge. The park gates were not opened until 5 A.M., and it could be shown that the closest gate to the discovery was at least 200 yards distance. However, no one was stationed at that gate, which was close to Albert Bridge, so entry could not be excluded. It was very close to the spot where a thigh had been recovered only days earlier. As he worked among the shrubbery, Davis discovered what he called "a curious looking bundle" about 25 yards from the wrought iron fence. He slowly opened the linen wrapped package and found, to his very great shock, some human remains. The remains could not have floated there, and had to have been carefully placed where they were found.

At first the humble gardener dropped the package, which was tied together with a white venetian blind cord, and stood back, not really knowing what to do. He quickly recovered, however, enough to find the nearest constable who patrolled the park perimeter. Police Constable Ainger, 502 V Division, would later testify that Davis "called me to the shrubbery and showed me the parcel, which contained the upper part of a woman's body." It would not take long for both men to convey this latest find to the police station. From there it was taken to Battersea Mortuary where it was examined by the assistant divisional police surgeon.

When the package, wrapped in brown paper, along with a section of a plum colored skirt, was opened, it revealed the upper section of a female trunk. The police surgeon would report, "The chest cavity was empty, but many internal organs, including the spleen, both kidneys, and a portion of the stomach intestines, were present. The lower six dorsal vertebra were in their place, but the five lower ribs were missing. A portion of the midriff above the breasts and the integumentary covering to the chest bone were cut down the center, as though by a saw. The ribs also were sawn through. Decomposition had set in, but had proceeded no further than was consistent with the assumption that the remains formed part of a living body not more than four, or at the most five, days previously."

Around noon on the same day a barge builder named Charles Martowe, who lived on Wye Street in Battersea, found more body parts as he worked on the river just off of Copington's Wharf. As he worked, he spotted "the neck, shoulder, the first and second ribs, and the liver, and these have been examined and pronounced to be part of the same body as the other portions. All that remains to be found now, in order to piece the various parts into a complete whole, are the head, the two arms, one thigh, and two legs from the knees downwards." (The report of a recovered neck was in error.) His discovery was given to Inspector William Law of the Thames Police at Waterloo Pier. Inspector Law stated that "…if the parcel had been put in at Battersea at the flood time, it would have had time to reach where it was found." A find of flesh was also reported to have been located by an engineer named David Keen in the river just off of Palace Wharf. It was also handed over to the police.

The *Times* of London—June 7, 1889

> In fact, the entire makeup of the ghastly parcel was exactly similar to the others, and the work was evidently done by the same hands.

The police felt they finally had a real clue to the woman's identity when they received a letter from Oxfordshire, a small town north of London. The letter informed the authorities that a woman named L. E. Fisher was a native of Oxford whose description was said to be identical to the published description of the body parts then being recovered at various locations along the Thames. The letter stated that "...this young woman, who came to London for the purpose of entering service in a good family some time ago [was missing]." With this information in hand, the Chief Commissioner telegraphed the Oxford Police requesting more data, sending Detective Inspector Turrell of the CID (Criminal Investigation Department) to investigate the matter. It would prove to be a false lead.

The next day more discoveries lead the Thames Police back to the riverbank. The first recovery of the day was made by a gypsy named Solomon Hearne near Wandsworth Bridge in Fulham. Mr. Hearnes was living at the time on the grounds of Lammas Hand, Townmead Road, Fulham, in a tent. He had discovered "...a woman's leg lying on the foreshore of the Thames on the Fulham side." The leg was apparently covered with a torn collar from an old dark check–patterned ulster. The ulster matched exactly the cloth that had been found with the human remains earlier discovered near Albert Bridge at Battersea. He soon located a constable, who took the remains to the local mortuary.

Before long the leg was reunited with other recovered parts at Battersea Mortuary. At the mortuary it was preserved in spirits and then closely examined by Dr. Felix Kempster, who compared it with other recovered parts and announced it was from the same woman. The cloth was also an exact match to pieces found earlier in reference to other body parts. According to the good doctor, the "...limb consisted of the leg and foot (entire), it having been cut off from the thigh just below the knee."

A few hours later a lighterman named Edward Stanton of Park Street in Limehouse, working on the river off of West India Docks, noticed a bundle floating in the river. It was wrapped in a dark material and tied with a string. This would later be shown to have been the sleeve of an ulster. After he plucked it from the river he brought his discovery to Inspector Hodson. Hodson had been placed in charge of the police galley ordered to keep an eye out for any more body parts. Stanton had not opened the parcel, knowing full well that pieces of a woman's body were being found all along the river; wanting to open the package himself, he gave it to the officer.

Also on the 7th a nitric acid maker named David Goodman, who lived at 15 Prairie Street, Queen's Road, in Battersea, found a piece of flesh on the riverbank at Palace Wharf, Nine Elms. This find also made its way to the authorities.

Once again Detective Inspectors Regan and Tunbridge made their way to Battersea Mortuary where Dr. Kempster was standing by to examine the day's recovered parts. Dr. Kempster found that the remains had been pushed inside a sleeve, which had been part of an ulster, and then tied with a locally common string. Inside the bundle he found the right leg and foot of a woman. All of the parts matched a single body.

The *Times* of London—June 8, 1889

A most careful search for the portions of the body still missing is being maintained. All along the foreshore of the Thames experienced watchers have been engaged, and every likely hiding place, such as the shrubbery of Battersea Park, where one of Thursday's discoveries took place, is being inspected.

The police forces were being overwhelmed at the time with requests for information on missing women. Friends and relatives of missing women, throughout London and beyond, wanted a detailed description of the woman, many believing that they were related to or knew the victim. Most of these inquiries led nowhere. One such request, however, seemed to be of great value at the time. A constable named Fisher, from the Hertfordshire Constabulary, had wired the London authorities about his missing sister and believed she may have been the latest victim of the Torso Killer. His sister's maiden name was L. E. Fisher, which matched the name found on the victim's clothes. His sister, just before she was married some four or five years earlier, had marked many of her new clothes with her name. The constable further related that his sister had married a man named Wren when she was 20, and would be around 25 at the time of this murder. His sister had left her husband, her child and her home on May 18, 1888, with another man and had not been heard from since. The police were quick to establish that a young woman named L. E. Fisher had indeed been in London and was working as a barmaid at the Old Dock Tavern near the Thames some months earlier. She was also missing!

On June 9 the only discovery would be "a small liver" found floating in the river. Found off of Wapping, it was very decomposed, to such an extent that the doctors on the case could not establish if it was human or not. It was then preserved in spirits and taken to Battersea Mortuary. In comparison, the day before had been a banner day.

Saturday, June 8, had begun clear and cool. Later that day, as the parts piled up, clouds would form over a wet and dismal London. The first discovery was made just before 8 A.M. just off of Bankside in Southwark on the south side of the river. Once again a Londoner had spotted a parcel floating downriver, held by the tide. When William James Chidley, a lighterman working on the Thames, pulled the package to shore he soon found that he was holding a piece of the woman that all of London had been reading about. The package, which had been wrapped in the now falling apart brown paper, was taken to the local Thames police station. It was wrapped around the left arm of a woman.

The remains were described as a "...limb, well molded, and the hand small and shaped with every appearance of having been well cared for. The arm had been severed from the body in a very skilled manner, and the person who cut it off must have had a very considerable knowledge of anatomy." With this information the suspect list could be cut down a great deal. This killer was educated and had at least general knowledge of the human body, as well as a certain amount of skill in the removal of certain body parts. The skills of this killer seemed to rival that of his contemporary — Jack the Ripper!

Later in the day, river police patrols came across another part floating downriver. The Thames police had spotted an unidentified object "...floating, half submerged in the river." They rowed out to the spot to find the buttocks, pelvis, and lower back of the missing woman, bobbing up and down in the current. This find was not wrapped in any covering, but since it had been in the water longer than most of the other body parts it is very possible that the covering had simply been washed away by the river. When interviewed, Sub-Inspector Joseph Churcher of the Thames Division would state that his discovery was spotted at around 12:25 P.M. "...between the Albert Suspension Bridge and Battersea Park pier in mid-channel."

The final discovery of the day was made by a newspaper reporter who had been assigned to the story. Mr. Claude Mellor was walking along the Chesea Embankment near the river, not really expecting to find any remains. At best he hoped for a human-interest story about which he could pen a few lines. As he passed the private estate of Sir Percy Shelley, near the waterside garden, at around 12:15 P.M., he noticed something a bit strange through the tall ornamental railings. The railings fronted an extensive belt of evergreens, which gave the residents the required privacy as well as a bit of security from the many individuals wanting to walk along the Thames Embankment on a daily basis.

As he drew closer and looked at the shrubbery he could see a large package partially concealed in the underbrush. The package had partially covered the remains, but there was enough open for Mellor to clearly see that he had made an important discovery. He would certainly have much to write about on this day.

Reporter Mellor soon located Police Constable Jones 182B and showed him what he had found. Both men then proceeded to the back of the estate through the stables and over to the railing. It was immediately seen by both men that the railings would not have allowed anything as large as that package to be simply pushed through. The bundle would have had to have been placed there from that side of the railings, or perhaps thrown over the structure. It was later discovered that the tops of the bushes were broken and bent.

Before long an inspector was called and the remains were taken to the mortuary. It was at the mortuary where the find was unwrapped from the piece of dark ulster, along with a costermonger's pocket handkerchief. It contained a piece of a woman's thigh. As before, the remains were examined by Doctors Bond, Kempster and Hibbert, who pronounced it to be positively from the same woman whose several body parts had been already recovered. If the killer was trying to hide his crimes he was doing a very poor job of it. Poor job or not, the authorities did not have a single clue as to who the killer was.

The press began to report that this fresh crime was the work of the same man who had killed in 1887 at Rainham and again in 1888 at Whitehall. Officially, however, there were no reports, to the public at least, that a second possible serial killer was working the streets and waterways of London. Privately, however, many involved with the case felt that these were the workings of the same man. The hunt was now on for a second serial killer in the very heart of London.

The Times of London—June 12, 1889

> The Thames Police and boatmen specially engaged by the
> authorities still continue actively to watch the foreshores of the
> river. Battersea Park has been thoroughly searched; special boats
> have been engaged in searching the "...holes in the bed of the
> river in Chelsea, Battersea, and Pimlico reaches."

On June 10, Bond, Hibbert and Kempster came together to conduct a complete examination of the remains so far recovered, with a view towards identification of the murdered woman. The men also hoped to discover exactly how she had been killed so as to provide as much evidence as possible to the police now combing the area for likely suspects and more remains. They would discover no likely suspects, but more remains would soon be on the way to the good doctors.

The continuing intensive search on June 10 soon yielded results along the river at Bankside in Southwark. It seemed for a while that no day could pass without the mutilated remains of a woman being found in or near the Thames. Londoners found themselves glued to daily newspaper reports of the hunt under the headline "The Thames Mystery." Many would join the search, most looking for the missing head, as fewer requests went into police stations trying to identify the victim. Mr. Joseph Squires, however, did not join the search. He had work to do on the river and had no time for such things, but he would be the next to find a piece of "The Thames Mystery."

In the early morning, Mr. Squires, who worked as a lighterman on the river, spotted "...an object floating in the water, and getting it out found it to be the right arm and hand of a female." There was no doubt in his mind that he had found the missing arm of the woman he had been reading about. This discovery, however, did not have any cloth or paper covering, as had the other remains. It did have a new twist. The arm had been folded up double "...with the wrist and shoulder tied tightly together with a piece of common string."

This arm, which had been found near the same spot where the left arm had been located, was immediately taken to the local constable on patrol from M Division. It was then relayed to Inspector Knight of the Thames Police. From the river it was taken to the by-now-familiar, mortuary at Battersea. The arm and hand were received and examined by Dr. Kempster, who confirmed that it was part of the same woman now coming together in the morgue. The authorities surmised that this part had been tossed into the river from Southwark Bridge. In fact, it was possible that most, if not all, of the remains located in or along the banks of the river had been thrown into the Thames from Southwark Bridge. The bridge itself was now under constant, but quiet, observation. The killer was not expected to return, but the police could not allow that chance to go by without some kind of effort on their part. After all, they had no real leads and did not know where to look for the head!

As for the new hand, it could be easily seen that the fist was clenched in a very tight grip. It was an indication that the victim had been in a great deal of pain when she was murdered. Unlike the Ripper victims, this woman had been fully aware of what her fate would be. It was also reported that "...some slight marks on the third finger, caused apparently by the removal of [her] ring...." had been found on the left hand of the woman. The killer had removed the ring — similar to what had been done to a Ripper victim less than ten months earlier. This killer was also a collector.

That evening the London papers listed which remains had been found to date and gave a day-to-day review of the recovery. In case any London readers were not familiar with the workings of the human body, the papers also listed which parts had yet to be recovered. To this they added a pregnancy report. "Besides the missing portions of the woman's body—namely, the head, neck, lungs, heart and intestines—there is reason to believe that the child to which she gave birth has also been thrown into the river."

Earlier that afternoon a meeting had been held between Assistant Commissioner McNaughten, Sir Robert Anderson (who had some oversight responsibilities in the Ripper matter as well), Detective Inspector Marshall, Detective Inspector Tunbridge and several other officers working on the case. The consultation was conducted to review all evidence thus far recovered in the current case, as well as to review the Rainham and Whitehall Torso murders. It had become clear that the London authorities were once again dealing with a multiple murderer. None of the officers believed that they were dealing with the Ripper, but it should be noted that the police did not know why the Ripper had stopped his bloody murders, so they could not be sure. For that matter, they had no evidence that he was even still alive. The possibility that he was the author of the Torso Murders could not, on the evidence alone, be fully removed. He was still a viable suspect, and he would be heard from again.

One mystery would be solved, however, that of the "L. E. Fisher" markings found on the woman's drawers. The police had continued their inquires into the missing barmaid who had disappeared after working at the Old Cock Tavern in Highbury. It was learned that she was very much alive and living in Ramsgate, outside of London. It was to be another dead end as the victim continued to be nameless. In order to move that part of the investigation along, police issued a request to London papers to reproduce the marking in their evening editions.

> The Commissioner of Police of the Metropolis requests us to
> publish the following facsimile of the name on the portion of a
> pair of woman's drawers in which part of the human remains
> recently found in the river Thames was wrapped.
> L. E. Fisher

The papers soon reported the fact that, despite massive efforts on the part of the police, very little in the way of real evidence had been gathered which could lead to the killer. The only real conclusion reached had been that the victim was indeed *not* L. E. Fisher. The victim had somehow acquired, possibly second hand, several pieces of old clothing, which made the markings of little value to the investigation. Or so it seemed at the time.

Once again the police, using everything at their disposal, called upon the use of tracking dogs on June 16 in an effort to uncover the location of the woman's head. As reported in the *Times*, "The police are extremely anxious to obtain this most important link to the woman's identification in order to increase their chances of bringing the miscreants to justice." Earlier, however, *The Weekly Herald* had noted that using dogs might not be effective. "The advisability of employing bloodhounds to trace the perpetrator of the crime has been eagerly discussed by the inhabitants of the district. It is considered, however, by experts that the time has gone by for such an experiment, and it is pointed out also that in the case of the Backburn murderer, who was discovered by such means, the circumstances were different, and that the present case does not admit of that."

As before, Mr. Waring's dog "Smoker" was called upon for search duties. The animal had been instrumental in locating several body parts in connection with the Whitehall Torso case, so the police had high hopes for new clues in this murder. The animal had done his work, even as the police had held little hope that any more clues could be found. Smoker was taken to the thick bushes in Battersea Park where remains, hidden in a package, had been found by the gardener. It did not take long for the dog to find a trail in and around the area, but after an hour's work it became clear that even this hearty animal could not locate a new trail out of the park, which had long since dissipated. There was simply no other area within the park which held any more remains. The police came to the very reluctant conclusion that "the head of the victim has either been burnt or buried, and the scene of the crime is believed to have been either Chelsea or Battersea." The Southwark Bridge ran between both areas.

The authorities also concluded that, due to the fact that no woman had yet been reported as missing who fit the description of the victim. she had probably arrived in London of recent date and had yet to find any close friends. They did not seem to feel that she might have been a simple prostitute who did not have any real close friends. There was also another theory being circulated, due to the woman's pregnant condition, that "...she had undergone an illegal operation," and that she had been killed during the procedure. This theory also concluded that her "friends" had subsequently cut her body up for disposal in order to hide their involvement in the death. The police were running out of ideas, and this new one would lead them nowhere; however, the "illegal operation" part of the theory did have merit.

The police were able to report to the general public, however, that Dr. Thomas Bond, F.R.C.S. and surgeon to Westminster, had, along with Doctors Hibberd and Kempster, completed their examinations of the remains and that they were being kept in alcohol for any future investigation. A report by these men was made to the Chief Commissioner of Police for the City. At first it was thought wise to keep the details of the doctors' inquiry secret, so as to avoid any copycat murders. But any individual who would copy these murders would have certainly killed anyway, so keeping details quiet would be of limited value. Thus, the London Metropolitan Police issued a lengthy report on the remains, as well as the pieces of clothing, which had accompanied many of the discoveries. What the doctors could not discover was an exact cause of death. This was becoming a hallmark of the Torso Murders and points to some purpose in keeping the method of death a secret. Without the head or neck, a cut throat or evidence of strangulation could not be fully determined. They knew that the woman had not drowned nor had she been poisoned. Beyond that, there was very little to go on.

In a further attempt to identify this latest victim of the Thames Torso Killer, the Metropolitan Police circulated a description of the remains then discovered, along with the clothing, to the London papers. The problem was that it could easily have fit many of the women in London who made their way in life on the streets of that great city.

The *Times* of London—June 13, 1889

The remains are those of a woman, age from 24 to 26 years, height 5 ft. 4 in. to 5 ft. 6 in., well built and fleshy, very fair skin, hair light brown or sandy, well-shaped hands and feet, bruise on ring finger probably caused by wearing a ring; nails on both hands bitten down to the quick; four good vaccination marks, about the size of a three-pence piece [5 cents U.S. or Canadian] on left arm; skin on palms does not indicate that deceased did hard work; considerably advanced (probably about seven months) in pregnancy. The articles in which the remains were enclosed are as follows: — The skirt of an old brown linsey dress, red sleevage, two flounces round bottom, waistband made of small blue-and-white check material similar to duster cloth, a piece of canvas roughly sewn on end of band, a large brass pin in skirt, and a black dress button (about size of a three-penny piece) with lines across in pocket; a piece of the right front, two pieces of the back, the right sleeve and collar (about 4½ in. wide) of a lady's ulster, gray ground, with narrow cross stripes of a darker colour, forming a check of about three-quarters of an inch square; ticket pocket with outside lap on cuff, upon which there is also sewn a large black button; the material of good quality, but much worn; a light blue flannelette bag, about 13 in. square, top edge unhemmed; a pair of woman's drawers (old); square patch on both knees, originally of a good material, band formed of several pieces joined; "L. E. Fisher" in black ink at right end of band; a piece of tape sewn on with black cotton to each end of band to tie round body. The various parcels tied up with black mohair bootlaces, pieces of venetian blind cord, and ordinary string. The various articles described can be seen between 10 A.M. and 4 P.M. daily at Battersea Station by persons who have missing female relatives. The clothes may not have been worn by the deceased.

It was also reported that the officer in charge of a Thames Police boat had spotted, the day before, a "large stove pickle jar floating near the foreshore." The jar, upon closer examination, contained a fetus, which had been sealed in and tossed in the river. Dr. Felix Kempster was of the opinion, however, that this was not the missing fetus carried by the latest Torso Murder victim.

ANOTHER TORSO MURDER INQUEST

On Saturday, June 16, the inquest into the latest Torso Murder began at the *Star and Garter* public house in Battersea. The proceedings were overseen by Mr. Braxton Hicks, Coroner for Mid-Surry, London. Present, as a representative of Scotland Yard, was Inspector Tunbridge who had charge of case at the street level. Coroner Hicks opened with the swearing in of the jury and then explained that they were there to look into the death of a woman whose body parts had been gathered together at Battersea Mortuary.

The first witness called was Doctor Thomas Bond, the Westminster surgeon who doubled as Divisional Surgeon for A Division of the London Police. He produced his medical report on the victim and stated that he had been called to the case by Sir Robert Anderson. This was a sure indication that the Ripper was on the minds of London authorities.

"I first examined a human thigh at Battersea. The thigh was the left one, and had been severed with three or more sweeping cuts from the hip joint. The head of the thighbone had been neatly disarticulated, and so had the lower portion. I am of opinion that the limb had only been severed a few hours, as there were traces of blood visible. On the same day I examined parts of the abdomen, which were found off Wapping. In my first report I stated that the body the body parts belonged to was that of a woman who had not been dead more than 24 hours. The deceased was apparently 5 ft. 4 in. to 5 ft. 6 in. in height, fair, and plump. She was pregnant at the time of her death—possibly in her eighth month; but she could not have been delivered before her death. It was evident that this was the woman's first child. There were no outward signs of violence to show whether the deceased died a violent death or from natural causes. The body must have been cut up, however, very shortly after death. In my first report I also stated that the age of the deceased must have been from 20 to 30 years; but I could not then decide more positively without making a further examination of the thigh bone, which at that time I had not deemed it desirable to do.

"On the 7th of June, in conjunction with Mr. Hibberd and Mr. Kempster, surgeons, I made a further examination of other parts of a human body—the shoulders, and upper and lower parts of the back, and on June 10, still further portions were submitted to me, and in my final report I stated that all the parts belonged to the same body; that the age of the deceased must have been from 23 to 25 years; and her height the same as previously given. The condition of the ring finger of the left hand showed that a ring had been removed shortly before or just after death. The hand showed that the woman was not accustomed to manual labour. The division of the parts showed skill and design; not, however, the anatomical skill of a surgeon, but practical knowledge of a butcher or a knocker. There was a great similarity between the condition, as regarded cutting up of the remains and that of those found at Rainham, and at the new police buildings on the Thames Embankment."

> CORONER HICKS: "In both these cases the heads were not found?"
> DR. BOND: "That is so."
> CORONER HICKS: "The head, if thrown in the river, would probably sink?"
> DR. BOND: "Yes."

The coroner also wanted to know if an abortion could have been carried out "by means of drugs and not by a surgical operation." Doctor Bond answered that he had no way of knowing that because the stomach, brain and throat were all still missing. Perhaps the killer had meant that to be the case. It did appear to be an effective way of hiding the cause of death, and perhaps with that cause a reason might have been discovered. If so, this was a clue—this killer had medical knowledge, and he was trying to hide that fact!

Dr. Kempster was then called to the witness stand where he went over the same details and corroborated Dr. Bond's statements. He further remarked that the victim had delicate hands and had not worked with them at any great length.

It was not long before the jury was hearing from witnesses who had, in one area of the Thames or another, located various body parts. The locations were marked on a map, giving the jurymen a very good idea of just how widespread the discoveries had been. One witness, a fireman named John Finchum who worked at the Battersea Park frame yard, stated that he had actually seen the package, which had been found on the 6th of June in the brush, a day earlier. He had not seen anyone near the bundle and had not been interested enough to go over and have a look at it. In fact, he had not even reported that a package was in the park and had only come forward after hearing of the discovery the next day.

With the discovery witnesses complete, Inspector Tunbridge was called, but he was "at present not prepared with any further information that would assist this inquiry." The authorities were still making their inquiries and needed more time to identify the victim. The coroner took this under advisement and adjourned the inquest until July 1 at 11 A.M., but not before he complained about the lack of "...accommodation for inquests in the district, and the necessity for providing a proper court." He felt that a district as large and populated as Battersea could surely afford a proper coroner's court, which was then being held in a local public house (bar)!

> Prostitute [Elizabeth] Jackson was identified by scars on her wrists. She lived in a lodging house in Turk's Row, Chelsea.

Finally, with a full description of the victim and her clothes, the nameless torso of London was identified. With her identification came a renewed investigation in and around the area of Turk's Row. Inspectors and constables spread out to locate any information they could on Jackson, and were soon rewarded. Mrs. Mary Minter, the old family friend, told police of her meeting with Elizabeth and informed them about the ulster she had given her to keep warm. She was able to identify it with ease. Before long it would also be confirmed that Elizabeth had indeed purchased some used clothes with the name L. E. Fisher on them. That part of the mystery had been solved.

Despite the victim's name then being known, the police were never able to locate a single likely suspect in Jackson's death. When the inquest into her death was reconvened on July 1, the police were unable to bring forward any new evidence to point to any one suspect. It was left to the jury to decide that in this case it was

> "Wilful murder against some person or persons unknown."

The Thames Torso Killer would escape to once again terrorize the women of London, all in the shadow of the Ripper. But the next time he hunted he would kill in the very heart of the Ripper's own territory and drop off the torso across the tracks from the home and workplace of the Ripper himself! The London police would once again come very close to catching this serial killer as they investigated the mystery of the Pinchin Street Torso.

Chapter 8

The Mystery of the Pinchin Street Torso— 1889

...the division of the neck and attempt to disarticulate the bones of the spine were very similar [to the Kelly Ripper murder].
— Doctor George Phillips, quoted in the Torso inquest papers

THE CENTRAL KILLING AREA

On September 3, 1889, a letter was found behind the East London Hospital. In that letter the writer announced that he was once again prepared to kill "immediately" on the streets of the East End. That letter, as well as many others which had come into the hands of the authorities, was signed "Jack the Ripper." The police would place no importance in that letter but would, nevertheless, investigate and place it into the Ripper files.

The death of Ripper victim Alice McKenzie was still on the minds of Londoners in September of 1889. The East End prostitute was stabbed twice in her throat, cut on her chest and left for dead in a dark putrid alley in Whitechapel on July 17. She would soon be joined in death by the fourth victim of the Thames Torso Killer, whose identity would never be discovered. The newspapers were quick to report that once again a vicious murder had occurred in Whitechapel, and that the police were nowhere near catching the killer. They were also quick to assume that this victim had been a prostitute, even through no evidence would ever come to light proving that theory, and that the Ripper had been the killer.

The *Times* of London — September 11, 1889

ANOTHER MURDER AND MUTILATION IN WHITECHAPEL

Early yesterday morning a discovery was made which leads to the belief that another horrible murder has been committed in Whitechapel, and that victim, a woman, belongs to the same class as the eight who have been murdered in the same locality during the last two years. The manner in which the body has been mutilated suggests that the outrage has been committed by the same person.

Police Constable William Pennett, 239H, had walked the same beat some 15 minutes earlier and had neither seen nor smelled anything out of the ordinary. He had been on regular beat duty most of the night and was making one more pass along deserted Pinchin Street. It was around 5:15 A.M. as he passed the railway arch, owned by the Tilbury, and Southend Railway Company, running along and just south of Pinchin Street. As he walked, the officer looked away for a moment towards Cable Street. Looking across the tracks at the old weather-worn buildings on Cable Street, he could see the barber shop of Severin Klosowski, who had moved there the year before from the center of Whitechapel. (The local barber would be interviewed later in the day.) Looking back towards the arches under the Great Eastern Railway, he first smelled and then visibly noticed "something unusual" inside one of the arches.

The area below the arches was well known to the constable, who knew it to be used "...as a receptacle for stones belonging to the District Board of Works." There was also some crude but sturdy boarding in front of the stones, part of which had been misused and damaged. As he worked the remaining boards with his bare hands, pulling them aside, the smell became overpowering. What he saw was even worse. To his horror he had found the rotting torso of a woman. "The head had been severed from the body, while both legs were missing, and from the lower part of the stomach was a deep gash through which the bowels were protruding."

Constable Pennett's first thought was "Ripper!" The officer had discovered a murder victim in the heart of the Ripper's central killing grounds, across the tracks from a future three-time serial killer, but with all the trademarks of the Thames Torso Killer. Could this one victim be the key to all three series of murders Klosowski may have been responsible for? The investigation into that question would come later.

From the *Illustrated Police News*, September 1889, "The Pinchin Street Mystery."

Pennett knew that he patrolled the Ripper's home ground. He was also fully aware that one of two women murdered in a single night by that killer had been dispatched only four short blocks away, just to the north! And he recalled that it was almost one year to the day since the Ripper had murdered Polly Nichols in a small backyard on Hanbury Street. With these thoughts on his mind he stood very still, knowing that the killer was close—very, very close. He had walked the same ground minutes earlier and he was certain that the torso had not been there at the time. He would have easily smelled the rotting corpse as he passed by.

Pennett looked around him, then to the ground near the gashed torso. He could see no pool of blood, nor were there any footprints in the soft dirt areas under the arch or near the victim. Again he stood still to take in the area in full in order to see if anything was out of place. He needed to see if any man looked just a bit out of the ordinary. He was however, alone, and the killer had made his planned escape, but it must have been a very close affair.

The torso was still partly covered by an inexpensive chemise, reminiscent of the one found on the badly mutilated corpse of Ripper victim Mary Jane Kelly. Kelly had been the only one in the series to have been murdered indoors, in her own room, and on her own bed. All of the Torso Murders, it would be surmised, were conducted indoors with ruthless efficiency, but with no known motive other than the pleasure derived from the kill. It should also be noted that with the greatly added danger of dumping a section of a corpse between police patrols, this murder greatly mimicked the risks taken by the Ripper himself. The murders were one thing, but the danger of being caught was a thrill which seemed to be greatly enjoyed by this killer. That too was in line with theories on the Ripper murders.

It was at that point that a street cleaner came around the corner, and Pennett directed him to go to the bottom of the street just to the east and find a constable on patrol. "Tell him I've got a job on, and make haste." He did not want to blow his whistle for fear he would alert the murderer, whom he felt was still nearby. But he had instructions to wait by any body found and call for assistance. In accordance with his instructions he reluctantly blew his police whistle.

Before long two constables came to his aid, and Constable Pennett went over the facts, as best he knew them. One of the officers immediately took off running for the King David Lane Police Station for reinforcements, which soon arrived. While at the station word was telegraphed to all of the local East End police stations, as well as to Scotland Yard, that a new murder had been discovered. Due to the murder rampage of the Ripper, the authorities had developed a short code to speed the information through in order to give the police the best possible chance of catching the killer. The message was only two words long, but all who saw it knew what it meant and what they had to do about it.

"Another Whitechapel"

This time the police were ready. This time they had a plan. As soon as the two-word message arrived throughout the district, "...every outlet in the immediate neighborhood was blocked." The top officers were also alerted, and soon Superintendent Thomas Arnold was on site, along with Detective Inspector Reid of H Division. These were some of the men who had worked so hard to find the Ripper, and if they had anything to say about it the killer would not get away this time.

Because this death showed all of the aspects of a Torso Murder, the Thames Police were also alerted. If there was to be any dumping of body parts in the Thames this time they wanted to be "Johnnie on the spot." Within minutes of the alert, Detective Inspector Regan was directing the officers of the Thames Police in a detailed search of any vessel in the immediate area moving along the river. Special attention was given to the many cattle boats presently docked just south of where the torso had been located. The plan was simple but direct—place as many officers as could be found into a search as soon as possible to minimize the possibility of escape or cover-up, and block off any and all escape routes. They were unaware that a future (or, more probably, active) serial killer lived just across the tracks and could see everything that was going on.

It was starting to become light as the officers on duty were questioned as to whether or not they had seen anyone carrying a sack in the area. None had seen any man of such description. The killer could not have traveled very far to dump the torso and could not have gone very far after. He was still close—very close, but he did not live on Pinchin Street, for it had been deserted for some years and not many would go into that area at night. It was simply not safe. The closest occupied street was Cable Street, just to the south.

The police were now working from the outside of the containment area inward when Constable Pennett heard a noise from inside one of the arches next to the dumpsite. He had been standing by the torso and quickly called out for assistance. If it was the killer he knew he would need all of the help he could get. As Inspector Charles Pinhorn arrived to take charge of the local investigation, a fast search of the arches revealed two sailors, one named Richard Hawk, and a shoeblack named Michael Keating. Keating lived in the area, at 1 Osborne Street, and had been sleeping off a night of drink. The men were found in the archway next to the dumpsite, but due to their obvious intoxication at the time they arrived in the arch they had noticed nothing. In point of fact, they had arrived hours before the torso had been dumped, so there would have been nothing to see, yet! The killer, however, had dumped his murderous cargo within feet of three sleeping men. It was a risk he may not have known he was taking until he read about it that night in the evening papers. As for the three sleeping men—they were detained at the location until they could be taken to Leman Street Station. Later, all three, after a meal and a bit of conversation, were released, having nothing at all to do with the murder.

The murder site was, of course, not on Pinchin Street, but the area where the torso had been dumped was gone over with great care. It did not take long for the police to see that the site was difficult to reach from the north. The northern entrance to Pinchin Street had been well fenced off by wooden palings, disallowing easy movement from what was the working yard of *Pinchin and Johnson's Paint and Oil Company*. It was a reasonable conclusion by the police that the killer had moved from the south or southwest to Pinchin Street from Cable Street, just across the tracks. And if the remaining body parts were deposited in the Thames River, as were the previous torso murder victims, then junior surgeon and barber shop owner Severin Klosowski could rightly claim that his home and business was literally "between the body and the parts!" It was an interesting place for a serial killer to be found.

Before long, Doctor P. John Clarke was called to the scene for his medical opinion on the wounds of this latest victim. Doctor George Phillips, H Division Surgeon, would have been called but he was on a much-needed vacation at the time. Doctor Phillips had, the year before, been called, to the murder room of Mary Jane Kelly and would later examine and compare her murder with this latest brutality. He had also investigated the body of Annie Chapman while it lay in the backyard of 29 Hanbury Street, another victim of "Jack." Along with Doctor Sargeant, who lived and practiced in the area, Doctor Clarke examined the body in great detail. It did not take long for both men to agree that the woman had been murdered "at least three days previously, as the blood was all dried and signs of decomposition were setting in." It was as complete and detailed an examination as could be obtained on the site. The usual pre–Ripper murder investigation, consisting of announcing that life was extinct and carrying off the corpse, had ended—at least as far as Whitechapel murders of women were concerned.

When the examinations were complete the police procured an ambulance and the torso was taken to St. George's Mortuary. At the mortuary the remains were preserved in spirits owing to the decomposition, and the doctors began a more detailed examination, recording all they had found in two separate reports. After this work, the police issued a notice to the newspapers and the general public.

> Found at 5:40 this morning, the trunk of a woman under railway arches in Pinchin Street, Whitechapel. Age about 40; height, 5 ft. 3 in.; hair, dark brown; no clothing, except chemise, which is much torn and bloodstained; both elbows discoloured as from habitually leaning on them. Post-mortem marks apparently of a rope having been tied round the waist.

The first reported information to be released about the identity of the killer came from comments made by Dr. Sargeant. He had been quoted, by the *Times* of London on September 11, as saying that the killer had removed the head in a "very skilled manner." The medical team was also reported to believe that the killer had been left handed and that this fact "points to the murderer being the same person who killed the eight other poor creatures, as in each instance the cuts are supposed to have been the work of a left handed person." The London papers were also quick to remind their readers that this murder did not stand alone in the slums of the East End.

The following is a list of the East End murders :

1. Dec. 1887.—Unknown woman found murdered near Osborne and Wentworth Streets, Whitechapel.

2. Aug. 7th, 1888.—Martha Turner [Tabram] found stabbed in 39 places on a landing of the model dwellings in George Yard buildings, Whitechapel.

3. Aug. 31st, 1888.—Mary Ann Nichols, murdered and mutilated in Baker's Row, Whitechapel.

4. Sept. 8th, 1888.—Mary Ann Chapman, murdered and mutilated in Hanbury Street, Whitechapel.

5. Sept. 30th, 1888.—Elizabeth Stride, found with her throat cut in Berner Street, St. George's.

6. Sept. 30th, 1888.—Mrs. May Eddowes, murdered and mutilated in Mitre Square, Aldgate.

7. Nov. 9th, 1888.—Mary Jane Kelly, murdered and mutilated in Dorset Street, Spitalfields.

8. July 17th, 1889.—Alice McKenzie, murdered and mutilated in Castle Alley, Whitechapel.

9. The woman whose mutilated body was found yesterday morning.

Within 30 minutes of the first murder report and the two-word telegraph code, the Chief Commissioner of Police, James Monro, was on the scene, along with Assistant Commissioner Colonel Monsell. These men were immediately briefed by Detective Inspector Donald Swanson of Scotland Yard. All three men had been involved with the Ripper investigation in one way or another and were greatly concerned with capturing the individual who had brought one more brutal murder to the East End of London. Swanson had served as the desk officer in charge of the Ripper investigation and had as much knowledge about the crimes as any man alive at the time, excluding the Ripper, of course.

It would be James Monro who would submit a detailed report to J. S. Sanders, the private secretary to Home Secretary Henry Matthews. It would be this eight-page report, marked closed until 1990, which would show conclusively that police and government officials did not know who Jack

PINCHIN ST. TORSO & STRIDE MURDER SITES

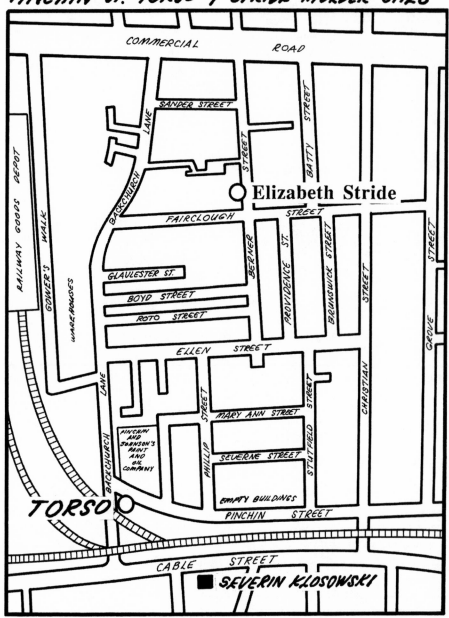

the Ripper was. Moreover, it was proof that when the police had stated that the Ripper was either dead or in an asylum they had clearly lied! It was held in Home Office File — HO 144/221/A49301 K.

Dated 11 September 1889   Closed until *1990*
                                                            A 0144/221/A49301 K
Subject: The Whitechapel Murder (Pinchin Street)
Mr. Sanders.

I communicated to you yesterday the finding of the trunk of a female, minus head & legs in one of the railway arches in Pinchin Street.

This street is close to Berner Street, which was the scene of one of the previous Whitechapel murders. It is not a very narrow street, but is lonely at night, and is patrolled every half hour by a constable on beat. The arch where the body was found abuts on the pavement.

The constable discovered the body somewhat after 20 minutes past five on the morning of Tuesday. He was in consequence of the pressure for men in Whitechapel just now, working part of two beats in addition to his own, but even so he passed and re-passed the spot every half hour. He is positive that when he passed the spot about five the body was not there. I am inclined to accept his statement thoroughly, for from another circumstance which has come to my knowledge he evidently was on the alert that night. It may therefore be assumed that the body was placed where it was found sometime between 5 and 5:30 A.M. of Tuesday the 11th.

Although the body was placed in the arch on Tuesday morning, the murder (and although there is not as yet before me proof of the cause of death, I assume that there has been a murder) was not committed there nor then. There was almost no blood in the arch, and the state of the body itself showed that death took place about 36 hours or more previously. This then enables me to say that the woman was made away with probably on Sunday night, the 8th September. This was the date on which one of the previous Whitechapel murders was committed.

The body then must have been concealed, where the murder was committed during Sunday night, Monday, and Tuesday up till dawn. This leads to the inference that it was so concealed in some place to which the murderer had access, over which he had control, and from which he was anxious to remove the corpse. We may say then that the murder was committed probably in the house or lodging of the murderer, and that he conveyed the portion found to Pinchin Street to get rid of it from his lodging where the odor of decomposition would soon betray him.

Why did he take the trunk to Whitechapel and what does the finding of the body there show? Is this a fresh outrage of the Whitechapel murderer known by the horribly familiar nickname of Jack the Ripper? The answer would not be difficult although this murder, *committed in the murderer's house* would be a new departure from the system hitherto pursued by this ruffian. I am, however, inclined to believe that this case is not the work of the Ripper. What has characterized the previous cases has been a/. death caused by cutting the throat—b/. mutilation. c/. evisceration d/. removal of certain parts of the body. e/. murder committed in the street, except in one instance in Dorset Street—In this last case there were distinct traces of furious mania. The murderer having plenty of time at his disposal slashed and cut the body in all directions, evidently under the influence of frenzy.

In the present case, so far as the medical evidence goes there is a/. nothing to show that death was caused by cutting the throat— b/. There is no mutilation as in previous cases, although there is dismemberment. c/. There is no evisceration— d/. there is no removal of any portion of the organs of generation or intestines. e/. The murder was undoubtedly committed neither in the street, nor in the victim's house, but probably in the lodging of the murderer. Here, where there was as in the previous case of murder in a house, plenty of time at the disposal of the murderer, there is no sign of frenzied mutilation of the body, but of deliberate and skillful dismemberment with a view to removal. These are all striking departures from the practice of the Whitechapel murderer, and if the body had been found _elsewhere than in Whitechapel_ the supposition that death had been caused by the Ripper would probably not have been entertained.

But the body _has been found in Whitechapel_ and there is a gash on the front part extending downwards to the organs of generation — and we have to account for these facts. I place little importance on the gash; it seems to me not to have been inflicted as in the previous cases. The inner coating of the bowel is hardly touched, and the termination of the cut towards the vagina looks almost as if the knife had slipped, and that as if this portion of the wound had been accidental. The whole of the wound looks as if the murderer had intended to make a cut preparatory to removing the intestines in the process of dismemberment, but then changed his mind. Had this been the work of the previous frenzied murderer we may be tolerably sure that he would have continued his hideous work in the way which he previously adopted. It may also be that the gash was inflicted to give rise to the impression that this case was the work of the Whitechapel murderer and direct attention from the real assassin.

As to how the body got to Whitechapel this is a great difficulty unless it be supposed that it was removed in some conveyance and placed where it was found, unless it be supposed that the murderer, being other than the "Ripper," had good knowledge of the locality. I may get some light on this point as the case goes on. Meanwhile I am inclined to the belief that, taking one thing with another, this is not the work of the Whitechapel murderer but of the hand which was concerned in the murders which are known as the Rainham mystery—the new Police buildings case—and the recent case in which portions of a female body (afterwards identified) were found in the Thames.

Sept 11, 89

Monro

Thank Mr Monro for
     This report
     H.M.
     12 Sept./ 89.

(The underscores are by the author of the report)

Once again, cries of "Murder in Whitechapel" could be heard throughout the district. It took only minutes for the residents of the East End to begin flooding towards the crime scene. With so many people converging on the area, the police plan to capture the killer in an ever-closing trap of officers would have no chance to succeed. Once again the killer would find luck on his side.

The *Times* of London—September 11, 1889

> Within a few minutes of the discovery the front of the arch, and, in fact, the whole of Pinchin Street, was crowded with hundreds of persons, and the excitement was intense. Indeed, it was growing during the whole of yesterday, and the discovery was almost the sole topic of conversation amongst those living in the East End.

As the police attempted to control at least the small area near the arches, the crowds continued to grow. The police and other officials at the scene were being "questioned" about this latest murder, with most wanting to know if this was another Ripper murder and why the killer had not been captured. The area of the arches was described as being "a very lonely one, and is only frequented by the poorest class, who seek refuge under some of the railway arches." Along with rocks and other debris could be found old barrows and carts pushed up against the walls. The police also found two pieces of old cloth that had partially covered the body. One piece of evidence which did become clear to the police very early was that the access to the area was a difficult one. There was only one entrance and exit to the darkly lit arch, and that was from Backchurch Lane. But patrolling officers and those interviewed in the area had seen no one come from that direction. Backchurch Lane had been deserted. That left only a southern approach from Cable Street to dump the torso. The police fanned out to the south, generally believing that the rest of the body parts were "...in the immediate neighborhood." It was also felt that the murder site was very close, perhaps within sight of the railway arches. If they could find the blood soaked room or smell the area this case was solved!

Before long the papers were full of reports covering this latest murder, as hundreds of onlookers crowded the local police stations. Many local women made requests to the constables in charge, posted in the front of nearly every station in the area, for permission to view the body. Many believed, from the brief description given in the morning papers, that they could identify this latest victim. They were, however, all refused. The authorities did not believe that anyone could simply look at the torso, which had no identifying marks, and give a positive identification. It was perhaps a missed opportunity.

News reports directly related to the torso's condition were brief, and fuller reports had to wait until the doctors could report their findings to the inquest. The police spokesman reported, "The difficulty in identifying the remains is obvious, owing to the absence of the head. There are no marks on the fingers of any rings having been worn, and it is evident that this latest victim belonged to the poorest class of woman. The hands presented a dirty and neglected appearance; but, as far as could be ascertained at the first cursory examination, there were no birthmarks by which the body could be identified."

It was also reported that the woman's hands were not clenched, as was the last victim in the series, indicating that she had been killed before she was cut into pieces. Without the head, however, the cause of death would be difficult to pinpoint. As for the gash in the lower part of the trunk, it was reported that this was the only "extra" wound from which to gage any possible mutilations. From the *Times* of London: "The police, after full investigation, give it as their opinion that the murder, if such it be, was not done by the person now known as 'Jack the Ripper.'"

The police were spreading the story around that the victim had died at the hands of some type of doctor during an illegal operation (possibly an abortion), and that in order to do away with the body, he had cut her up for disposal and nothing more. Yet why leave the torso where it could easily be found? And surely the police did not believe that the other Torso Murders were of the same origin. This was a weak cover story by the authorities, even though it may very well have been true. In private, however, they debated whether or not Jack the Ripper was back at work in Whitechapel.

In the meantime, the detailed search continued in the general area, as it developed into a house-to-house and room-by-room search south of Pinchin Street. It would be of no use. The killer, it would seem, may have been close, but he had taken the time to clean-up his murder room with great care. In point of fact, no evidence of any kind would ever come to light in this case. The missing head and missing legs would never be located. Unlike the earlier case of Elizabeth Jackson, there was simply nothing out there to find in the way of body parts. The only find in the neighborhood was a bloodstained piece of cloth, but it could never be connected to the victim.

For his part, Monro requested and received 100 more men to saturate the area. He was not going to let the killer "go to ground" if he could help it. He even went on patrols himself as his "secret force" combed the area for any clue to the man who had fully beaten London's finest.

The *Times* of London—September 11, 1889

> All persons living in Pinchin Street area have been closely questioned, but these deny all knowledge of having seen anything unusual in the street on the previous night, or, in fact, at any time.

One of the London news agencies reported on the cuts and other wounds on the victim and speculated on whether or not this murder should be placed in the Ripper's column. As reported in the daily London papers, "The cleanness of the cuts and knowledge of surgery displayed in dissecting the body would suggest that this crime is not the work of Jack the Ripper. He did all his terrible work firmly, but without any approach to scientific knowledge. The present crime bears a closer resemblance to the mysterious outrages at Rainham, on the Thames Embankment near Whitehall, and at Battersea than to the terrible deeds of the Ripper. In each of the foregoing cases the heads were missing and the manner of mutilation was very similar. It is most probable that the murderer took advantage of the scare produced by the Ripper tragedies to dispose of his victim in a way and such a place as should throw all suspicion upon that unknown person." The source of this report was not given, but it could easily have been someone in government!

Later that evening a conference was held at Leman Street Police Station. Present were Dr. George Bagster Phillips, who had arrived back in London just in time to examine the corpse, Chief Constable Colonel Monsell, Chief Superintendent Thomas Arnold, and selected officers from Scotland Yard. Most, if not all, of these men had been fully involved with the Ripper investigation the year before, and it was still very much an active case.

The meeting began at 6 P.M., and the assembled teams were briefed on the facts as they were at the time. At 7 P.M. Chief Commissioner Monro, fresh from a meeting at the Home Office, arrived by private carriage and joined in the discussions. By 8 P.M. the meeting had ended with the firm determination to place as many men as possible on this latest investigation. It was also generally decided that, as far as the public were concerned, this would not be considered a Ripper murder. The facts, however, did not point either towards or away from the Ripper.

By nightfall the police could correctly state that they had arrested "a seafaring man on suspicion," but they would soon clear the suspect then being held at Arbour Square Station. The night would also bring to the police a note found in Whitechapel.

"I told you last week I would do another murder"

It would be reported the next day that "The police, after full investigation, give it as their opinion that the murder, if such it be, was not done by the person now known as 'Jack the Ripper.'" After one day, with no suspect, no Ripper in hand, no clue as to where the woman had been killed, and indeed no identification of the victim, it could be said with reasonable confidence that the police were a bit too quick to dismiss this as not a Ripper crime.

The effect of such announcements were felt very quickly, however, as the London papers soon took up the cry. "The excitement was not so great as on the previous day, owing no doubt to the fact that the inhabitants of the district begin to doubt whether the deceased met her death at the hands of the so-called 'Jack the Ripper.'" It was well played propaganda, but was it the truth?

At the same time, the New York City police received a letter from "the Ripper" dated "from Hell." It was mailed from the city of London. Was the writer having fun with the "Yanks" or planning his next move?

A Torso Inquest in Whitechapel

Once again the flamboyant coroner for the South-Eastern Division of the County of London, Mr. Wynne E. Baxter, opened a murder inquest at the Vestry Hall on Cable Street, St. George-in-the-East. It is noted that Pinchin Street is on the edge of Whitechapel, as Cable Street is just inside St. George-in-the-East. Present and representing the police was Detective Inspector Edmund John Reid, who headed up the H Division (Head of CID), replacing then retired Detective Inspector Frederick Abberline. Abberline had become famous for his work on the Ripper case, and Reid was now in charge of that investigation. Also present was Chief Inspector Henry Moore.

First to be called was the man who found the torso, Police Constable William Pennett, 239H of the Metropolitan Police.

I went on duty at 10 o'clock on Monday night. Nothing attracted my attention that was unusual. I was on a regular beat during the night and morning. I had to go through Pinchin Street about every half hour. I entered it from Christian Street and Backchurch Lane. I occasionally turned down Frederick Street, to where the stables were. I then returned to Pinchin Street. Once or twice I cut it short, and simply went into Backchurch Lane.

About 25 minutes past 5 [A.M.] I came from the direction of Christian Street to Pinchin Street. I went across the road from the northern side, in the direction of the railway arch, and had no particular reason for so doing. As I was crossing I saw, in the arch, something that appeared to be a bundle. The arch, which was filled with stones belonging to the Whitechapel District Board of Works, led to a piece of waste ground, on which three arches abutting on to Pinchin Street. Two of these arches were closed in with fencing to some considerable height. In front of the arch that I just referred to there remained only the uprights for some fencing, which had been taken away. The archway had a large quantity of paving stones in it, and these were piled up. There was also a carriage entrance to the arch from Backchurch Lane.

The bundle was, I should say, from four to five yards in the archway, measuring from the pavement. The bundle was near the wall of the arch, on the western side. On going up to it I found that it was a portion of a human body. It was covered by two or three pieces of rag, but what these were I could not say at this time. With the exception of these it was naked. I noticed that the head had been taken from the body, and that the legs were missing. The trunk was lying on the stomach, with the shoulders towards the west. It was very dusty inside the arch, but I did not notice any marks of wheels or footprints. I do not think the impression of footprints would show. There were no clots of blood about.

I did not blow my whistle, as I thought it might cause a crowd to assemble. Knowing it was a lifeless body I waited a minute or two. A man came along with a broom on his shoulder. I said to him, "You might go and fetch my mate at the corner." He replied, "What's on governor?" I answered, "Tell him I have got a job on, make haste." The man then went up Backchurch Lane towards the adjoining beat.

I next saw two constables running towards me. Constable 205H was acting sergeant at the time, and he was the first to get up to me, and Constable 115H was behind him. I said to 205H, "You had better go and see the inspector, as there is a dead body here." He ran away in the direction of the station, and 115H remained with me. It was not very long before I saw Inspector Pinhorn, who at once gave directions for the arches to be searched.

After a few more questions were asked of Constable Pennett and others, Inspector Charles Pinhorn, also of H Division, was called to give his account of events that morning.

Shortly after half past 5 on Tuesday morning I was called to the railway arch, and went to the spot at once. When I arrived two constables were there, and I ordered and assisted in a search. Statements were taken from the men who were found in the arches. I had the street cleared of persons who were passing through on their way to work. The statements of the men, with the exception that the body was not there when they had entered the arches, had no bearing on the case. Two of the men went into the arch at 4 in the morning, and the other one at 2 o'clock. The arches were used by casuals, and as far as possible they were prevented from doing so by the police. Night after night people were turned out. The class of persons who used the arches and were accustomed to the neighborhood would know there was a probability of persons being in the arches. The ground belonged to the Whitechapel District Board of Works, and was got in exchange for another piece of ground. It was used for stone breaking. The police had no right there, as it was private property.

At the same time all isolated spots were searched during the nighttime by the police. The arches were fully open to the road, but, with the exception of this one, were guarded with some boarding, which, however, was only of a temporary character. No constable on duty near the spot on Tuesday morning saw anyone with a bundle. A bundle of that nature, if seen, would have certainly attracted attention. Costermongor's barrows would not have been passing in that direction, but in quite another direction. Those going to Spitalfields Market would not leave until after 6 o'clock.

A general search of the whole neighborhood had taken place, but up to the present time there was no clue at all. The men found in the arches stated that they then saw no bundle when they entered, but their condition might have been such as to cause them not to notice it, even supposing it to have been there. There was a lamp about nine feet away and the light from it would have been sufficient to show the bundle during the nighttime. The condition of the trunk was such as it would have been had it been carried in a sack. The arms were close to the body and the hands close to the abdomen. The left hand was evidently resting where the gash was. There was no dust or sawdust on the back. The body was lying breast downwards. The chemise was entire, although at first sight it had the appearance of being in pieces, as it had been cut open from top to bottom. The armholes were cut right up to the neck. There was no name on the garment or lettering of any kind.

> The men who were found in the other two arches would have
> to pass the one in which the body was found. The front of the
> arches near Pinchin Street where the men were found was some
> 30 yards from the spot where the body was discovered by the
> constable.

It was at that point in the hearing that Coroner Baxter informed the
jury that Dr. Clarke was engaged with another case at the Old Bailey and
Dr. Phillips had yet to complete his full examination of the torso. With
that, the inquiry was adjourned until September 24. This would give the
authorities two full weeks in order to complete their investigations and
possibly come up with a suspect.

As before, with the Ripper series, unofficial patrols of men from the
area began looking for likely suspects. Once again strangers in the area were
taken to local police stations—some the worse for wear! And any man stupid enough to claim the Ripper mantel (and there were a few) were severely
beaten before they were half-dragged to any constable the crowd could find.
As before in 1888, crowds gathered on the streets for days after the murder,
many demanding to know what was to be done.

The police, for their part, did their very best to convince the "East
Enders" that this latest business was not the work of the Ripper. They continued to play on the idea that it was simply an illegal operation gone bad,
ending with a body needing to be disposed of. After a while many of the
people of the area allowed themselves to believe that story, even as the
police had no evidence to show that it had any basis in fact.

After a week of constant Thames River searches, both on the water
and along the banks, the number of men working the case were cut back.
Not a single body part had been recovered besides the discovery of the victim's torso. It was in great contrast to the earlier murder of Elizabeth Jackson, who seemed to have been deposited all along a very large section of
the river.

The *Times* of London—September 20, 1889

> Nothing has occurred to throw any light upon the circumstances
> attending the finding of the trunk of a woman under one of the
> railway arches in Pinchin Street, Whitechapel. Without the
> head, all hopes of the body being identified will have to be aban-
> doned, as on the body there are no birthmarks of any kind.

There was one incident, which occurred in connection to this murder, that does bear examination—however briefly. A newsman named John
Arnold made a most interesting statement to the authorities about a man

he had encountered as he was leaving the *King Lud* public house in Whitechapel. Arnold had run into a soldier, later identified as John Cleary. The soldier had told Arnold that he better "Hurry up with your papers. Another horrible murder in Backchurch Lane." Arnold told the police that the soldier was "between 35 and 36 years old, standing five feet six inches, fair complexion and mustache." He also reported that the man carried a parcel. It may have been a good lead, but it had only one problem—the incident occurred on September 7, fully three days before a body turned up on Pinchin Street around the corner from Backchurch Lane! After the murder several walls near the crime scene would carry the words "John Cleary is a fool." Fool or not, the police were most interested in speaking with the good Mr. Cleary.

The police had also become aware of a prostitute named Lydia Hart. Hart had come up missing around September 8. Hart was a well-known East End character with many friends. She had even been mentioned in the *World* newspaper out of New York as the possible Pinchin Street victim, but no evidence could ever be produced to prove this claim. As far as the Lydia Hart matter was concerned, she was just one of many women who went missing each week from the wicked East End of Victorian London.

As promised, Coroner Wynne Baxter resumed his inquest into the Pinchin Street matter on September 24. It was a packed room at the Vestry Hall on Cable Street, St. George-in-the-East, just down the road from Mr. Klosowski's new barber shop. Constables stood inside and out to insure that order would be kept. Representing the police were Superintendent Arnold, Detective Inspectors Moore and Reid, and several officers from Scotland Yard. The first to give testimony was Doctor Percy John Clarke, assistant to Dr. Phillips, who had been called to the scene by the police.

> A little before six A.M. on the morning of September 10, I was called by the police to Pinchin Street. Under the railway arch there, about eight feet from the road, and about a foot from the right wall of the arch, I saw the trunk of a woman minus the head and legs. It was lying on its chest, with the right arm doubled under the abdomen, the left arm lying at the side. The arms were not severed from the body. There was no pool of blood, and no signs of any struggle having taken place there.
> On moving the body I found that there was a little blood underneath where the neck lain. It was small in quantity and not clotted, and evidently had oozed from the cut surface of the neck whilst lying there. Covering the cut surface of the neck and right shoulder were the remnants of what had been a chemise, of common make, and of such a size as would be worn by a

woman of similar build to the trunk found. It had been torn down the front, and had been cut out from the front of the armholes on each side. The cuts appeared to have been made with a knife. The chemise was blood stained nearly all over, I think from being wrapped over the cut surface of the neck. There was no clotted blood on it, and no sign of arterial spurting. I could find no distinguishing mark on the chemise.

Riger mortis was not present, and decomposition had set in. The body was taken to the mortuary, and an examination there showed that the body was that of a woman of stoutish build, dark complexion, about five feet three inches in height, and between thirty and forty years old. I should think the body had been dead about 24 hours.

Besides the wounds caused by the severance of the head and legs, there was a wound 15 inches long through the external coats of the abdomen. The body was not bloodstained, except where the chemise had rested upon it. The body seemed to have been recently washed. On the back were four bruises, all caused before death. One was under the spine, on a level with the lower part of the shoulder blade. An inch lower down was a similar bruise. About the middle of the back also, over the spine, was a bruise about the size of a half a crown [about the size of a U.S. half dollar]. On a level with the top of the hipbone, and three inches to the left of the spine, was a bruise two and a half inches in diameter, such as might be caused by a fall or a kick. None of the bruises were of old standing. Round the waist was a pale mark and an indentation such as would be caused by clothing during life. On the right arm there were eight distinct bruises, and seven on the left, all caused before death and of recent date. The back of both forearms and hands were much bruised. On the outer side of the left forearm, about three inches above the wrist, was a cut about two inches in length, and half an inch lower down was another cut, both caused after death. The bruises on the right arm were such as would have been caused by the arm having been tightly grasped.

There was an old injury on the index finger of the right hand over the last joint. Two vaccination marks were on the left arm. The arms were well formed. Both elbows were hardened and discoloured, as if they had been leant upon. The hands and nails were pallid, and the former were not indicative of any particular kind of work. The breasts were well formed, and there were no signs of maternity about them.

Next to give testimony was Divisional Surgeon Dr. George Phillips, who had been away at the time of the murder. He had been called back to London in order to aid in the investigation.

I first examined the body at six o'clock on the day the remains were found. I confirm, so far as I have observed, the evidence given by my colleague, Mr. Clarke, who was present with me when I first examined the body. Decomposition of the body had been fairly established. There was an oozing of blood from the cut surface of the neck. The cut surfaces where the thighs had been removed were nearly dry. The cut surface at the neck was not so dry, but it impressed me greatly with the general even surface. The skin was beginning to peel and the decomposition of the trunk was greater about the upper than the lower part of it.

There was not a head, and the thighs had been removed from the body. Next morning, in the presence of Dr. Gordon Brown and Mr. Hibberd, I further examined the body. Decomposition had extended greatly. The cut surface of the neck was much drier at the ends of the muscles, but more moist underneath. The neck had been severed by a clean incision commencing a little to the right side of the middle line of the neck behind, leaving a flap of skin at the end of the incision. It had severed the whole of the structures of the neck, dividing the cartilage of the neck in front, and separating the bone of the spine behind. The walls of the belly were divided from just below the cartilage of the ribs. The two small cuts upon the forearm appear to me as likely to have been caused when the sweep of the knife divided the muscles covering the upper part of the thigh. Both thighs were excised by the extensive circular sweep of the knife, or some sharp instrument, penetrating the joint from below and separating the thighs at the hip joint, but the cartilages within the joint and those which deepen the joint and surrounded it had not been injured.

The marks upon the fingers had been made some time previous to death. I think the pallor of the hands and the nails is an important element in enabling me to draw a conclusion as to the cause of death. I agree especially with the remarks made by Mr. Clarke as to the date. I found the length of the trunk to be 2 ft. 2 in., and the measure went round the nipple 34 in., and below the breast 31 in. Dr. Phillips, having given some further measurements, said that the deceased was about 5 ft. 3 in. There was throughout the body an absence of blood in the vessels.

The heart was empty; it was fatty, and the vessels coated with fat, but the bowels were healthy. The right lung was adherent, extent at the base, the left lung free, and, taking them both together, fairly competent, and especially considering the decomposition of the remains. The stomach was the seat of considerable post-mortem change, and contained only a small quantity of fruit, like a plum. In my opinion the woman had never been pregnant. I believe her to have been under 40 years of age.

There was an absence of any particular disease or poison. I believe that death arose from loss of blood. I believe the whole of the mutilation to have been subsequent to death: that the mutilations were effected by someone accustomed to cut up animals or to see them cut up; and that the incisions were effected by a strong knife eight inches or more long. The supposition—(and only a supposition)—which presents itself to my mind is that there had been a former incision of the neck, the signs of which had disappeared on the subsequent separation of the head. The loss of blood could not have come from the stomach, and I could not trace it coming from the lungs. I have a strong opinion that it did not.

CORONER BAXTER: "Is there anything to show where the loss of blood occurred?"

DR. PHILLIPS: "Not in the remains; but the supposition that presents itself to my mind is that there was a former incision of the neck, which had disappeared with the subsequent separation of the head."

CORONER BAXTER: "The drawing of blood from the body was such that it must have been a main artery that was severed?"

DR. PHILLIPS: "Undoubtedly; and was almost as thorough as it could be, although not so great as I have seen in some cases of cut throats. I have no reason for thinking that the person who cut up the body had any human anatomical knowledge."

The jury was then invited to hear testimony from the three men who had taken their leave under the arches of the railway line just south of Pinchin Street. First before the assembled group was Michael Keating. "I live at 1 Osborn Street, Brick Lane, and am a licensed shoe black. On the night of the 9th, between 11 and 12 o'clock, I went to sleep in the railway arch in Pinchin Street. I went there because I had not the price of my lodgings. When I went there I did not see anyone, and neither did I see anything under the arch. I was not sober. I do not remember noticing anything in particular, but there were people about Pinchin Street when I went in. I soon fell asleep, and was not awoke during the night. The police woke me up, and when I came out of the arch I noticed the trunk of a body in the next arch. An inspector was in the act of covering it up with a sack in which I kept my blacking box. I could not say if I was sober enough to have noticed the body if it had been there when I went in. I did not go into the railway arch in which it was found. I do not remember anyone else coming into the arch in which I was, but when I woke up I saw two more men coming out from the other side. I had never slept there before. I happened to be passing by, and finding the arch open and thinking it was a quiet place I went in to have a sleep."

From seaman Richard Hawke came an account of his night spent under the fated arch. "I am a seaman, and I live at St. Ives, in Cornwall. I was paid off in London some seven or eight weeks ago, and have since been in Greenwich Hospital. I came out of the hospital last Monday fortnight [two weeks earlier], and at the time had no money. I walked up to London, and knocked about the streets until 20 minutes past four the next morning. I then went to have a rest under the railway arch. At that time I did not know the name of the street. It was very dark at the time. I was not exactly sober. I had about three pints of beer about shutting-up time. I know the time because a policeman who was close by told me. When I entered the arch I did not see anything. I think I lay down on the right hand side of the arch in which I slept. There was another man with me when I went in, and he was just about the same condition. To get to the arch in which we slept we had to go through the one in which the body was found, and did not see anything there at that time. The other man with me was a seaman, and I picked him up in a public house somewhere near the Sailor's Home. During the night I did not see or hear anyone, and I was awoke by the police."

The third man found under the arch was not required to testify at this early stage, as he would have added little, if anything, to the inquiry. Instead, the jury was read a written statement taken by the police from one Jeremiah Hurley, a cabman who lived in the area, and who had seen a possible suspect leaving the area at the critical time. "I live at 10 Annibal Place, Annibal Street, and am a cabman, and am in the employ of John Smithers of Well Street. A policeman called me at 5 o'clock, and I am always called in that manner. When there is a change of policeman they continue to call me. I have to be at work at half-past five. On the morning of the 10th I left home at 25 minutes to six. As I was coming round Phillips Street into Pinchin Street I saw a man, who had the appearance of a tailor, standing at the corner of Pinchin Street. The man appeared as though he was waiting to go into work. I saw no one else until I got to the arch where the body was lying. I then saw an inspector and an officer in plain clothes. At that time the body had been found."

The man with the appearance of a tailor would be the only other individual seen in the area around the dumping site, and it was soon established that he had no knowledge of the events which had come to pass on Pinchin Street.

Detective Inspector Henry Moore, who briefed the jury on the area of the crime, then represented the police. He had with him, as all good inspectors would, a hand drawn map of the area. "I have charge of this case under the direction of Superintendent Arnold. I produce a plan of

Pinchin Street and surrounding neighborhood, and it is an accurate one. The red cross on the plan denotes the position in which the body was found. Every effort had been made to identify the body, but without success. There was nothing to show how the body came there or who placed it in the position in which it was found."

Doctor Phillips was then recalled by the coroner and asked if the wounds had any similarity to those found on the Ripper victims. Phillips had worked on the Ripper victims, and his opinion would carry great weight at the hearing.

> CORONER: "I should like to ask Dr. Phillips whether there is any similarity in the cutting off of the legs in this case and the one that was severed from the woman in Dorset Street?"
> DR. PHILLIPS: "I have not noticed any sufficient similarity to convince me it was the same person who committed both mutilations, but the division of the neck and the attempt to disarticulate the bones of the spine are very similar to that which was effected in this case. The savagery shown by the mutilated remains in the Dorset Street case (Jack the Ripper) far exceeded that shown in this case. The mutilations in the Dorset Street case were most wanton, whereas in this case it strikes me they were made for the purpose of disposing of the body. I wish to say that these are mere points that strike me without any comparative study of the other case, except those afforded by partial notes that I have with me. I think in this case there has been greater knowledge shown in regard to the construction of the parts composing the spine, and on the whole there has been a greater knowledge shown of how to separate a joint."

The coroner then gave his summary and noted that the authorities had not been able to "produce any evidence as to the identity of the deceased, but the evidence of both medical gentlemen engaged in the case clearly showed that the unfortunate woman had died a violent death." After a brief remand to the jury, the men returned a quick verdict of:

"Wilful murder against some person or persons unknown."

On October 4, 1889, after a brief debate in government whether or not to bury or cremate the torso, the remains were placed in a specially constructed and sealed container preserved in alcohol and buried. And, in a small plot in the East London Cemetery, Grange Park, Plaistow, Essex, the remains now lie awaiting their final identification. Henry Moore would report on October 5, 1889, "I attended at the cemetery at time specified and witnessed the internment. It was placed in grave number 16185, and upon the metal on box was the following:

This case contains the
body of a woman (unknown)
found in Pinchin Street
St. Georges-in-the-East
10th Septr. /89."

Although no other evidence was ever brought to light in this case, the killer seemed to have ended his series of death—at least for the time being. Was it a close call on Pinchin Street or did he have other "work" to do? Did he simply change his preferred killing method or was he actually caught for other crimes and imprisoned for a few years? All is speculation except for one fact. It would be 13 years before the Thames Torso Killer struck again, and that would be the last death he could claim under that mantle. The question is asked—what was he really doing for 13 years, and was he really a serial killer?

Chapter 9

The Serial Killer Up Close

What kind of person do you think I am?—
serial killer Jerry Brudos, quoted in *Serial Murder* (2d ed.;
Ronald H. Holmer and Stephen T. Holmes, eds.)

WHAT IS A SERIAL KILLER?

Authors Ronald and Stephen Holmes defined a serial killer or serial murder as "The killing of three or more people over a period of more than 30 days, with a significant cool-off period between the killings." This seems a fair enough way to define this type of predatory animal, and both the Ripper and Torso Killer would have fit right in. In the Ripper series the killer took six in 13 weeks and then slowed down, ending with a possible total of 9 from August 1888 through February 1891. In the Torso Murder series the killer took one in 1887, one in 1888 and two in 1889. But then a period of 13 years passed before the same man murdered a final victim. Two different patterns from what is reported to be two different men, yet both are defined as serial killers. It is clear from these two cases alone that there must be many things that play into the time frame and methodology of serial death. Certainly there are no two serial killers that are alike, and therefore each series becomes a unique signature of the killer himself.

In both the Torso and Ripper cases there is a definite sexual connotation in the killings. Body parts of generation were taken in one series, while the other involved attacking the sexual organs. These attacks, however, are not consistent throughout either series. Yet there is overlap, and in this overlap there may very well be evidence of one man with two separate

murder requirements at the time of the murders and therefore two separate ways needed to kill. What is clearly the same, however, is the need to
control the victims and then kill with speed. And, as stated earlier, both series
seem to have targeted one particular segment of Victorian society—prostitutes. And are we really dealing with two men, or are these the manifes-
tations of a demented split personality—both of which happen to be serial
killers?

A sexual background or motive is the base driving force for most serial killers—although not all of them, killing with that driving force, actually engage in some type of sexual activity with the victim either before or
after the murder. In the Ripper series there was never any actual sexual
activity reported with any of the victims, despite the fact that it would have
been an easily obtainable goal, as all were working prostitutes. There is
less certainty with respect to the Torso Murders due to the decayed nature
of the victims when found and the fact that most, if not all, of the victims
appeared to have been killed while in bed or at least in their bed clothes.
Once again we are faced with two different sides of the same need to control and finally destroy. And the need to be the one in control of the sexual situation is primary in both series. It is also ritualistic in nature.

The choice of victim—smaller, weaker, in a state of alcohol or sleep—
shows that the killer of both sets of victims was a coward, and he knew it.
He could never escape that fact no matter what risk he took. By dominating
weaker individuals who were unable or unwilling to defend themselves,
the serial killer (or killers) in the Torso and Ripper murders was attempting to prove himself a man. Yet that justification and gratification never
lasted very long, thus the need to continue killing. He would also never
have attacked a larger, stronger woman in full possession of her faculties.
And certainly he would never have attacked a man of any size, unless the
man was fully unable to protect himself, and even then it would have been
a risk this (or these) killer would have avoided at all costs. Capture—if the
authorities had the right suspect—would have been easy!

Power and Control

To be able to control and ultimately decide the fate of the victim is
the fantasy behind the crime. Power and control over one individual who,
in normal social situations, would be impossible for the serial killer to
obtain are two of the motivations behind the murders. At times, in order
to show, at least to himself, how much control the serial killer really has,

he may even decide, "Today I will not kill. Today I will allow this one to live." However, even if the killer does not admit it to himself, the need to kill will override any desire to show he can let any victim live. In the end, the desire to kill controls the serial killer. He is the ultimate fantasy victim, and the subjects of his rage become the innocent throwaways he is simply using in his closed and disturbing world.

After a while the serial killer turns his needs for control into a ritual. The ritual of death becomes a safe and familiar place to which he may go to once again live out his fantasy of power and control. Part of that ritual would be to take his selected victim to his comfort zone. For the Torso Killer his comfort zone seemed to have been the bedroom, or at least a home/dwelling situation. It would have been a place or room in which he had full and complete control over all aspects of the murder act. There is, however, evidence to show that a particular room in one location was not necessary. Only "a" room in which he felt in full control was needed, as he can be shown to have moved around a great deal during the murder periods. Perhaps it was one death per room?

It would appear that in the Ripper series the comfort zone, for the most part, was a geographic area of east London. In that series it can be shown that the killer took his first victim very close to his home (same apartment building), which is classic serial killer behavior. It was only by circumstance, however, that the first Ripper victim, Martha Tabram, was killed inside of a building. The Ripper's true comfort zone was along darkly lit small streets and back alleys during the early morning hours of the weekend. And he was always on the hunt, even when he was not actively killing.

The Torso Killer seemed not to have been on the hunt but was an opportunistic serial killer who would take advantage of the situation if the right victim fell under his control in the right place and only at the right time. "Jack" was an adventurer looking for the thrill, whereas the Torso Killer was a full coward only killing when he was positive that there were no chances taken during the act of murder. And yet, great risks were taken as the Torso Killer disposed of his murderous bounty. Two sides of the same man coming together or two men? The Torso Killer may have planned his murders well, but his disposal methods left something to be desired. The dumping of a body is *the* most critical period and the most dangerous for a serial killer. And make no mistake — these killers knew the difference between right and wrong. They, or he, knew the need to get away from the dump or murder site as fast as possible.

Methodolgy

In these two series we see evidence of individual methodology. In the Ripper series it can be seen that the victims seem, at least on the surface, to have had the ability to control movement — until, of course, the killer took over and began his death ritual. The prostitutes were, so to speak, on the job in their selected locations and aware of the potential dangers. And it seems they were able to move about relatively freely before the final encounter. It was a false freedom, but it shows how confident and secure the Ripper was during his stalking and tracking of his prey. The other side of the coin may be viewed in the methodology of the Torso Killer, as he always insured that no one was able to interrupt his efforts as he went to work. His work was always done outside the possible view of others, and he took as few chances as possible. He probably selected his victims very carefully and may very well have done some research on them before he acted.

During the Ripper murders it is thought that the killer may have had only the slightest knowledge of his victims. He knew, of course, that they were prostitutes, but may not have known much more than that. Careful study into the Torso victim's background could have shown the killer how many people his victim knew, how long she may have gone missing before anyone noticed, if at all, and how vulnerable his victim was. The Ripper killed strangers, but the Torso Killer may have "only" killed women he knew, or even women he had sex with. The possibility that the Torso Killer knew his victims is borne out by the fact that he went through great lengths to hide their identities after he had disposed of their lives. It would have been a wasted effort on the killer's part to go through such lengths if he did not feel that it was absolutely necessary to do so. Time spent with the victim is always a great risk.

The Torso Killer would have known his victims' names, and therefore the killings could have been a much more personal event to him. In his mind he may have felt that he had some kind of personal relationship with each victim. The question is asked: Whom was he really killing when he acted? The Ripper killings, in contrast, show an individual using cold-blooded efficiency in his operation. The Ripper did not waste any time at all during any of his street murders. He did, however, have plenty of time with Mary Jane Kelly, whom he killed and butchered in her small dirty room off of Dorset Street. That murder, however, was not the norm, but it did show how much damage the Ripper was capable of doing if he had the opportunity. After that murder the Ripper never killed inside again, perhaps only because the opportunity never presented itself again. He certainly did not seem to search for that opportunity. Did he know Mary Jane Kelly?

From the surviving photos one is able to see that Kelly's murder was a major overkill. The killer did just about anything he wanted to do to the corpse, including the almost total destruction of her face. Because this was the last of the "spree period" Ripper murders, and because it was the one with the greatest time separation during that period, the overkill aspects may have been brought on by the frustration of the killer unable to find a safe victim to kill. At the time the authorities were conducting a major house-to-house search of his prime killing ground. When he was finally alone with Mary Jane Kelly it would not have been long before he killed her. The attack must have been vicious, very fast and overwhelming.

It can also be seen in the total destruction of the victim in the Kelly case that not only did the killer return to his normal method of killing, but also he began to spread out his murders over a much longer time period. In fact, the Ripper would take "only" three more from the streets of the East End during the next three years. By that time the series was complete—but only in London. It was becoming too hot in London to continue, and he may very well have finally been placed under the watchful eyes of Scotland Yard.

In both cases it can be generally stated that the killers were collectors, but care must be taken in the Torso Series because he may have only possessed the body parts for a short while before he disposed of them. With body parts being thrown in the Thames, it is possible that the Torso Killer never kept any body parts at all. There is, however, the problem of the heads never being found in four of the five cases. The fifth and final head was on top of the pile of body parts being prepared for disposal. So the question of collection in the Torso Murders is up for debate. There can be no question, however, about the Ripper. The Ripper was very much a collector of body parts on the first order. It may very well have been one of, but certainly not the, primary reason for him to kill. And a serial killer does need to have a reason to kill, if only a demented one taken out of fantasy.

Another aspect that separates the Torso and Ripper killers is the length of time spent with each victim both before and after their deaths. The Ripper, in most cases, spent as little time as possible with the victim. He knew that his time was very short, and he did not wish to be seen with the victim. In fact, when the killer was seen on at least two confirmed occasions with a woman who would soon be murdered, he did his best to cover his face and look away. The Torso Killer had no such problem and probably spent a great deal of time with the victim both before and after the murder. Certainly it would have taken time for him to cut up and clean the bodies, and, in at least one case, cook or boil a victim. Gratification may also have been achieved using the victim's body after death during acts of necrophilia. Documentation of modern serial killers has shown that several who had taken heads later used them in sex acts when they could relive the original murder to obtain further gratification. The longer a serial killer is in possession of the body or body parts, the longer he is in control of that victim—the longer he has the ultimate power over life and death.

Experimentation with death can be a most powerful source of pleasure to the serial killer. That includes experimentation with the corpse after death. And if change becomes pleasurable, then the only method will be a constant change—or perhaps two separate methods at the same time, testing which method brings the most pleasure to the killer.

Movements

Although many serial killers choose locations they feel are safe and preferred, that does not mean the area they work in must necessarily stay the same. The location may change, as long as it is familiar to the killer. It must be comfortable and controllable to be preferred. As stated before, the Torso Killer killed indoors, yet he seems to have been on the move, given the pattern of deaths and the locations of his dumping areas. Even though his dumping spots changed, he could feel somewhat safe as long as he worked near the Thames River. This closeness to and familiarity with the river allowed the killer the freedom to move around a very large area — as long as he was within easy dumping distance of the Thames.

The closeness to a single area is also shown in the Ripper case, as he killed for the most part in a single square mile of London's East End. However, the size of the area is much smaller than first thought. When viewed from the perspective of victim location, the area shrinks to no more than 300 square yards! It was an extremely small area to work out of, and in fact the Ripper may well have lived on the southern end of the area and had a regular job on the northern end. Even the one victim who was taken in Poplar, East End, fully two miles east of the central area, lived within that 300 square yard area. Yet when the police finally searched nearly every cubbyhole in that area, and beyond, the killer, or evidence of him, could not be found. The reason is easy to understand—he moved when he needed to. Where he lived, as long as it was close to the killing and hunting grounds, did not matter. What was critical was the area he hunted in. That area *never changed*, and the police reports do not reflect any realization of that fact.

It is evident that comfort zones can and do change as the need arises, and the need arises whenever capture or exposure becomes probable or even possible. Serial killers are very good at what they do, and if this were not the case then both of these killers would have been discovered and probably hanged. Most serial killers are by no measure stupid or generally careless. They learn with every murder and adapt as they go from victim to victim. Some even change to specifically put the police off the trail. The police need to keep this in mind whenever they are investigating a serial killer. And this also relates to the method of murder as well. When the killer feels the authorities have somehow caught on to his method, style or location, he will move on to other areas and/or other methods.

Even though a serial killer learns from experience and becomes an even more lethal killer over time, some become over-confident. Carelessness will creep in—which is exactly what happened to the Ripper. Even though he was not tried or convicted in the Ripper series, the most likely suspect was caught when he began to speak of killing his final victim. He did not come right out and tell anyone, that we know of, that he was going to kill her—which would have been particularly stupid. But he did the next best (or dumbest) thing—he began to hint at it to her family! It would eventually cost him his life, with a drop of six feet on the gallows.

THE CRIME SCENE

It is at the crime scene where the two series differ most, not only in relevance but in the amount of evidence which the police can glean. In the Torso series the police never located the actual crime scene. If they had found any of the five actual murder sites, it is very possible that they could then have solved the murders with a great deal of speed. What they did find were the dump sites, and, for that matter, not all of these sites were located either. Since none of the Torso victims were killed where they were found, these sites left little or nothing in the way of collectable evidence upon which the late 19th century authorities could base any investigation. The only real evidence to be collected was the body parts and what they could tell the police. It was a secondary evidence site.

Quite to the contrary, the Ripper murder sites were all soon discovered and were very intact as far as evidence was concerned. Much was lost, however, by a police force quite unprepared or fully trained to handle anything but the simplest murders or other criminal acts. Gathering evidence for future examination was—to say the least—in its infancy as far as crime location investigations were concerned. At most times the police surgeon would be called, death would be certified and the hapless victim hauled away to be stripped at the makeshift morgue. This was, in fact, how the first two Ripper victims were handled. Before long a pail of water was splashed over the pool of blood and the crime scene investigation was complete. However, by the time of the Hanbury Street murder the police were sure they were dealing with a madman who was killing time after time. More time would be spent on the rest of the Ripper crime scenes, although very little real evidence would be recovered. And no weapon was ever found which could ever be exactly tied to any Ripper—or, for that matter—Torso murder.

In both murder series the true crime scene would not be any one small geographic location. The true crime scenes would have been the bodies of the victims. They would have to tell the story. In the Torso series the bodies were, for the most part, uninjured as far as excessive mutilation beyond what was necessary to cut up the victims into easy-to-move pieces. There was, to say, purpose, in most of the cuts. The killer did not go into a great deal of unneeded cutting, even though he clearly had a great opportunity to do so. It was almost as if he was just doing a job. In contrast, the Ripper seems to have been all over the place as far as mutilations were concerned. At times he would be all business, cutting only as much as was required to kill and then remove whatever organs he was after. At other times the murder was all he seemed to be after, with a quick kill and an escape. But at his most brutal he mutilated Kelly well beyond anything needed to kill or to take any body parts he wanted. For some unknown reason he wanted to fully destroy Mary Jane Kelly.

Of the Man

The serial killer who is looking for control and ultimate power over others is a deadly predator for more than one reason. However, the most compelling reason is his ability to be charming and open at one moment, and deadly the very next. It is possibly *the* trait which allows him to appear normal and move through society without being suspected of crimes. He is the man who would be overlooked as the police hunt for their killer. He would even go to great lengths to aid the police in their search. He is the friendly barber who is quick with a joke, or the bartender who laughs at the bar, but he is also the one who would escort the lady on her last walk home.

The serial killer is a perfect human chameleon, never showing his true face until it is time to kill. And for the most part he is above average in intelligence. He enjoys the risks his path presents, and he moves around as much as needed to get the job done. He is not one to be tied down to one place or one person, unless it is part of his plan or cover. And he is very hard to capture, as he is constantly thinking of how he can avoid capture.

The killer (or killers) in both series in this work had an above average education. This is borne out by the way the victims were killed, and in the Torso series, how the bodies were sectioned for disposal. The Torso and Ripper killers knew the workings of the human body; therefore, both men had at least some medical education or better than average knowledge of the subject. Both killers paid very close attention to detail in not only the murders but also their escape routes and method of disposal. These murders were planned to the point that the killer (or killers) had worked out a method of operation before he went hunting. There were no spur of the moment deaths in either series.

Both killers must have met a great deal of women in social situations, but these relationships would have only been superficial. They were unable to establish any real long-term relationships with women and would have remained single unless a wife could provide cover for their crimes. The charm they may have used to "capture" a wife, however, would have soon worn off. Before long they would begin beating their wives to enforce a continued control, and over the frustration of not being able to murder them without being caught.

The wife would be expected to keep his home (castle) in perfect order, to the point of being unlivable. She would have suffered greatly for anything out of order, and dust and dirt would not have been tolerated. And she would probably have been expected to earn some type of money, even if he was not always employed. His time and activities would have been — in his view — fully more important than hers. She would, in effect, have worked only for him. His job was to kill, as all other work would have been in the way of his "true" job. And he would never stop killing unless he was captured or killed.

It was shown from the time of the Ripper murders that the killer was a night person. (No time known for the Torso Killer, but night is suggested.) The Torso killer can fit this trait due to the times his "packages" were found — mostly in the early morning. These finds point to a nighttime drop-off of body parts. In fact, three torsos were found in the middle of the night, which rules out daytime movement of the Torso Killer in those cases. The night naturally affords a great deal of cover, but these men enjoyed the night for many reasons, much more than the bright light of day.

The Victims

The selection of a victim in many serial murder cases is part of the detailed planning necessary to succeed not only at the crime, but to achieve the thrill and control the killer requires. As stated earlier, the victims of the Ripper and Torso Killer were most likely all prostitutes. However, there had to be other criteria used by the killers in order for any one victim to be selected. What look or movement, what body language or other trait caused these few women to be selected when 1200 others never met these killers?

In the Ripper series we find a very small area in which all of his victims could be found. Why the police never focused on that fact is a matter of speculation, but it is a geographical artifact of the case nevertheless. This information shows that although both the Torso and Ripper killers were killing the same type of victim, the Ripper could not or would not, for whatever reason, move very far away from his home ground. Perhaps because he knew he needed to get off the streets as soon as possible after the murders were done, he stayed in the area. The Torso Killer had no such restrictive situation, moving around a much larger area of the East End. However, even the Torso Killer stayed in the East End, which in and of itself shows some restriction, but it may not have been due to any lack of funds. The East End itself was an area of great cover for many criminals, a fact of which both killers must have been well aware.

There could have been a particular walk or a particular type of personality, which was seen as exciting to the killers. But in both series the only known link seems to be the fact that these victims were small women who were also prostitutes. In the end it may very well have been a situation of "targets of opportunity" that were simply in the wrong place at the wrong time. All the victim had to do was fulfill the killer's fantasy, and that could be accomplished if she was weak or drunk or, for that matter, asleep when the attack and control began. In effect, the victim had lost control, but the killer had only marginal control and only for a short period of time. It was, however, enough of a margin to accomplish his fantasy. The victims had, by their own actions, unknowingly delivered themselves into the hands of their killers.

The potential victims of these killers, even during the most active time frame of the Ripper and Torso killings, never stopped walking the streets, nor did they stop going into the many pubs in the central killing zone. For most it was a numbers game they felt unable or unwilling to walk away from. The records show that any one prostitute working the streets of the Victorian East End was far more likely to commit suicide or die by other means than meet up with the Torso or Ripper killers. There was a general fatalistic view held by many of these women that it could not happen to them. Many felt that they could spot trouble and walk away from it. This may have been correct, if they were in control, but they were not in control—the killer was. And in all cases the killer, or killers, showed how much they were in control by the very fact of their continued successes.

No one was ever tried for a single Torso or Ripper murder, and that is perhaps the final judgment on the success of these serial killers. But the question remains, can anyone, 100 years or more after these murders, solve these crimes? Is there any trial or other evidence as yet uncovered, or unrecognized, which will finally point to one man as either the Thames Torso Killer or possibly even Jack the Ripper? Perhaps there is!

Chapter 10

On the Trail of a Victorian Serial Killer — George Chapman

> *It would be interesting to discover when the idea of murder for gross personal gratification first germinated in the brain of this unscrupulous Polish adventurer.*
> — Hargrave L. Adam, *Trial of George Chapman*

ALIAS GEORGE CHAPMAN

No one was ever brought to the bar of justice in any of the cases related to the Thames Torso Murders. Considering the fact that only one victim was ever identified, this is not a surprising result. Even today it is nearly impossible to solve a murder when you do not know who the victim was. There is, in fact, not even a list of suspects from which to match time frames, motives and opportunities in the Torso Murders. Just the opposite appears to be the case in the Ripper series, as suspects continue to pop up out of almost thin air. Anyone from a gay royal prince, the queen's doctor, a cabby, a boyfriend of one of the victims, several other doctors and the famous three found on a confidential internal police memo, and many others, have been put forward as suspects. None seem to have filled the shoes of the Ripper. There is no such internal police memo in the Torso files. In fact, most of the Torso case files no longer exist. All is speculation when it comes to suspects.

Before we look at one possible suspect, however, it is necessary to review what must have been part of the killer's makeup. Point one, which must be stated even though it is quite obvious, is that this man (I think we are on firm ground here) was a serial killer, and there were very few known serial killers in the East End of London at the time. Murder was not a daily event in the crime-ridden East End. Murders did occur, but serial murder was very rare indeed. The killing of strangers for "gross personal gratification" was not well known by any means. And if newspaper accounts are to be trusted, there were "only" two serial killers operating with knives in the East End at the time, the Ripper and the Thames Torso Killer. They were enough, however, to spread terror throughout London.

So with no solid evidence that points to any listed suspect, it is time to speculate by looking closely at one known serial killer who would never admit to being himself, let alone admit to murder. However, he was tried, convicted and executed for the deaths of three women he called his "wives." None could truly hold that mantle, as his real wife (which could have been his second) never divorced him. This minor detail, however, would not stop him from entering into phony marriages with three women who were more than willing to play along to the point of fooling their friends and families. His name was Severino Antonovich Klosowski, Severin to his friends (but by his own admission he had none). He would later acquire the name George Chapman, but we are getting ahead of our story.

HIS EARLY YEARS

Severin wrote a short biography of himself as he looked for more training in the surgical skills. "I was born in 1865, in the village of Nagornak, district of Kolo, Government of Kalish. I lived with my parents until the age of 15, attending at the same time the primary school." Indeed, young Severin was born in the tiny Russian/Polish village of Nagornak on December 14, 1865. His father was a hard working carpenter of 30 years named Antonio, and his mother was Emilie, who bore him at the age of 29. It is not known if he was an only child, but his short biography fails to mention any siblings, so it is a possibility that he was alone. A demented serial killer was alive and well.

He was an average student who attended the rural public school with regularity but not with any distinction. It would have been difficult for anyone to point to this young man and see any greatness. He would, however, be given the chance for a real career, as well as a very good education, at the age of 15. Having completed his public school studies, young Severin found himself apprenticed to Senior Surgeon Moshko Rappaport in December 1880 for the purpose of studying the fine art of surgery. His parents had sent him to Rappaport's medical facility at Zvolen where he would study for the next 4½ years.

In November of 1882, Severin had progressed sufficiently to become registered as a student of surgery. He, along with other students training under Dr. Rappaport, began work in the town of Radom, some 60 miles south of Warsaw. On the 16th of that month Severin obtained a document, which in part reported, "Severin Klosowski, resident of the village Zvolen, is a well-behaved man, and was never found guilty of any crime whatever." It is not recorded if any of the other students of the good doctor were also required to obtain such documentation.

> October 23–November 4, 1885.— The Radom Surgical Society, of the town of Radom, hereby certifies that the surgical pupil, Severin Klosowski, was entered at the registry of surgical pupils by the Senior Surgeon, Moshko Rappaport, in the town of Radom, November 22 — December 3, 1882. Subject No. 8, and in accordance with Article 17, letter b, of the Surgical Society. One ruble in silver was paid by him into the Treasury of the said Society.— In witness whereof, Brodinski, the Chief of the Society, testifies by affixing his signature and the seal of the Surgical Society.

On June 1, 1885, 19-year-old Severin completed his primary apprenticeship in surgery and was rewarded with documentation stating that he had been "diligent, of exemplary conduct, and studied with zeal the sciences of surgery. [He] discharged accurately all duties." Dr. Rappaport signed the paper. It would soon be added to by a second document attested to by medical practitioner O. P. Olstetski that Severin had "in the capacity of a practicing surgery pupil, and under the doctor's instruction rendered very skillful assistance to patients ... in cupping by means of glasses, leeches, and other assistance comprised in the science of surgery." Surgical student Severin Klosowski was now well on his way to a most promising career, but in order to advance further he would need to leave the back roads and villages of rural Poland and travel to the ancient city of Warsaw.

In 1885 Warsaw was becoming a major industrial center with a population of over 400,000 and was growing with great speed. It was a center of learning, focusing on the Imperial University of Warsaw and its many colleges. Nineteen-year-old Severin could have easily been overwhelmed, but before long he was training under Senior Surgeon Krynick. Severin never did take long to adjust to new situations or surroundings, a trait which would serve him well in years to come.

Before long Severin was adding to his resume by working part-time in the nearby city of Praga as an assistant surgeon to C. F. Olshanski. The good doctor's report on Klosowski's duties would state that from August 20, 1885, until February 1, 1886, "...during the whole of the time he fulfilled the whole of his duties with zeal, and was of good behavior." At the same time, Severin had taken a practical course of surgery at Praga Hospital. Severin Klosowski appeared to be on the fast track to a long career as a doctor of surgery in his native Poland.

> Certificate issued to the surgical apprentice, Severin Antonio Klosowski, to the effect that he, Severin Klosowski, was in my surgery for the purpose of studying surgery from December 1, 1880, till June 1, 1885, and during the whole of the time he, Severin Klosowski, discharged accurately all his duties. He was diligent, of exemplary conduct, and studied with zeal the science of surgery.— In testimony thereof I affix my signature, Moshko Rappaport, Senior Surgeon and proprietor of the surgery in the village Zvolen, June 1, 1885.

By December of 1886, Severin had completed hospital training under C. F. Olshanski and soon found a position as a surgeon's assistant under Dr. D. Moshkovski. He would report that Severin, now living at his own apartment at 16 Muranovskaja Street, had "performed his surgical functions with full knowledge of the subject and his conduct was good." There was only one final step to be taken, so in December of 1886 Severin petitioned the medical faculty dean of the Imperial University of Warsaw for an examination which would advance him to the position of Junior Surgeon.

> Warsaw, December, 1886
> His Excellency, the Dean of the Medical Faculty
> of The Imperial University of Warsaw.
>
> Petition from Severin Klosowski, surgical pupil,
> residing at No. 16 Muranovskaja Street.
>
> Sir;
> I have the honor to request your Excellency to grant me permission to undergo the examination for the purpose of receiving the degree of Junior Surgeon. I enclose herewith the required documents.
>
> Yours faithfully, Severin Klosowski.

The response was swift and the results were successful. On December 5, 1886, he received a document signed by the Collegiate Councilor and Inspector stating, "In consequence of the application presented by

Severin Klosowski, surgical pupil, the medical administration hereby testify to the effect that they do not see any reason to oppose his receiving the degree of a Junior Surgeon."

> Passport, given on November 24, 1886, to Severin Antonovich Klosowski, residing in the Radom Government, district of Ilshetsk, county of Khotche, village of Tyshenitsa, Nova Nil to travel to the city of Warsaw from the above date till November 1–13, 1887, upon the expiration of which the said document shall be returned to me. The civil and military authorities shall allow the bearer a free passage, and if necessary render him legal assistance. Given in Khotche, November 24, 1886. Physical description. Age, 21; born in 1865; height, medium; hair, of a dark shade; eyes, blue; nose and mouth, medium; chin and face, longish; birthmarks, none. Passport within the limits and the Kingdom of Poland. Free.—[Signed] Mazur, Magistrate of the County of Khotche. [Seal] Godlevski, County Clerk.

On February 28, 1887, Severin's membership to the Warsaw Society of Assistant Surgeons was paid. He was then a member of a select group of surgeons who would be expected to advance the science of surgery at the Imperial University of Warsaw. The receipt for fees paid would be the last documented evidence that Severin Antonovich Klosowski was ever in Poland. The record simply and completely ends there. He would next surface in one of the worst, and most vicious, ghettos in Europe, the East End of London!

THE EAST END

Why would a young man well on his way to a successful medical career suddenly remove himself from his home, his family, his studies and his country to an uncertain future in a foreign country? Any answer at this point would be pure speculation, but it does not take a great deal of logical thought to realize that Severin Klosowski was, for whatever reason, running for his very life. However, with no official documentation, we are left only with questions and very few answers. One question can be answered, and that is whether or not he ever contacted anyone in Poland after he left. According to those who were questioned about him, he never made contact again with anyone in Poland. As for his Polish wife he is reported to have left behind, she simply "disappeared" after finding Klosowski living with his new "wife" in London. (How did she find him in London, and who might have told her?)

Did he murder and possibly decapitate a woman in Warsaw before he escaped to London? Perhaps he attempted to perform an illegal operation, which ended in the death of his patient? The record is silent, but murder would seem to be the best motive for running as fast as he could away from his life in his native Poland.

> *It is possible that he may have committed murder before he left Poland.*
> — Hargrave L. Adam, 1923

Klosowski's arrival in London was not marked with any fanfare. Indeed, it is not possible to ascribe any particular date to his arrival. There is, however, a time frame in which he is most likely to have come to the East End — between March and June 1887. He would have arrived as a 21-year-old Polish immigrant, posing as a Jew, and reportedly speaking very little English. He did, however, speak fluent Yiddish, which would serve him well in the mostly Jewish area he had come to. And, if the timing was right, he was just in time to participate in the Rainham Torso Murder of May 1887.

After a few months of what must have been a trying period in his life, Klosowski found work as an assistant hairdresser in Poplar, East End. At the time, the jobs of assistant surgeon and hairdresser were mixed in an ancient position known as a felcher. It was a holdover from a much earlier time. Abraham Radin, the shop owner, would later testify that he had hired Klosowski in late 1887 or early 1888 for his shop located at 70 West India Dock Road.

For a period of five months, at least, Klosowski performed his duties at the shop. At one point he even helped nurse Mrs. Radin's oldest son back to health using the medical skills he had acquired over the 6½ years of training. He had even showed the Radins his medical papers, of which he was justly proud. During that period it must be said that there were no Torso or Ripper murders in the East End, or, for that matter, any unsolved or mysterious murders in London. After all, Radin's shop was a full two miles away from the heart of Whitechapel. There were, however, two strange attacks.

Before long he would be on the move. For whatever reason (it can be surmised), he never seemed to stay in one place for very long. It almost seemed as if he was always looking over his shoulder. Perhaps he needed to keep looking out as he went from place to place. As he was moving, it seemed a new crime wave moved with him.

On February 25, 1888, the first of two seemingly unrelated attacks occurred in the heart of "Thieves Kitchen," the locally given name for

Spitalfields. 38-year-old widow Annie Millwood lived at 8 White's Row, Spitalfields, and may have supported herself by prostitution. On that Saturday "a stranger who stabbed her numerous times on the legs and lower torso" attacked her. It was an unskilled attack using a clasp knife and seemed to have no motive other than the pure excitement the attacker obtained from the assault. A little more than a month later, on March 28, 39-year-old "seamstress" Ada Wilson was attacked in her home at 19 Maidman Street, Mile End. A stranger, described as around 30 years old, sun burnt face, moustache and standing about 5 feet 6 inches, forced his way into her home and demanded money. When the attacker was told that she had no money he stabbed her twice in the throat. It would be her screams that finally drove him off and almost into the hands of Ada's neighbors, who lost him in the darkness and fog of a cool London night.

By then Severin had ended his work at Mr. Radin's hairdressing shop and was looking for work in Whitechapel. He would soon find work as a floating barber and move into a cheap room in George Yard Dwellings. He was now firmly established in that "wicked quarter mile."

Jack's Place

It is interesting to note that the Ripper chose to begin his work in George Yard about the same time as Severin Klosowski moved into the area. It is even more notable when one finds that the first victim, Martha Tabram, was murdered on the first floor landing of the very same building Severin lived in!

Martha had last lived at 19 George Street at Satehell's Lodging House, just one street over from Severin's place. On August 7 she had gone off once again with an individual she had met at a local pub to conduct a bit of "street business." It was around 2 A.M. in the morning and it would be the last anyone would see her alive. Within the hour she was dead. At 4:45 that morning one of the building residents, John Saunder Reeves, discovered her body "lying on her back in a pool of blood." In point of fact, he had slipped on the blood. It was soon discovered that she had been stabbed 39 times, once with a bayonet type weapon and 38 more times with a short-bladed knife, possibly a penknife. The Ripper series had begun.

It would not be long before a second East End prostitute fell under the knife of the Ripper. Polly Nichols lived at a common lodging house at 18 Thrawl Street, just around the corner from George Yard. During the early morning hours of August 31, 1888, Polly had walked down a dark street called Buck's Row with a man she had hoped would become her last

customer of the night. He turned out to be Jack the Ripper. After he strangled her, the Ripper drew his knife twice across her throat deeply from ear-
to-ear. Lowering her to the ground he then began the first detailed mutilation
in the series.

> *...the lower part of the abdomen had been ripped up, and the
> bowels were protruding. The abdominal wall, the whole length of
> the body had been cut open.*
>
> Illustrated Police News— September 8, 1888

The East End was now up in arms as the press began to play the events
for all they were worth. Newspapers were selling as fast as they could fly
off of the presses. The public wanted answers, and the police were starting to see that a madman was living among the poor of London's ghettos.
He was a different kind of killer. The East End was faced with the task of
locating one of the world's first recognized serial killers. And they had yet
to acquire any description of the killer.

With the police lacking any description to go on, the Ripper felt quite
safe to continue his bloody work. As the police began to gather their strength,
the Ripper struck again. It must have been a long night for the killer, as he
would wait until nearly dawn before a target of opportunity walked his
way; but walk she did. At 5:30 in the morning of September 8, prostitute
Elizabeth Long walked past 29 Hanbury Street and saw her friend and fel-
low prostitute Annie Chapman speaking with a man. He was a stranger
as far as she could tell. As she passed, Long heard Annie say, "Yes" to a question. She had agreed to go into the back yard of the building with Jack the
Ripper. Within minutes the Ripper had strangled and ripped Annie's throat
before laying her on the stones and dirt of the very small yard. He would
need to work fast, as the sky was starting to lighten and he did not want
to become trapped in that very confined space.

> *...Left arm resting on the left breast, legs drawn up, abducted,
> small intestines and flap of the abdomen lying on right side, above
> right shoulder, attached by a cord with the rest of the intestines
> inside the body ... throat cut deeply from left and back in a jagged
> manner right around the throat.*
>
> — Inspector Joseph Chandler

As for Severin Klosowski, the *Daily Chronicle* of March 23, 1903 (he
was well known by then), would report, "The police have found that at
the time of the first two [Ripper] murders Klosowski was undoubtedly
occupying a lodging in George Yard, Whitechapel Road, where the first

murder was committed." At this particular time Klosowski felt safe enough to stay in the central Ripper area, but he would soon change his mind.

The people of London would not have long to wait for the Ripper's next attack on humanity, as he would deliver a "double event" during the early morning of September 30, 1888. The first to taste his blade that night was a 44-year-old prostitute named Elizabeth Stride. Stride had spent the afternoon earning her keep at a local lodging house cleaning two of the rooms. Later that evening she could be found going to one pub and then another, but it would appear that prostitution was not on Elizabeth's mind that night.

It has been suggested that she may have planned to meet someone on Berner Street, near the International Workingmen's Educational Club, as she had rejected the advances of at least two men as she made her way to the club. It would be in a side passage leading to a small backyard next to the club that she would meet her death. Just before 1 A.M. the Whitechapel Killer pushed her to the ground and produced a "fearful rip across her throat, killing her in a second."

> I could see that her throat was fearfully cut. There was a great gash in it over two inches wide.
> — Mrs. Diemschutz

Louis Diemschutz, the steward of the small club, discovered her still warm corpse. He had come very close to seeing the Ripper in the middle of his work, but this time the Ripper did not mutilate his victim. This was a hit! Did Stride know who the killer was? Only silence moves across the years on that question; however, one question may be answered. When Diemschutz finished his nightly sales of cheap jewelry using his pony-drawn cart he would place the cart in the backyard next to the club known as Dutfield's Yard. He would then walk the few blocks northwest towards the stable. It was located on the other side of George Yard *directly across the street from the George Yard Dwellings and the rooms of Severin Klosowski!* Earlier that evening one of the club's American guests, Joseph Lave, had seen "a man pretending to be a Polish barber, and that he was living in George Yard." The police, it would seem, never followed up on that clue!

The terror of that September night had just begun, as the killer calmly walked the dark streets towards the west and the edge of the central city of London, past George Yard. At 1 A.M., as the damp and cooling corpse of Elizabeth Stride was being discovered, 46-year-old Catharine Eddowes was being released from one of the local police station's drunk-tanks. She was by no means sober, but at least she could walk. She should have headed north towards her usual lodging house; instead she walked south towards Mitre Square for a meeting with Jack the Ripper. Earlier she had told friends, "I think I know him." By 1:45 A.M. she was dead and badly ripped up by the Whitechapel Killer.

After a six-week break the killer would strike again with the bloody murder of Mary Jane Kelly on November 9. She would become the worst mutilated of the Ripper victims. Again a break would occur until December 20, with the death of Rose Mylett in Poplar, East End. And once again the killer would slow down his attacks, perhaps due in part to the many forces desperately trying to find him. However, he would come out of hiding on July 17, 1889, to stab Alice McKenzie twice in the throat and cut her on the chest from the left breast to her navel. McKenzie would be found dead but still warm in the heart of Ripper territory in a dark passageway known as Castle Alley. It was one short block from George Yard.

By then, however, Klosowski had made one of his many moves to 126 Cable Street, St. George-in-the-East. His new lodgings were about 1/2 of a mile southeast of the central Ripper area, and just outside of the great search area. In fact, he had probably moved to that location just before the massive search effort began. It would have been a very good time to move. The 1889 issue of *The Post Office Directory of London* lists 126 Cable Street as his working address. It was not an area known to be particularly safe. Much of the area was uninhabited and known for being a very dangerous place to live.

It was soon medically shown that the killer of McKenzie was just as skilled as the Ripper, whether this was the same man or not. He had killed with speed and very quietly, as witnessed by a woman up late that early morning, reading, with her bedroom window open to the alley only feet from the body. If this was not Jack it was a very good reproduction.

> [He] knew the position of the vessels, at any rate where to cut with reference to causing speedy death.
>
> — Dr. Phillips, Police Surgeon

In both the Torso and Ripper cases the police were looking for a single man who would somehow not fit into the East End. It is difficult to know exactly what type of man this could possibly be, as there were a great many different and strange type of people, from all over Europe, living or passing through the East End at the time. Very little has changed in that regard, even today. The single man theory, living alone, however, could be the key. If the killer was to complete his "tasks" he would need the cover of responsibility, and that would mean marriage.

Only days after the final body parts of Torso victim Elizabeth Jackson washed up on the banks of the river Thames, and just days after the murder of Alice McKenzie, Severin Klosowski decided that he would visit a local social club. *The Polish Club* on St. John's Square, Clerkenwell, London, was a meeting place for single men and women. It was a place to find a wife of similar social standing and background.

At the club Klosowski met a Walthanstow tailor by the name of Stanislaus Baderski. Baderski would later recall the meeting and state, "He was introduced to me as Severin Klosowski and said that he had a barber shop." A short time later Stanislaus would introduce his sister Lucy to the young Mr. Klosowski. As in most matters, it would not take long for Klosowski to make his move. Within five weeks, Klosowski and Lucy were living together at 126 Cable Street. Just across the tracks, which ran in front of his barber shop, was Pinchin Street, known locally as "Dark Lane." It would soon hold the decomposing torso of the third victim of the Thames Torso Killer.

As was the case with Ripper victim Martha Tabram, whose body was found literally on Klosowski's front steps, the Pinchin Street corpse (or portion found there) was located just across the street from his home and business. No other suspect could ever claim to have been so close to both cases. It is also interesting to note that in the police report filed on the Pinchin Street murder, mention was made that the authorities did not know whether the Ripper had finished his work or not. The report also made mention of the fact that this body was found around the corner from where Ripper victim Elizabeth Stride had been killed.

> *We may say that the murder was committed probably in the house or lodging of the murderer, and that he conveyed the portion found to Pinchin Street to get rid of it...*
> — Home Office file 144/221/A 49301 K, September 11, 1889

The Pinchin Street murder would be the last Torso case for 12 years, and the Ripper would not kill again in all of 1890. During the next 12 months Klosowski and his new wife moved several times. He seemed to always be on the run, moving in and around Whitechapel several times— to Commercial Street, Greenfield Street and others, ending up by September 1890 at 89 Whitechapel High Street. In the basement of that dilapidated building Klosowski began work as an assistant barber. Just above was the *White Hart Public House*. Before long Klosowski became the sole proprietor, but the reason for his "promotion" has been lost.

He was soon able to move his wife and new son, Wohystaw, to a house on Greenfield Street. With her move to Greenfield it would give Klosowski the freedom he needed to pursue his "hobbies." As for the East End population, they were quickly getting back to business as usual as less and less could be heard on the streets about the Ripper. Even with the newspapers trying their best to keep the story alive, and several Ripper letters coming to the police and newspapers, no one was interested in him anymore. Most believed that he had been killed, moved away, or had somehow lost the urge to kill. The Ripper had other ideas.

On February 13, 1891, 25-year-old constable Ernest Thompson was walking his first night beat on his own. At 2:15 A.M. on that foggy morning, Thompson was patrolling in a westerly direction on Chamber Street. Ahead he could hear, but not see, the steps of a man walking away from him, but not in a hurried manner. Thompson was 300 yards away from Klosowski's new barber shop as he turned into a short passage called Swallow Gardens. Under the railway arch he found Frances Coles with a deeply cut throat lying on the wet ground. Coles would become the final victim to fall at the hands of Jack the Ripper. The series was over, but only the killer knew that for certain.

Once again the hunt was on for the Ripper, but many involved in the search felt (at least officially) that this was a copycat crime and not the work of Jack. Nonetheless, this murder would find its way into the Ripper file as the East End geared up for yet one more search.

Klosowski was also very busy at the time. He was doing a fair amount of business in "his" basement shop, storing away as much money as he could. But he had family problems. He was staying out late at night, at times coming back home as late as 4 A.M. He was continuing his late night "walks" around Whitechapel and would not tell his young wife where he would go. At the same time his son was gravely ill.

On March 3, 1891, 5-month-old Wohystow Klosowski died of pneumonia asthenia. His death certificate would state, "father was present at death." As the years would pass, Klosowski would find himself present at many deaths, and this one could not have meant much to him. Klosowski was a stone cold serial killer who had just had the burden of his son removed. He was now free to travel, and travel he did, or perhaps a better word would have been run!

After the Coles murder several detectives who had worked on the Ripper series would write that the killer had indeed been caught. Some of them had reported in later years that he had to be released because a witness had refused to testify, but that with his identity thus known to the police he was unable to continue his bloody work. It has been further written that the Ripper then left London for new killing grounds in America.

On April 3, 1891, the national census was conducted. That survey is reported to have found Klosowski and his wife living at 2 Teakesbury Buildings, Whitechapel, at the time. Within days, however, he and his wife boarded a ship and crossed the Atlantic, landing in New York City sometime in April 1891. Perhaps the detectives were correct when they said the Ripper had left the country. One point is clear, after Klosowski's departure there would never again be a Ripper murder in England. That cannot be said of the United States.

America Calling

The exact date of Klosowski's arrival in the United States has yet to be determined, but if he left on the day after the British census it would have given him 19 full days in which to cross the Atlantic. At the end of the 1800s even slow ships were making the crossing in less than 12 days. There would have been plenty of time for the couple to arrive and find a place to stay by April 23, 1891. Why is that date so important?

During the early morning hours of April 24, an aging prostitute named Carrie Brown, known to her friends as "Old Shakespeare," was murdered in a hotel room near the East River in New York City. She had been strangled, stabbed and disemboweled in a manner very much like that of the Ripper victims. She was found laying in a bed very much like Mary Jane Kelly. The suspect, seen by at least two witnesses, was described as a man looking very much like Klosowski. After the murder the killer walked a short distance to another hotel but was unable to acquire a room for the night.

> He asked me in broken English if I could give him a room. His right hand rested on my desk and I noticed it was all bloody.
> — Glenmore Hotel night clerk Mr. Kelly

Before long Klosowski and his wife were on the move once again. This time he would set up a small barber shop in the front of his living quarters in Jersey City, New Jersey, just across the river from New York. It would not, however, be a pleasant move for Mrs. Klosowski. She would soon find that her husband's roving eye had not settled down at all, and he was soon out at night without any explanation. Adding to his evening activities was his thug-like behavior to his wife. At one point during an argument Klosowski held her down on the bed and pressed his mouth against hers to prevent her from screaming. He fully intended to kill her. It was only the entry of a customer in the front shop which prevented him from continuing his "work" on his wife. Cash carrying customers were always of great importance to Severin.

That evening Klosowski explained to his wife that he meant to kill her by cutting off her head. She would later find a very large knife under his pillow on the bed she had been pinned to. Klosowski meant business and she knew it. When he pointed to a spot in the room where he planned to bury her, Lucy stated that the neighbors would wonder where she had gone. Calmly Klosowski replied, "Oh, I should simply have told them that you had gone back to New York."

At that point Lucy knew it was time to leave. It is not recorded whether or not she suspected her violent husband of being the Ripper or perhaps the Torso Killer, but she was not about to test the theory. Whatever her thoughts, she did not share them with the police. After only ten months in the United States, the six-months-pregnant Lucy left her husband and returned to the East End of London in late January 1892. Severin Klosowski had lost control of his home life, was alone and was very angry.

On the morning of January 31, 1892, 70-year-old watchman Joseph Senior returned home from his job as a night watchman in Milburn, New Jersey, to find his wife of many years dead on the kitchen floor. Blood and the signs of a battle were everywhere. 73-year-old Elizabeth Senior had been brutally attacked by a knife-wielding man. Her throat had been ripped open and her breasts were stabbed eleven times. Mrs. Senior did not go down easy, as witnessed by the deep defensive wounds on her arms. "...Both arms were frightfully gashed."—The *New York Times*.

After her murder the killer calmly washed his hands and his knife in the sink as he waded in her pool of blood. He then carefully ransacked the house. As was the case before, no one would stand before a jury for this murder. It would be "Murder by person or persons unknown."

As for Klosowski, business was not what he felt it should be. Perhaps he paid too much attention to his sexual needs and not enough to his barber shop. Whatever the reason, he was fast running out of money. If he did not find some way to raise cash he would soon be out on the street. With no other woman in his life, he made plans to return to London. Perhaps his wife, who was about to give birth to their second child, would take him back?

ENGLAND ONCE AGAIN

On June 8, 1892, Herta May Anderson met her death at the hands of a mad killer as she walked along the tracks near her home in Perth Amboy,

New Jersey. She was dragged to a wooded area just off the tracks and her throat was cut from ear to ear, but this time a new twist was added. She was also shot through the heart by a 32-caliber pistol. It was a new touch in a long series of death. By mid–June, Klosowski was making his way back to London for what he planned would be a reunion with his wife. He *needed* to re-establish control. Before long Klosowski would arrive in London in the heart of Whitechapel and was able to convince his wife to take him back. He had very little money, a few documents, some medical books, a few barber tools and a brand new American 32-caliber pistol!

Within a month he had again departed, this time without his wife. He would begin a period of nearly 16 months where the records of his movements have yet to be found. As for his wife Lucy, she would not see him again until his 1902 trial for murder eleven years later. At that last meeting Klosowski would state that he "did not know the woman nor had he known her eleven-year-old daughter."

By the end of 1893, Klosowski re-surfaced in South Tottenham at Haddin's Hairdresser's shop using the name Schloski. While working at the shop he met and began living with a woman named Annie Chapman. She could very well have been Annie Georgina Chapman, the daughter of Ripper victim Annie Chapman. Before long this union would also fail, as Annie refused to live with Klosowski and his new girlfriend. There would be two lasting results from this period of his life. Klosowski would take the name George Chapman and Annie would have a child.

Chapman/Klosowski was now free to move about once again, as next he finds employment in Leytonstone. He was also looking for a woman to share his "lifestyle." He would find her in the guise of Mrs. Mary Spink, former wife of humble railway porter Shadrack Spink. She would become the ideal victim for this serial killer—not overly intelligent and mostly drunk. Before long she would cease to amuse the abusive "Mr. Chapman" as he looked for the best way to dispatch his now unwanted "wife." After her cash had run out, Chapman decided on a little boat trip. On that trip Mary, who could not swim, ended up in the water with Chapman and almost drowned.

With one eye on a new lady named Alice Penfold, Chapman went to local chemist William Davidson. Davidson had a business at 66 High Street in Hastings. On April 3, 1897, "George Chapman" purchased a small bottle of white powder. He would turn away from the knife and pick up the poison.

Poison, Tartar-emetic. Dose, 1/16th grain to 1/4.
To be taken with caution.

Alice would not stay around Chapman for long. She seemed to know that he was just not right for her. Chapman, however, was still tired of the usually drunk Mrs. Spink, who just had to go. She would become the first *known* victim of the Borough Poisoner, as Chapman was once again reinventing himself—this time as a publican in Barthotomew Square. He was also slowly administering poison for months to the once healthy Mary Spink. Mary finally died on Christmas day 1897. For Chapman it was a gift, called by Dr. Rogers "natural causes"; for Mary, a final release from slow torture.

Not to be held back by a "death in the family," Chapman soon recovered and was on the lookout for a new wife/barmaid/victim. Before long Elizabeth "Bessie" Taylor came to the rescue of the widower Chapman. Bessie had answered an ad for a barmaid placed in the local paper. Many women applied, but only one would suit the special needs of the Borough Poisoner.

Before long Bessie would enter into a bogus marriage with Mr. Chapman. For some reason, time and time again, women would fake marriage with this killer. Bessie would not be the last. She would, however, last three years in the "position." Chapman would soon tire of the new Mrs. Chapman and plans would need to be made. He knew that the deaths of two wives at the same location and from the same apparent cause would be just a bit too much, so a move was in order. In late 1898 he gave up his lease on the Prince of Wales and moved to Stortford. There he continued his cover as a publican with a lease on the Grapes Public House. He now had enough time and space to do a little work on Bessie, who soon fell ill.

In March of 1899 the "happy" couple once again moved, this time to Union Street in Southwark. Chapman had taken another lease, this time on the Monument Tavern. As Chapman was intercepting money sent to Bessie from her parents, he continued to slowly poison his new wife. Despite a slight recovery, noted by Dr. J. Morris Stoker, it was soon evident that Bessie would not recover. The many months of slow poisoning were about to pay off.

As Chapman carefully detailed her slow and painful decline, the doctors reported that it was only a matter of time. They had no clue as to what was really killing Bessie. The end came in the early morning of February 13, 1901. Chapman ensured that the nurse and doctor were not present at the death. He wanted to enjoy his work alone, but one nurse insisted on staying. She would later report that the "husband cried bitterly." If anything, Chapman was quite an actor. He had to be to be a successful serial killer.

In order to properly tie up loose ends he needed a death certificate stating that poor Bessie had died of natural causes. The most accommodating Dr. Stoker, who would never look past the surface of the case, soon issued it. The final act in Bessie's "play" was for Chapman to portray the grieving husband by sending out cards to all those who had tried to help his wife. He would also send a card to the gravesite ceremony with not a single truthful word on it.

In loving Memory of
Bessie Chapman
Wife of George Chapman

By afternoon the pub was open for business, with Chapman explaining that it was best to keep working at a time like that. He would later begin his nighttime walks around the area looking for companionship. These were all right for one-night stands, but Chapman was getting older now and needed a more convenient way to spend his time. He needed a new wife. After a respectable six months of public mourning, he began to advertise for a new barmaid/victim.

THE FINAL VICTIM?

After a detailed search through the many letters Chapman received in response to his ad, he was ready to make his choice. The woman who caught his lustful eye was 18-year-old Maud Marsh, who had written from her parent's home in Croydon. It was August of 1901 and Chapman had found his final poison victim.

Before long Maud was working at the Monument and living upstairs with George Chapman. As would be expected, Chapman soon began "paying her attentions" and giving Maud gifts such as a gold watch and chain. The gifts meant nothing to Chapman, as he knew they would be returned upon the sudden death of Maud! Within weeks the always fast moving Chapman had proposed to Maud, who conveyed the proposal to her parents. They were not amused, to say the least, and began to mistrust the good Mr. Chapman. However, Maud would soon enter into a bogus marriage with Chapman. She knew full well that it was false, going off with Chapman to drive around town for a while to fool her friends and family.

On the surface, which was about all anyone ever saw of Chapman, it seemed that the marriage was doing well. The couple looked happy and business was up. However, in late 1901 Chapman's lease on the Monument would be up for renewal, and there was a possibility that he would not get a new one. This would not do, so Chapman decided to empty out his goods and cash and simply set the place on fire. It was not a very good job. That morning the *Morning Advertiser* reported that it had indeed been arson, with Chapman being by far the best suspect. Chapman was quick to "issue a writ for libel," but it would not hold up in court. The facts, as known by the police, were brought to his attention and he dropped the matter. It would also seem that the police dropped the matter as well. No charges were ever brought forward in the case. If they had been, perhaps Maud would have survived her short and deadly encounter with the Borough Poisoner. But he may have spent time in jail and never been convicted of other crimes.

Despite the problem with the Monument fire, which damaged but did not destroy the pub, Chapman was able to once again acquire a pub lease. Just before Christmas of 1901 Chapman and Mrs. Chapman number three moved into the Crown Public House at 213 Borough High Street, Southwark, London. It would be his last business venture as a publican.

For a few months nothing of note was occurring, other than the slow poisoning of Maud Marsh. Once again a wife of Chapman's had taken ill and several doctors could not come up with any satisfactory reason. It would be a very slow process, with Maud passing through periods of general good health and then going into a rapid decline. In the background of his slow torture another body would drop only 1200 yards down the road from the Crown Public House.

In June of 1902 the final Torso Murder would come to the attention of London police. As before, the killer cut off the head, arms and legs, but this case had a twist or two. The killer would cook or boil the head, the only one found in the series, and he would pile up the body parts to be found. The question is asked whether or he intended the corpse to be found with the head placed on top of the pile, or was he interrupted during the disposal? History is silent on the matter.

It was time to finish off Maud. But Chapman had been killing for a very long time and he was getting a bit sloppy in his work. He was talking a bit too much as well. During a visit by Maud's older sister Louise, as Maud was slowly dying, Chapman made a very stupid remark. "I could give her a bit like that [snapping his fingers] and fifty doctors could not find out." It was a statement which would be recalled at his trial but did not seem to push Maud's family to remove Maud from the "care" of Chapman. No one wanted to accuse Chapman of slowly killing his "wife," such was his ability to fool those around him even as all clues pointed to him.

On the day before Maud took her last breath, Maud's father Robert called a new doctor into the case. Dr. Graspel would finally come to the proper conclusion that poison was the agent of her long illness, and he suspected Chapman of being the culprit. He telegraphed his grave concerns to Dr. Stoker, who had been acting as Maud's physician, but it would arrive too late—Maud was already dead. Chapman had suspected that his game was about to be uncovered, but rather than step back from killing he gave Maud a massive dose of tartar-emetic. Chapman could not allow a victim he had been working on for so long to escape, even if it cost him his life.

Dr. Stoker was stunned. He knew Maud was very sick, but her death on October 22 was still a surprise. He refused to issue a death certificate until he could show what had caused the vomiting and diarrhea which had contributed to her death. Chapman demanded he issue the certificate so that he could have control over Maud, but the doctor stood his ground. Chapman was trapped but still felt that he could fool any doctor. He ended his protests and allowed a limited post-mortem. It was a fatal error. Chapman was unaware that Dr. Stoker now suspected him of murder and was about to prove it.

The day after Maud's death her mother and younger sister, Alice May Marsh, visited Chapman. They were suspicious of Chapman but wanted to be supportive in case he had not been the cause of Maud's death. Chapman, never one to let a good opportunity go by, asked Alice if she would come to work at his pub. After all, he had a fresh opening. "There is a chance for you as barmaid now, will you come?" It was later recalled that the shocked Alice could only reply, "I said, no thanks, London does not suit me." As for Maud's mother, she was unable to say anything. Chapman had by then regained his composure and was attempting to control the women around him. The grand serial killing misogynist was back, and he was looking for a new wife! He would, however, find little time to look, as the authorities, slow to react, were about to finally catch up to his game of serial death.

On a bright Saturday morning, October 25, 1902, as all levels of London society were watching the coronation parade for Edward VII, Severino Antonavich Klosowski, alias George Chapman, was arrested at the Crown Public House. Inspector George Godley, who fifteen years earlier had been involved in both the Ripper and Torso investigations, took into custody a man suspected in the death of a single woman. He would soon find all the evidence he would need to convict Klosowski of at least three murders.

Opposite: The old Crown Public House, 213 Borough High Street, the final address of Severin Klosowski, where he was arrested for serial murder. (The London Institute of Technology and Research no longer exists; it went out of business, and the building is presently unoccupied.) Photograph by Debbie Gosling, 2000.

Godley would also be one of the first to suspect that he had arrested the man known to criminal history as Jack the Ripper. He was not alone. The inspector who had headed up that investigation, Chief Inspector George Frederick Abberline, also believed that Klosowski could indeed have been the Ripper.

There was no doubt that "Chapman" was Klosowski. Documents found at the Crown pub clearly proved this as fact, yet the prisoner would never admit who he really was. Even as he was clearly identified by individuals who had known him for up to 15 years, including his wife Lucy, Klosowski stuck to his story that he was the American George Chapman.

Klosowski soon found himself standing before Mr. Paul Taylor at Southwark Police Court. He was cynical to his surroundings and appeared disinterested in the proceedings. The air of contempt had yet to leave him, but it would not last. He was remanded to custody without bail. The court had heard enough evidence to show that the police finally had the right man.

> *He has had three deaths in five years— two Mrs. Chapmans and Marsh.*
>
> — Inspector Godley

By the time the police court and coroner's inquest had done their work, Klosowski knew he would not escape the justice he so richly deserved. On March 16, 1903, Severin Klosowski, 36-year-old serial killer, went on trial for the "willful murder of Maud Marsh." All three poison victims had been exhumed, and all three had been literally saturated with antimony, an extract of tarter-emeric. It would be an easy case for the prosecution.

The trial of the Borough Poisoner would consume barely four days, from the time Klosowski declared in a very weak voice, "Not guilty, Sir," until jury deliberations. Most of the time was spent by the crown, which put forward an iron-clad case. The defense, however, put forward no case at all. There was none to present! There would be no witness for the defense and Klosowski would say nothing.

The jury of twelve was then instructed to "think over the evidence which has been given and come to a proper conclusion." They were then escorted out of the courtroom to a small side room for their deliberations. The men soon came to their decision. In less than eleven minutes the jury signaled that their work was done. It was left to the foreman to declare:

"We find the prisoner guilty."

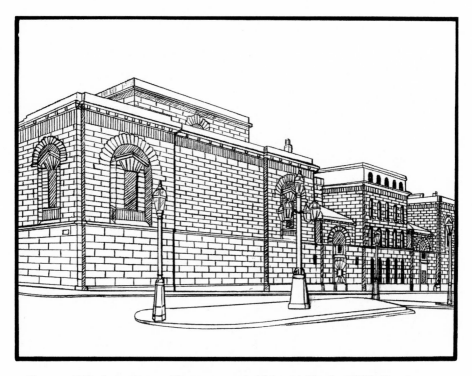

Newgate Jail where George Chapman was held for trial in the Old Bailey. It was demolished in 1904 to make way for a new Central Criminal Court for London.

The judge took little time going over the case and immediately brought the trial to its expected conclusion. He addressed Klosowski by his real name. "I decline to call you by the English name you have assumed...." Before a packed courtroom the now much hated and convicted serial killer faced the justice he had escaped for over 15 years.

"I have but one duty to perform—and it is not necessary for me to say more. It is the duty of sentencing you to death."

All eyes were on Klosowski, including Maud's mother, father and sisters, as the sentence washed over him. He turned white with fear as his eyes darted around, looking for some way out like a trapped animal, and he began to tremble noticeably. Barely able to stand, he could not speak, and was soon lead, half supported by guards, out of the courtroom and loaded onto the police vehicle.

I see you've got Jack the Ripper at last!
— Chief Inspector George Abberline to his friend Inspector George Godley

On April 7, 1903, Severino Antonovich Klosowski, poisoner, serial killer and misogynist, was hanged on the scaffold of Wandsworth Prison. His years of murder had ended. A reporter from *The South London Press* who had closely covered the story would report to their evening readership his firsthand account of Klosowski, alias Chapman's, execution. The final scenes were reported on April 11, 1903.

From the 1903 trial of Severin Klosowski, alias George Chapman, at the Old Bailey.

"The convict was aroused shortly after 6 o'clock, when he dressed and took mass, after which, at 7 o'clock, he was offered his breakfast of bread and butter and coffee, but scarcely ate anything. He was then very moody and depressed. As the dread hour approached, Chapman displayed a nervous fear of his approaching fate, and the slightest sound caused him to start. Shortly before the time appointed, the condemned cell was entered, and as Chapman was told to stand up he faltered, but soon pulled himself together. Billington [the executioner] quickly proceeded with the pinioning process, and the melancholy procession walked slowly to the execution shed, about 50 yards across the yard. As Chapman went to the scaffold, he was ashen pale, and almost stumbled more than once, and the dread of his rapidly approaching end seemed too great a strain to his nerves.

"Just before leaving the cell he appeared faint, and drank a glass of water, and during the pinioning process he appeared to tremble. When actually on the scaffold Billington quickly strapped his legs and adjusted the cap, and instantly on the signal pulled the lever, death being instantaneous.

"On the way to the scaffold, and also on the scaffold, Chapman made frequent ejaculations, and muttered inaudibly, rendering the last scene a peculiarly painful one.

"After the execution Dr. Beamish examined the body, and pronounced life extinct, and it was left to hang for an hour.

"Chapman was of ordinary build, and was given a drop of 6 ft., 6 in.

"In the crowd outside the gate were seen many of the foreign witnesses who figured in the case, and Chapman's reputed wife, Lucy Klosowski, was said to be in the immediate vicinity with her brother and sister."

What began with his death was nearly a century of speculation that this three-time serial killer and woman hater was a great deal more deadly than that. Was Severin Klosowski the killer who brought terror to the East End of London in more ways than can be imagined in the late 1880s? His patterns of movement and training certainly place him at the top of anyone's list of Ripper suspects. But was he also the Torso Killer? The evidence, such as it is, makes this claim a great deal more difficult to sustain. It can only barely be shown that he may have been in the East End in 1887, about the time the Torso Murders began, and yet he was moving through Europe towards England when the Paris torso was dumped in the heart of that great city. He was also firmly established in London for all of 1888/89, when three other torsos were discovered. He was also living in a house, which would have given him a well-hidden "work" area.

More critically, he was a proven serial killer with documented surgical skills. These facts cannot be denied. It must also be said that the Torso Murders were suspended while he was in America and did not continue until he moved south of the Thames River. It would be in Southwark where the final "pile" of body parts would be found some 1200 yards from his final home. And he had a carriage of his own.

We must not forget that a torso was found within sight of his barber shop on Pinchin Street, literally across the tracks from his shop on Cable Street. The Pinchin Street torso could indeed be the key to the Torso series. Find the killer of this victim and the Torso series is solved, once and for all!

As stated earlier, the torso from the Pinchin Street case was placed in a container of alcohol in order to preserve it for later investigation. If the container is still there, and is still intact, DNA material could be extracted and matched to family members alive today. The problem is—what family to look for? I would suggest that the first place to begin any search would be the family of Klosowski's first wife in Poland. If the Pinchin Street Torso was his original wife, then Klosowski was the Thames Torso Killer—case closed!

But was he also the much more publicized serial killer known to history as Jack the Ripper? The Ripper's skills, movements, time frames and description all seem to point, once again, to serial killer Klosowski as the

Chapman's barber shop at 126 Cable Street, St. George-in-the-East, London, his home and workplace at the time of the Pinchin Street murder.

best suspect. If he was "Jack," then he had the almost amazing ability to continuously reinvent himself seemingly at will. He was a most deadly and singular serial killer, to be sure. If true, he would not be matched for originality until the Zodiac Killer walked the dark paths of California in the late 1960 and early '70s. This was an individual who fully lacked any real human emotions, save those of a lower animal. And he only killed the weak or the helpless—a true coward if ever there was one.

Serial Killer and Borough Poisoner—Yes
Jack the Ripper—Very Possibly
The Thames Torso Killer—Just Perhaps!

I will cut off your head and bury it in the room.

— Severin Klosowski to his wife Lucy,
quoted in *Trial of George Chapman*

Chapter 11

The Torso of Salamanca Place, 1902

The flesh on the face had quite disappeared!

— News report

THE FINAL DISCOVERY

In June of 1902 George Chapman was making plans for another quick change of address. He had consolidated his funds and was actively looking for a new woman with whom to once again escape to America. By this time he had moved south of the Thames, still in London, to the district of Southwark. He was now the respectable, but not well liked, married proprietor of the Crown Public House, and he had much "business" to attend to. Just over a mile down the road from his new pub would soon be found the final victim of the Thames Torso Killer. And this would be the only murder in the series that would show the killer had lived nearby and probably on the south side of the river at the time the murder was committed.

Salamanca Place was not an area you would find yourself in unless you lived or worked there. It was out of the way, yet near enough to the river to feel its presence; but the area was not a very healthy location. The area was described in the *South London Press* to its readership who woke to read of yet another murder in Old London: "Salamanca-alley is a short passage 20 ft. wide and 50 yards long, uniting Broad Street and Salamanca Street. It is close to the Albert Embankment and the Lambeth Bridge, and behind part of Doulton's works. It is a small thoroughfare of back entrances and blank walls, in a neighbourhood teeming with workmen's dwellings. In the daytime swarms of children play in the gutter. At night few people can have use for it, and the patrolling constable's visits are few and far between. Nearby rush the South-Western Railway."

Charles Whiting, who lived at 16 Neville Street, and his friend Robert William Muntzer, worked for Messrs Doulton's Pottery Works. Whiting was a stoker and Muntzer worked as a general laborer on the night shift. It was a little after 4 A.M., June 8, and well enough lit by an early cool Sunday morning sunrise as the men walked out of Doulton's across Broad Street parallel to the Albert Embankment. They turned into the darkened Salamanca Alley to fire up a new kiln and spoke of the work ahead.

Whiting was the first to spot the pile as he stopped dead in his tracks, grabbing Muntzer by the arm. "Oh, what's that?" It did not take long for William Muntzer to see, with a short gasp, exactly what his friend had called to his attention. The men had nearly walked into a pile of human remains which had been piled up in front of the back door of Doulton's Works. What had stopped the men in mid-sentence and mid-stride was the sight of a woman's head laid on top of the torn flesh, with her dead eyes staring directly at the astonished workmen. For a short while both men just stared, not really knowing what they were looking at or what to do.

Later in the day, Mr. Whiting, then somewhat calmer, was interviewed by the *South London Press* for details of his discovery. He told the reporter that "The head was lying partly on its side. In addition to the head, I saw what appeared to be legs and arms all piled together, the head being on top. It looked as though the remains had been placed there carefully, and not as if they had been shot out of a sack. The body was really in three pieces. First came the legs, then the lower part of the body, and the head was in the pelvis. The remains were by the first gate on entering the alley from Broad Street. I drew my mate's attention to it by saying, 'Oh, what's that?' and Muntzer looked at the pile and remarked that it was a human being." It was later reported that "He turned the head over with his boot and saw a small ear, and that was how he judged it was a woman."

Both men took the time to regain their breaths, as well as their wits, deciding to report the matter to the night watchman, John Cox. The good Mr. Cox was reported to have "attended the kilns in Salamanca Street," and upon hearing the calls of the two excited men quickly opened the gate. His posting was in the lobby of Doulton's Works near gate number two, and the corpse pile had been located some 70 yards from where he watched by the first gate. The first gate was the first door anyone would come across as they entered the alley. It was clear that the killer had moved with his body bag down Broad Street and had ducked into Salamanca Alley to relieve himself of his criminal burden. He was not able, for whatever reason, to make it all the way to the river close-by.

Cox would later state that he had "previously passed down the alley at 10 P.M. on Saturday night and did not think the remains could have been there then, and some men told him [later in the day] that they passed there at 1 A.M., when there was nothing to see." John Cox had also left his lobby posting for a brief walk in the cool night air down the alley at around 3 A.M. and was certain that there was no body pile there at the time. He had also seen no one in the alley.

Mr. Cox instructed Charles Whiting at the time of discovery to "go and prepare your coke and coal for the fires, and I will go and report the matter." Before long Cox was off down Broad Street in search of the local beat constable who was not often in the area. It was a very good place to dump a body, as the patrols were few, but only a local would be well enough aware of that fact to use it with any reliability and confidence. The Thames Torso Killer was now local to the Southwark area!

Police Constable James Birton, 155L, Lambeth Division, was working his usual beat along the Albert Embankment. It had not been a particularly unusual night's patrol that cool Sunday morning until he saw an excited man running up to him at 4:40 A.M. It was now light enough to see that the man had some urgent business that the constable would soon be involved in.

John Cox was very agitated when he saw the officer and called, "Come here, I want you." He was not able to explain to the now confused officer exactly what he wanted as Constable Birton tried to calm him down. Soon, however, the message came across that a murder had been committed and the constable was needed in Salamanca Alley.

Birton had himself patrolled that very alley not 30 minutes before the pile of human remains had been located. "I am positive the bones were not there then, or I must have seen them. It was rather dark during the night." This was further evidence that the remains had simply been dropped off with speed. Perhaps the killer had seen the constable patrol past the spot and simply followed behind, certain that no other officer would soon pass that same way. It was later learned that a local gas lamp lighter had been through the area where the body was located at 3:10 A.M. This walkthrough had confined the time frame to dump the body.

It is also possible that the killer fully intended to drop off his body parts in the same manner as before—in the Thames River. However, if he had seen too many people about that early Sunday or simply became concerned about discovery he may have panicked and dropped his load as soon as he could. But why did he not simply leave the body parts in the bag he most probably carried them in? Did he carry them this time in a private carriage? If he had a carriage he could not have been poor. He was skilled in surgery; perhaps he was a local successful businessman as well!

While Cox was looking for a constable, Muntzer stayed to guard the remains. As he waited for his friend to return, two medical students walked by on their way to a local medical training facility. As they calmly walked down the alley they came across the pile of body parts and began to examine them. Muntzer heard one of them say, "Oh, it's a woman's head." The two young men then continued on their way, seemingly uninterested in the events which had recently transpired to create the pile of mutilated remains in the alley. They were never identified and would never come forward to explain their strange reactions to this brutal crime.

As Constable Birton entered the alley, with Cox fast at his heel, he approached Muntzer, asking, "You are the man who first found the body?" He then turned in the early morning light of a new day to view what he would never forget. P.C. Burton soon called for assistance and more officers, as an inspector joined the small group of men behind the factory of Messrs Doulton's Works. They began what would become a house-to-house search of an area fully ½ mile around the alley. The search, however, would miss the *Crown Public House*, Severin Klosowski's new business.

Before long Constable Birton and others loaded the remains, which he felt had been purposely placed in a small pile, into a cart, which carried them to the local mortuary. At Lambeth Mortuary the remains would be met by Police Surgeons Dr. George Nicol Henry and Dr. Rowe at a little before five A.M. "Upon examination by the divisional surgeon of police found that the hands and feet had been sawn from the trunk. Altogether, the body was in 10 pieces, and these had been apparently boiled or baked with the object of making identification a work of difficulty. [Other reports included, "The other portions of the trunk had apparently been burned, for the bones and flesh showed evident signs of charring."] Part of the scalp and hair were missing, but there were one or two peculiarities about the features which were not effaced, and which should help the police to identify the unfortunate woman. Not a particle of clothing was found on the body. Her face being practically destroyed."

Confidential memo

June 15, 1902   Several persons who have missing relatives have been permitted to see the body, but so far without any identification.

Once again a serial killer had taken a life on an early weekend morning. He had killed with silence at a location thought to have been close by.

And once again the killer had escaped—unseen—into the early morning mist of south London. Again the press asked if this could be the return of Jack the Ripper, but the police did not believe it was so. They would, however, need to wait for the coroner's inquest to discover if this murder had been committed by the same madman who had begun his work in 1887 in Rainham. Would he best them once again, or did he make any errors which would lead to his arrest?

As if to show that the East End had changed little during the 15 years since the first Torso Murder, a second body would be found later that morning. On Ferry Street, only three minutes walk from the torso pile, lay the fresh corpse of a child barely one month old. The child had been clearly murdered with a blow to the back of the head and simply thrown away with the rest of the trash. This was, of course, not a Torso Murder, but it did much to illustrate that the killer had chosen his area well.

The *South London Press*—June 14, 1902

GRUESOME DISCOVERY
Alleged Murder and Mutilation in Lambeth
A horrible discovery was made during the early hours of Sunday morning in Lambeth by Charles Whiting, a stoker in the employ of Messer Doulton who on leaving the works leading into Salamanca Alley, a narrow, ill-lighted thoroughfare, came upon the remains of a young woman scattered about the roadway. A constable was immediately called, and the remains were conveyed to the Lambeth Mortuary, only a short distance away.

Detective Inspector McIntyre, from Scotland Yard, was soon assigned to the case. Because of the report about the medical students, and the fact that a surgical college was within easy walking distance, his first thoughts were that this was some kind of practical joke by the very medical students who had walked by before the constable had arrived on the scene. It would not take long, however, for this veteran investigator to realize "that a crime of the most revolting character had been perpetrated." The body had "never been under medical supervision and was thus not preserved as would be the case if the woman had been used in a medical college or school." It was clearly a murder, and one that would be very difficult to solve.

THE LAST TORSO INQUEST

On Wednesday June 11, the acting coroner for the southwest district, Dr. Michael Taylor, called to order a coroner's inquest into the Salamanca

Place matter. Dr. Taylor informed the jury that this case "was of a very unusual character. The principal difficulty it at present presented was the question of identification, but the matter is in very good hands, and if anything could be made out of it I am sure the police would do it."

On hand were Chief Inspector Mackintosh and Detective Inspector McIntyre of the "Yard." They would be present to take down any new information, and both were ready to testify if the need should arise. Police Constable Birton was also there. He would be one of the first to be called, as he was the first authority on the murder scene.

The court was informed that early on the Monday following the discovery, acting coroner Taylor and the divisional police surgeon, Dr. Henry, had gone to the Lambeth Mortuary. There they met a medical expert from Scotland Yard and went over what could be learned about the case and the victim. The examination had taken three hours and a half, including time to consult on the matter. When the work had been completed the men released a statement to the press that "It was inadvisable to give the result of their inquiry until the inquest had begun." These men wanted to give the police time to look into as many investigative areas as possible before the medical information became public knowledge. That time had now come, and the court became very quite as Dr. George Henry rose to give evidence.

This police surgeon to L Division lived at 175 Kennington Road in Lambeth, not far from the murder site. He was very familiar with the area and had served many years in his position as police surgeon. "Shortly before 5 o'clock on Sunday morning I was called to the Lambeth Mortuary to examine the remains which formed part of a female body. Three front teeth were missing from the lower jaw—two having been wrenched or knocked off, and one broken off level with the jaw. [Similar missing teeth were reported on several Ripper victims as well!] The skin on the face had the appearance of having been subjected to moist heat; in fact, that applied to the whole skull. The other parts were the left arm and left shoulder blade, the right forearm, the left collar bone, the left tibia, the left fibula, the right fibula, the whole of the pelvis, with the lower part of the spine, the middle part of the backbone, seven lower ribs in one piece, and the upper part of the backbone, with the first rib on either side attached. A good many of the bones were missing."

When asked directly by Dr. Taylor, "Are these human remains?" Dr. Henry replied, "Yes; and they form part of one and the same body—that of a female." The court would hear more from Dr. Henry at a later session.

Charles Whiting, the man who had first spotted the body pile, was called to give his evidence in the case. He was still not clear on what he had seen or done even days after the event. The press reported on what he testified to, even as it seemed at bit confusing at times. Once again from the *South London Press*: "Witness had previously passed down the alley at 10 P.M., and he did not think the remains could have been there then, and some men told him that they passed there at 1 A.M., when there was nothing to be seen. Cox returned with somebody, but witness was so upset that he did not know who it was. Very few people passed up and down Salamanca Street at nighttime. At 10 o'clock he had noticed two persons in the alley, but he saw nobody when he found the remains. While working inside they would not be able to hear anything that went on in the alley. He could not recognize the head as belonging to anybody he knew or had ever seen. He had seen the remains in the mortuary, and recognized them as being those he found."

To confirm what Mr. Whiting had testified, the coroner called Mr. Robert Muntzer to report on what he had seen that morning. Mr. Muntzer confirmed Whiting's testimony on how the remains had been discovered; however, "I do not share Whiting's opinion that the remains had been carefully deposited, but favoured the theory that they had been shot out of a sack, and that the skull had been placed on top... I saw a man and woman in the alley at 10 o'clock on Saturday night, and they walked into Broad Street. I do not think I would know the man again, but the woman was wearing a white straw hat, which I believe had a black band. I should say that she was about 5 ft. high. I only saw the back of the man, who was wearing a cap. He looked like a working man in his best clothes, and was a trifle taller than the woman."

The general area of the dumpsite was described by the *South London Chronicle*: "The district in which the discovery was made is a densely populated one, and mostly let out in tenements, and the event caused the utmost excitement, many people likening it to the horror of the Ripper murders which startled London some years ago. The neighborhood is noisy enough at night, and there were people moving about as late as two in the morning, so that the gruesome bundle can hardly have lain in the spot where it was found more than a couple of hours when it was discovered."

In answer to a question about when he had contacted the police, Muntzer stated, "A constable who came up with Cox said to Whiting, 'You are the man who first found the body?'" Later Mr. Muntzer would correct that statement by stating that it was Mr. Cox who had volunteered the information. Finishing up, Muntzer said, "It was so dark [at 10 o'clock] that I cannot furnish any further particulars about the man and woman."

After a brief recess the coroner called forward Police Constable James Birton, 155L, Lambeth Division. It had been a cool and slightly foggy

Sunday morning, without rain, when Constable Birton spotted a very agitated man rushing up to his post as he walked along the Albert Embankment within easy sight of the river. "The man could not explain what he wanted me for, as he was very much agitated." As Mr. Cox began to calm down he began to explain to the officer that "he and a chum had found a woman cut to pieces." When the officer learned that the body had been dumped in Salamanca Alley he knew the killer had to be close—very close. The constable had passed that way earlier and had seen nothing out of the ordinary.

When he arrived on site he questioned the small group of men and sent one of them for an inspector. As he waited by the pile, he surveyed the remains and came to the conclusion that "they had been carefully placed there, and not thrown down." The constable himself may have been a bit put out by the whole affair, as he was not able to remember who had called him to the scene. At first he testified that it was Mr. Whiting, but when he was called back to re-testify, Mr. Whiting cleared the matter up by re-stating that it was Cox who had located the officer. The evening papers reported, "The constable, on being pressed by the coroner, admitted that he did not know whether it was Whiting or Cox that called him, nor could he say who was present besides Muntzer in Salamanca Alley. Coroner Taylor pressed hard for any little detail he could, stating, 'It is rather important, and I want the constable to make it clear if he could.'" It had been a very disturbing morning for all involved—except of course for the two medical students!

The inquiry was then adjourned for a week. The police had been unable to discover the identity of the young woman, even though several individuals had been reported as missing in the general area of late. Most of the women eventually surfaced, and even the relations of those who did not, could not positively identify the body then being held in the Lambeth Mortuary, by then preserved in spirits.

The London *Times*– June 19, 1902

The Discovery of Human Remains at Lambeth
Yesterday Dr. Michael H. Taylor, the acting coroner, resumed his
inquiry at Lambeth into the circumstances attending the death
of an unknown woman, whose mutilated remains were found ...
in Salamanca Alley.

When the inquiry resumed on June 18, Dr. Taylor once again called upon Dr. George Henry to describe, as best he could, the woman who had been murdered and dumped piecemeal in the small and narrow turnoff from Broad Street. "I am Dr. George Nicol Henry, divisional surgeon, residing at 175 Kennington Road. I have on three different days, in conjunction with Professor Popper, lecturer on medical jurisprudence at St. Mary's Hospital [an institute very near the murder site], made a thorough examination of the remains." At this point Dr. Henry went into great detail about the wounds and cuts made on the victim. It was clear from his description that an unskilled hand of little training had dismembered the victim. But was this done to disguise a medical man's training? The killer was smart enough to cover his tracks for 15 years and to disguise the identity of the victim. Was he also clever enough to disguise his own medical background?

The good doctor concluded, "The body was that of a female from 25 to 30 years of age, about 5 ft. in height, slim, but well-developed muscularly. She had very dark brown hair, straight, and probably roughly cut shortly after death. Her eyebrows were well marked, her nose somewhat short, and probably turned up at end. She had high cheekbones and a well-marked short-pointed chin, and very small ears. Her teeth were very regular and well preserved, only one being deficient in the lower jaw. The mutilation and cooking took place soon after life was extinct, and the head was undoubtedly boiled. The left upper limb was undoubtedly dismembered before roasting, and the bones of the left leg showed evidence of moist heat, and subsequently dry heat. Death was probably due to suffocation, but how that took place it was impossible to say. It was difficult to say whether the body was cooked in one place. The work showed no anatomical knowledge whatever. I saw no signs that a chopper had been used [the killer was probably not a butcher by trade], only a saw and a knife. I am certain that a surgical saw was not used. I think it quite possible that the work was done with an ordinary carpenter's saw. The roasting must have occupied many hours. The hair was probably cut off to prevent identification. The body [torso] had been cut into three pieces."

The medical men had now done all they could do. The investigation now lay in the hands of the police. Detective Inspector John McCarthy was then called and testified, "A house-to-house inquiry within a half-mile radius had been made to see whether anyone was missing. Seven women had been reported as missing from the area, but six of these had been accounted for, and I am anxious for a further adjournment to enable me to complete the inquires with reference to the seventh woman. I have made inquires at all the hospitals and medical schools where dissection went on, and was informed that it was absolutely impossible for a corpse to be removed without the knowledge of the treasurer or secretary, although a portion of a body might be taken out."

At that point, at the request of the police, Dr. Taylor called for a two-week adjournment of the proceedings. The London papers did what they could to inform the public and published a description of the woman in the case.

The *South London Chronicle* — June 14, 1902

**OFFICIAL DESCRIPTION OF THE
REMAINS**

The human remains, which were found in Salamanca Place, Lambeth, on the morning of the 8th inst. are those of a small woman, aged between twenty and thirty, height about 5 ft.; complexion dark, hair straight and very dark; the teeth are in an excellent state of preservation. Prominent cheekbones and upper part of jaw. Chin somewhat pointed, giving an angular appearance to the face. The nose was probably somewhat turned up. The patch of hair was verminous.

A Final Look

"All the inquires have failed to afford any clue to the mystery."

Although the authorities would never publicly link this final Thames Torso Murder to a single killer who had worked the London area for 15 years, many believed one man was responsible. However, coroner Dr. Michael Taylor, who had suspected suffocation as the cause of death, would state that the "latest torso murder was on all fours [same kind of murder in design and execution] as the murder of Elizabeth Jackson committed in 1889." By inference he had stated that the same man committed all five over a long span of time. What he could not know was whether or not that very same killer was also responsible for one or more other murders, not part of this series, using different methods.

It would be left to the coroner's jury to render the final words on the last murder in this series of deaths. It did not take very long for the men of the south bank to render...

"Murder by person or persons unknown."

No suspect was ever in the hands of the police for this series, yet the murderer seemed to simply quit with "only" five victims, and yet true serial killers rarely, if ever, end their deadly sprees by their own accord. What then was the reason for this vicious killer to stop? Perhaps an answer may be found in Elliott O'Donnell's 1928 book *Great Thames Mysteries*. Writing of the Torso Murders, Elliott would impart, "With the Salamanca Place murder, however, the Thames Dismemberment cases seem to have come to an end. Possibly the fiend who was responsible for them (It is, I think, generally agreed that one person did them all) died in 1902 or about that time, but at all events, so far as we know, there have been no cases of the same description since that date."

Dead? Or just perhaps this insane killer was taken off the busy streets of south London by police inspectors working on a completely separate set of murders, with poison as the method of death. And just perhaps there really was a simple motive linking these five deaths after all!

Chapter 12

A Possible Motive as a Dark Horse Emerges— Wolff Levisohn

I kept getting the notion that maybe our man had a little sideline as a back street abortionist.
— Debbie Gosling, from a letter to the author

WAS THERE A CONNECTION?

What set of events or circumstances connected these women to their killer? They were, to be sure, all strangers from one another, at least as far as any investigation can determine. Time and location would tend to support this conjecture. They were certainly wider spread, at least in death, than the very closely situated Ripper victims. Then what was the link which brought these women into the deadly grip of the Thames Torso Killer?

If we are to assume that all or most of these women made their way in life as prostitutes, at least part of the time, then a possible link may indeed have been established. But is there any real physical evidence, that can be examined which would point to that link? Indeed there is, and the victims themselves would supply the answer. Their clothes, their wounds and their missing body parts would serve to light the way.

A look at the Rainham Mystery victim shows that she had been cut apart by "a very fine sharp-edged instrument," according to the doctor who examined the located body parts. The dissection was not done at a hospital, but was accomplished by someone who had "a thorough knowledge of surgery." There were, however, no marks or wounds on the body which would show how this young woman had been killed. There were also no clothes on this first victim.

The victim in the Whitehall case would add much to the evidence files. Once again, someone with anatomical and surgical skills had dismembered the victim. He had also taken the full contents of the pelvis; in fact, the lower body cavity had been emptied, to include the removal of the uterus, which was never located. And again, as in the Rainham Mystery, there were no indications on the body which could point to a cause of death. All the doctors would say was that she had not drowned or been suffocated. Only hemorrhage was likely, but no primary wound could be located. In fact, it is recalled that the inquest jury came to the conclusion that the remains were "found dead" and were not one of willful murder, at least a murder could not be proven to have occurred.

Next came Elizabeth Jackson, whose identification allows for at least partial explanation of victim to killer. We know for a fact that she was a working prostitute, and she most likely died in bed or somewhere very close to that area. Bedclothes were associated with her remains. Her body parts would show much to the medical men. On one thigh there were four small bruises made by the fingers of an individual as she was held while still alive. She was at least seven months pregnant at the time of death, and the baby had been taken and probably (according to police reports) thrown into the Thames. Her body had been cut up very soon after she died, but once again there were no marks on the body to indicate how she had died. It would be the coroner who would ask the critical question, "Could an abortion have been carried out?" The doctor did not know, but he did state that the vital organs, which could have answered that question, were missing! The doctor did state, however, that a "killer" who knew how to do the job separated the body. The patterns were starting to fall into place, but were these murders or something else entirely? One thing was becoming clear — the killer knew what he was doing and had acquired some type of medical background or knowledge to do the job.

From the fourth victim, found on Pinchin Street on the edge of the Whitechapel district, came a torso dumped with the remains of a chemise, torn, and bloodstained, still attached. The killer had taken the body apart very soon after death and had done so in a "very skillful manner." Again the doctors could find no definite cause of death, and, significantly, there were no mutilations on the corpse before or after death. This victim did, however, show signs that she had been beaten shortly before she had died. Did she somehow change her mind and struggle, or did her killer know her and need to keep her quiet? Had there been a violent argument, shown by the much-bruised hands of the victim? The physical evidence would suggest yes.

The entire cutting had been done to help remove the body to the dumping locations rather than the pleasure it may have given the killer. Even with this discrepancy, when viewed against the background of the other previous murders, the police were quite sure that one man had been connected with all of the murders in the Torso series. It was at this point the London papers began to speculate on a possible motive in the Torso cases. The police were openly speculating that an illegal operation, such as an abortion, had failed, killing the woman in the Pinchin Street Mystery. The authorities were pleased that the Ripper would not be given credit for this death—but were they correct?

Finally, from the body of the victim in the Salamanca Place Mystery we learn that she had been hacked into 10 major pieces and "placed" in a scattered pile on the street. The body parts did not have any clothes with them, and the features of the last victim had been completely destroyed. This work seemed to have been much cruder than the four other "murders," but the time interval between victims four and five may have had something to do with the change in "style." The killer may simply have decided to chop her up and not worry about it. It is perhaps significant to note that a corpse of a child was found only three minutes from this victim. A link perhaps? One thing is very clear in this case—the killer did everything he could to remove the victim's identity. He must have known that this woman, if identified, could be linked to him, so destroying her identity was a must.

THE MOTIVE?

The question must be asked whether or not these five deaths truly fall into the category of serial murder. Or were they serial mistakes borne out of a medical or former medical man's lack of skills in the "operating room?" Upon closer examination of the medical evidence, such as there is, it would appear that we might be dealing with a series of failed abortions, at least in a majority of the cases. We may never know if the killer knew these victims well, or if they just came to him because they knew he could perform the abortions they may have all required. The motivation could have been as simple as the need to cover up the deaths of women who had come to him for help and died in the process. It becomes clear at that point that a series of women killed and identified could have easily been linked to an individual backstreet doctor. These women must have had friends they confided in, and these people would have talked to the police—if they knew their friend was dead instead of just missing. But who could this backstreet abortionist have been?

Certainly there were many men in or near the East End of London who could have easily performed an abortion. But the numbers become smaller when one realizes that in most cases abortion was illegal at the time. For any prostitute requiring such services, a trip to a local hospital would have been out of the question. Not that many of the locals really trusted the hospitals to be anything more than death traps. Then where would a woman seek this type of help in the Victorian ghetto? The answer must have been the local clinic!

These clinics were sprinkled throughout the area and were generally used by the mostly immigrant population. Patching up the many wounds of these working class residents was a daily occurrence, as was the dispensing of medications. There were few real doctors working in these clinics, but many could lay claim to being a feldscher or barber/surgeon and being available mostly on the weekends. It would be to these barber/surgeons that the prostitute population could turn to end an unwanted pregnancy.

A BARBER/SURGEON NAMED PEDACHENKO

Although much of the basis for information on a man named Alexander Pedachenko, operating in the London area, is second hand and hard to prove, there are some facts which can be known. It is, therefore, valuable to go over what is known or suspected about this infirmary assistant and allow the reader to make his or her own judgment on its value.

Most information on the mysterious Mr. Pedachenko comes from the reported work of Dr. Thomas Dutton, who lived at 130 Aldgate High Street in the East End of London. He lived very close to the murder areas at the time of the Torso and Ripper murders. The young doctor, reported to have been a good friend of famous Ripper investigator Frederick Abberline, the chief inspector on the street side of the investigation, was most interested in local crimes and wrote of them in a personal journal. His writing took the form of a three volume work he entitled *Chronicles of Crime*. This work was never published and may never have been meant for anything other than his own entertainment. After his death in 1935 his work was said by the family to have been either lost or destroyed. There are, however, other reports which state that it has been kept in a family vault. The reason is not given as to why it would be held in such a manner.

SOUTHBANK

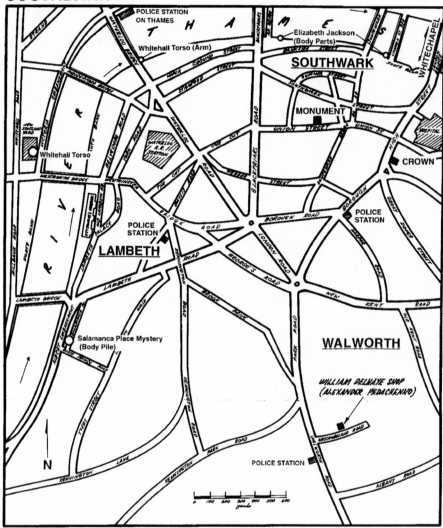

Writer and researcher Donald McCormick reported that in 1932 he was given the opportunity to read and take notes from the *Chronicles* before Dutton's death. He described the volumes as "not a single narrative, but rather a collection of impressions and theories which he noted at various periods." The works were then reported to have been given to a Miss Hermione Dudley. Miss Dudley is said to have been a friend of the aging doctor. "I knew the doctor when I was quite a young girl. By far the most interesting document he compiled was his *Chronicles of Crime*, three volumes of handwritten comments on all of the chief crimes of the past sixty years. Dr. Dutton gave it to me some time ago." So there are at least two eyewitness reports of the *Chronicle*—but what of "Doctor" Pedachenko?

The story goes that the good Inspector Abberline had suspected that Severin Klosowski might have had some involvement in the Ripper murders, as early as 1888, but could not act on his suspicions. McCormick writes that 14 years later, as Klosowski was ready to be hung for three poison murders, Abberline reversed himself. "What finally convinced Abberline that he had made a mistake in thinking Klosowski was the Ripper was his discovery that the Polish barber-surgeon had a double in London and that this double, a Russian and also a barber-surgeon, sometimes posed as Klosowski for reasons which were not apparent." The name given for Klosowski's supposed double was Alexander Pedachenko.

Dr. Dutton had done some of his own research on the matter when he interviewed Dr. John Frederick Williams. Dr. Williams was able to confirm that he did indeed have an unpaid assistant named Pedachenko who was a Russian barber-surgeon when Dr. Williams worked at St. Saviours Infirmary. Further, he confirmed that Pedachenko, who looked exactly like Klosowski, worked in other areas in the east and south of London, "removing warts and treating skin diseases." Those were the exact areas of the Torso murders!

It can be shown that both the infirmary and Dr. Williams did exist at the time of the Ripper and Torso murders, so there is some provable truth to the story. Also, it has long been reported that at least four Ripper victims at one time or another went to St. Saviours Infirmary—Tabram, Chapman, Nichols and Kelly. McCormick also wrote that Dr. Dutton had reported that Pedachenko was working part-time on Westmoreland Road in Walworth for a hairdresser named William Delhaye. Both the establishment and the good Mr. Delhaye also existed, so there is much meat on those old *Chronicle* pages.

The question must then be asked whether it is more likely for a serial killer named Severin Klosowski to have used just one more alias to further his own twisted needs or that an exact double really existed. It is much more likely that Klosowski and Pedachenko were one and the same man. And Klosowski, three-time serial killer, is the best suspect ever to come to light as the author of the Ripper murders. Was he Pedachenko when he took the lives of the Torso victims? Perhaps, but there was at least one other, a long shot in the dark and foggy mix, a dark horse if you will, on the edge of murder.

From Dr. Dutton's writings comes a name and a relationship which seems to stand in the deep shadows of Victorian crime, never really step-ping into the full light yet always near enough to feel the sting of its ever present demands. Dutton wrote that a man named Wolff Levisohn had told Inspector Abberline that "he should look for a Russian who lived some-where in Walworth."

From the Shadows a Dark Horse Emerges

The moment I see the name Chapman I knew this is the man.
— Wolff Levisohn

Wolff Levisohn seemed to always have a window into the world, and perhaps the dark mind of Severin Klosowski, or so it would appear as he testified at Klosowski's murder trial in March of 1903. "There he sits! That is his description. He has not altered from the day he came to England; he has not even a gray hair. Always the same—same la-di-da, 'igh 'at and umbrella. Two wives he had while at Tottenham—one English, one foreign."

Certainly these were the words of a man who had known the "Bor-ough Poisoner" for most of the time he had spent moving around the East End of London and beyond. But was Wolff Levisohn just a bit more than an acquaintance of Klosowski's? Was he possibly a friend at one time, a partner, or was he also a serial killer who, even though he was never sus-pected of any serious crimes, was responsible for one or more of the Rip-per or Torso murders?

For at least 15 years Levisohn had run into Klosowski time and time again, as Levisohn worked as a traveling hairdresser supply salesman. Lev-isohn, in trial testimony, was described as a Jewish commercial traveler, but he was much more than that. Levisohn was also a trained junior sur-geon with much the same training and background as Klosowski. Both men had trained in that demanding field by cutting up bodies. Levisohn would go on to serve in the Russian military for seven years as a feldscher, or assistant surgeon, before moving on to his sales route.

It would be in Warsaw, Poland, that the older Levisohn, fresh out of the army, would meet the then 22-year-old Klosowski. Klosowski was "working at a clinic," preparing for his junior surgeon examinations, when the ever-present Levisohn came by on one of his sales trips. It is not known if any business was transacted as the two men conversed in Yiddish. What is known is that by that time Levisohn had settled in the East End of Lon-don—in Whitechapel. It was early 1887 and a murderous crime wave had not yet begun in the world's metropolis of London. What Levisohn would also discover was that the young man's real name was Severino Antonovich Klosowski, yet in the years to come that name would become lost in the dark abyss of the mind of a serial killer. That secret Levisohn would keep for the next 15 years! Why?

As with Klosowski, the question is asked—why would a trained surgeon with as many years in the field as Levisohn surely had, spend many lonely days and nights on the road when he could have easily applied for work at one of the many hospitals in and around London? Certainly he would have had the contacts because of his many sales trips, yet he did not continue in that line of work. Wolff Levisohn seemed to have needed the ability to move about, and maybe that was the point. As a surgeon he would have been set in one place with no reason to keep on the move. As a commercial traveler he would not have seemed out of place to always be, shall we say, on the run.

Wolff Levisohn, from Chapman's 1903 trial. This is the only known likeness of the man who may very well have killed one or two of the Ripper victims, and perhaps committed one of the Torso murders as well. He is the dark horse of *all* these murders.

Before long Klosowski would also move to the East End of London, finding work as a feldscher and barber in Mr. Radin's hairdressers in Poplar. It was a location which seems to have been missed by Mr. Levisohn, as he was not to come across Klosowski again until Severin moved to the central killing grounds of Jack the Ripper—Whitechapel!

It would be late 1887 or early 1888 when both men would again meet. Klosowski had spent only five months with the Radins and was now working as a floating barber in Whitechapel. It is not known if this was in the barber shop on Whitechapel High Street below the White Hart pub or another location. If it were, it would help confirm that Klosowski worked only yards from where the first Ripper victim's body would be discovered in a few short weeks in August of 1888. By that time, according to Levisohn, he was using the name Ludwig Zagowski and would only speak to him in Yiddish. Klosowski was hiding in the hyper-crowded Jewish section of London, passing himself off as a Jew. He was, however, a Roman Catholic. What Klosowski was hiding from would only be a matter of speculation; however, the favor he asked of Wolff Levisohn is a matter of court record.

Levisohn would later testify that Klosowski, alias Zagowski, asked him to acquire some poisons for his personal use. Klosowski obviously felt he could trust someone from the old country, and since Levisohn was in the medical business why not get the needed white powders from him. Perhaps it was the new alias Klosowski was using, or even direct knowledge of how Klosowski planned to put the poison to use, that stopped the sale, but stop it it did. All Levisohn would say on the stand was, "I talked to the accused [Klosowski] about medicines and he asked me for a certain medicine. But I said no, I did not want to get twelve years."

At the time, most drugs seen as illegal today were readily available, so the request could not have been of a true medical nature. The only "medicines" that would have landed Levisohn in prison if he had sold it "under the table" would have been deadly poisons. It should also be noted that not long after Klosowski attempted to purchase poisons and failed— the Ripper murders began. A sharp knife would do just as well.

Further word comes from Robert Nash's *Almanac of World Crime.* Nash reports that "he [Klosowski] was secretly trying to obtain poison from underworld sources in Whitechapel at the very time of the Ripper murders." Is this a reference to other attempts to acquire the deadly powders, or was Levisohn "the" underworld source? Certainly Levisohn had secrets of his own to protect. Was serial murder one of them?

During the Ripper and Torso murders, Levisohn was generally in and around the killing grounds of the East End. And although he must have traveled for business reasons out of London during that period, he did seem to be in Whitechapel at critical periods of time. A case in point would be the night of November 15, 1888. By that time there were circulating some very good descriptions of the Ripper, as well as a very good drawing of the supposed killer in the *Illustrated Police News.*

Five East End prostitutes had been cut down by the Ripper, and, as would be expected, the local women were on the alert. None were more on the alert than prostitutes Johnson and DeGrasse. As reported in the *Illustrated Police News* of November 24, 1888, Levisohn was walking home in central Whitechapel when he was confronted by well-known prostitute Mary Ann Johnson. It was half past 11 when Johnson solicited Mr. Levisohn for services, but for whatever reason he declined the offer. Perhaps he did not have any money or it may have been a very long day. It was, after all, a cold November night, and the prospect of a sexual encounter in a back alley may not have been as appealing an offer as it may have normally sounded.

Not one to easily accept a fast dismissal, Johnson decided to verbally attack Levisohn by loudly declaring, "You are Jack the Ripper." At the time, Levisohn looked nothing like the descriptions being circulated or the drawing published in the local papers. Nevertheless, the cry had been made, which alerted those around, and before long a second prostitute, DeGrasse, took up the clarion call. Wolff Levisohn took off at a dead run, knowing full well that there would be no justice at the hands of the mob. The East Enders wanted blood and his would do nicely.

Levisohn knew he had only one chance as he ran. "Fearing that the consequences might be very unpleasant for himself, he took refuge in the Commercial Street Police Station," and then police took the women into custody. It did not take long for the police to see that the small-sized Levisohn was not the man they were looking for. At least he did not "look" like the Ripper. Once the mob had been cleared away, Levisohn was allowed to go on his way, a wiser man perhaps, but the two prostitutes were held for a while longer. Johnson would tell the officers that she felt Levisohn had attacked her because "he looked like the Ripper with his shiny black bag."

It had been widely reported that the Ripper carried a black medical bag, but those reports were false. In fact, no one who actually saw the Ripper or a suspected individual ever reported that he carried a black bag. The only real report was of a young doctor who was seen near one of the murder sites at the time with a black bag. But he came forward the day after and was never accused of any crimes. It is clear, however, that Levisohn did carry a shiny black bag. Was he also doing a bit of midnight surgery on the side?

This was the incident which may have brought Levisohn to the attention of Inspector Abberline. As the leading investigator at the street level it would be Abberline who would have questioned Levisohn about his movements and what he may have known about the murders in Whitechapel.

There are other statements that seem to indicate an interest in Levisohn by Abberline, which comes once again in the form of the chronicle written by Dr. Thomas Dutton. Reportedly, Inspector Abberline visited with his friend the doctor many times during the search for the killer or killers in the East End. It was from these visits that Dr. Dutton wrote his passages on this and other famous crimes of the day.

Dr. Dutton reportedly wrote about the meeting his friend Abberline had with Wolff Levisohn, reporting that Levisohn told Abberline that "he should look for a Russian who lived somewhere in Walworth, did a certain amount of illicit doctoring and attended barber's shops to cut out warts and moles." Upon further questioning, Dutton reportedly wrote that "Levisohn told Inspector Abberline that Severin Klosowski was not the Ripper."

It is unlikely that the good inspector would have left it at that, but Dr. Dutton does not seem to have given any more details along those lines, at least none are presently known. It is not known how Levisohn would have discovered this information nor what follow-up the police may have conducted. What history does show is that Levisohn was never held in connection to either murder series. So it is possible that his information was not held in very high regard and must remain so until other sources can be found to verify his reported statements.

There is one additional event reportedly described in Dr. Dutton's chronicle. It occurred on the night of September 29–30 of 1888. This was the cold and wet night of the Ripper's "double event" in which two East End prostitutes met their fates at the practiced hands of Jack the Ripper. According to Dutton, Levisohn was once again out that night on the streets of Whitechapel and he spotted a man Levisohn knew as Dr. Pedachenko on Commercial Street. That location was a half block away from where both Elizabeth Stride and Catherine Eddowes lived. These two women would both become victims of the Ripper that night.

The man known as Dr. Pedachenko was said to have been a junior surgeon working illegally in the field in the general area of the East End of London. Klosowski or his double? Clarification on the man's identity has never been settled, but a logical explanation would be that Klosowski was simply using another alias to work in the field he was trained in. History and police statements already place Klosowski living in the area at the time. It would seem that Levisohn's own words place him there as well.

Wolff Levisohn would continue to work as a commercial traveler for at least the next few years. During his travels he would continue to meet up with Klosowski. During Klosowski's murder trial Levisohn would relate to the court that Klosowski seemed to always be on the move during 1894–95. "He [Klosowski] moved around quite a few times during 1894–95." There was no mention of what name or names Klosowski used at the time, but by that time other witnesses firmly reported the new alias as George Chapman.

When Levisohn was asked by defense council why he had such a long interest and great feelings on the matter before the court (that being the serial murder case of three women by Klosowski/Chapman), he stated, "Not at all, why, bless your heart, the moment I see the name Chapman I knew this is the man." This confirms that he knew Klosowski was using another alias much earlier than the authorities, but Levisohn did nothing about it.

Clearly the man known to history as Wolff Levisohn had and kept many secrets about himself. Self-preservation can be a most powerful driving force. But there are no clear answers as to why Levisohn would keep secrets about a man he certainly disliked, if we are to believe the tone of his court statements at Klosowski's trial. The only answer would seem to be that some form of powerful bond between these men secretly kept them from turning each other in to the authorities. Illegal activity surely, but was it also serial murder that neither man could talk about and which neither would be called to the bar of justice to pay for? The final chapter of the secret lives of these two men may never be written, but one thing is clear—death would surely fill those bloody pages!

Postscript of Terror

We stepped up security and we are patrolling all bridges.
— Scotland Yard spokesman, quoted in the *Times* of London,
March 6, 2001

THE TORSO MURDERS OF 2001

As Londoners celebrated the passing of the 20th century a new killer was starting his series of death in the ancient city. Once again a sexual serial killer had made London his home, but this time the killer would add a strange twist to his work. He would drop off the products of his deadly craft in and around the exact same areas which had once held the victims of the Thames Torso Killer of Victorian London. Was this merely a coincidence of need or a deadly game being played on the prostitutes of London by a new demented killer? And would Scotland Yard be able to use this information to catch a modern day Jack the Ripper before he could kill again?

Her name was Zoe Parker, but she was also known as Kathy Dennis, which was not unexpected for a woman in her line of work. She was a 24-year-old occasional prostitute from Hounslow, Middlesex, who had come to London to make her way in the world, but she ended up on the streets of London selling herself for a few pounds. And in that work she would become the first victim of the Copycat Torso Killer.

Zoe had "gone missing" around November 25, 2000, from her "usual work area" in Battersea. And although a missing persons report had been filed, no one could understand what had become of her. That question would be answered on December 17 when her "severed torso was found in the Thames near Church Road in Battersea." Only the upper half of her body was found, which was subsequently examined and found to have been in the Thames for around three weeks. It had been "worked on and dissected by a large, sharp knife." The torso had been located where a portion of Elizabeth Jackson's body had been found in June of 1889.

On December 28 it was reported in the London papers that Detective Chief Inspector Andy Baker had released a preliminary report on the victim in the hopes of achieving identification. "Red rose tattoo, scrolled with the name Zoe. Distinctive twisted lateral incisor. White woman between 5 ft. 3 in. and 5 ft. 7 in. tall. Slim to medium build and could have been in the Thames River since November 25." Along with this description the police released a photo of the unique tattoo. Leading the investigation was Detective Chief Inspector Richard Heseldin, who was quoted as saying, "Through the unique top [a white or stone colored blouse which had limited sales in London], the tattoo and the tooth, someone must be able to recognize this woman."

It did not take long for the police to identify the corpse after Scotland Yard released the description. The killer did not take the head and did not seem to care whether or not his victim was eventually identified or not. Disposal of the body appeared to be his primary concern as he made his cuts. However, he may have had one other reason for cutting up his prey—he was a collector. The lower half of Zoe's body was still missing!

At this point investigators had very little to go on and certainly were not thinking "serial killer." After all, "only" one body (half of one at least) had been found in the river. And in a city as large as London a new murder or two did not elicit a great deal of excitement in either the halls of justice or the general population. There were, of course, many other stories to tell as the new millennium was just getting started. However, women were starting to "come up missing" and there may very well have been a connection to the torso at Battersea.

The police began to review missing persons reports and found that three women had gone missing in the same general area of West London. The first was Elizabeth Chau, a 19-year-old student. Chau had last been seen outside Ealing police station on April 16, 1999. She had "been in a spot of trouble" and was seen making a call at a nearby payphone. The second woman to possibly meet this latest serial killer was 20-year-old Iwona Kaminski. Kaminski was from Poland and had been in London for only four days when she disappeared on July 13, 2000. She had disappeared, according to police reports, in "similar circumstances" and in the same general area as Elizabeth Chau. She had also been to the police station.

An American-born computer school graduate named Lola Shenkoya followed Chau's vanishing act. 27-year-old Shenkoya had also been in the West London area of Ealing when she disappeared on January 3, 2001. She had been last seen making a phone call on a public payphone in Ealing. By this time the police knew they had a problem, and it was about to get worse. Things were starting to pile up near the payphones of Ealing police station. Could the killer have a possible police connection?

The *Times* of London—March 3, 2001

New Ripper fear as second body is found
SCOTLAND YARD fears that a new serial killer who preys on prostitutes could be on the loose after discovering a second severed torso in the capital's waterways in less than two months. Detectives believe that the latest Ripper may be keeping some of his victim's dismembered limbs as trophies as some body parts are missing from both women.

With reports of a new Ripper now flowing over London's population the police announced that a 10-year-old boy had discovered, on February 19, the remains of a second torso victim while playing near Regent's Canal in Camden, North London. Her name was Paula Fields and she was a 31-year-old prostitute originally from Liverpool. She was at the time of her disappearance "working" out of a hotel in Highbury Grove, London. She had been a drug addict whose drug of choice was crack cocaine, and she was also a mother of two.

For this murder the killer had gone to great lengths to dispose of his victim. The police reported that he had "taken his time to dissect the body, possibly using an electric saw." The killer must have felt very secure in what he was doing as he loaded six plastic shopping bags (or hold-alls, depending on which source is quoted) and prepared them for disposal. He weighed each down with old tiles and bricks, which could very well point to who this killer was—or at least his general location or workplace. The tiles could point to a single location.

As the police intensified their search of the area where the body parts were found, they added an investigative tool unavailable to Victorian police. Specially trained police underwater search teams were soon moving along the floor of the canal, searching for more body parts. As before, the killer was not disposing of the entire body. He was still collecting his trophies from the kill, and he was far from finished. There were, after all, plenty of targets of opportunity for the modern serial killer in the fast moving city of London.

The *Times* of London—March 7, 2001

**Ripper fears as another body
is found in the Thames**
THE discovery of the third woman's body in one of London's
waterways in three months has led to fears of a Ripper-style serial killer, who murders prostitutes before throwing their bodies
into the capital's rivers or canals.

The police would not have long to wait for the killer to add to his body
count, even though official government sources were not yet prepared to
admit that they had a serial killer on their hands. On March 7 a Scotland
Yard spokesman took the question of serial murder and quickly brushed
it aside. "As is normal, those leading the separate inquires will work with
each other, but at this stage there is nothing to link the three cases." This
comment could easily have fitted right in during the early days of the original Ripper murders a century ago. However, one thing was very clear, the
police had very little to go on and very few theories.

On March 5, at around 1:45 in the afternoon, the Thames Police were
called to an area near Lambeth Bridge on the Thames River. Reports had
come in of a woman's body floating in the river, and the police soon arrived
to pull a corpse out of the water. The unknown woman, thought to be "in
her late thirties to fifties," was pulled to the shore by police diving spe-
cialists. It was soon discovered that she had not been in the water for long,
possibly less than a week, and that she had been carried to the river and
dumped, "wrapped in a carpet."

Detective Chief Inspector William Chambers was placed in charge of
the case. He had been assigned to the Serious Crime Group out of Scotland Yard, and he was certain a murder had occurred. He was not sure it
was the new "Ripper." What he did know, from a post mortem which had
been conducted at the Westminster Mortuary, was that this victim had
died due to "a compression of the neck." She had been strangled and then
tied up in the carpet.

The Serious Crime Group would only state that "investigation officers
in all three cases will be conferring to probe whether the murders are
linked." They would also report that this as-yet-unknown victim had not
been "hacked up like the previous victims."

That is where the official reports would have to sit until this new serial killer introduces the people of London to his next murder victim, most
likely to be found floating down the "Bloody Thames." The only question
left is not if, but when the next victim would be found!

A VOICE FROM THE PAST

As if on cue to fill the murder void between these new deaths, a letter written in 1888 resurfaced for the entire world to see on April 24, 2001. It was signed Jack the Ripper, and had originally been sent to Dr. Thomas Horrocks Openshaw. Dr. Openshaw was at the time of the original Ripper murders on staff at London Hospital's pathological museum. He was the doctor who examined the kidney which had been sent by the killer of Catherine Eddowes to George Lusk of the Mile End Vigilance Committee. A letter "from hell" had accompanied that body part, which had been preserved in red wine.

The "recently released" Ripper letter which had been posted in the East End of London on October 29, 1888, was an attempt to take credit for the kidney and warn of other murders to come. It was, however, not written by the killer, as the handwriting and syntax did not match the letter which had come with the kidney.

> Old boss you was rite it was
> the left kidney I was going to
> hopperate agin close to your
> ospitle just as I was goin
> to dror mi nife along of
> er bloomin throte them
> cusses of coppers spoilt
> the game but I guess I wil
> be on the jog soon and wil
> send you another bit of
> innerds
>
> Jack the Ripper
>
> O have you sein the devle
> with his mikerscope and scalpul
> a looking at a kidney
> with a slide cocked up

The letter had been kept in the files of the Public Record Office, where it had been held for the past 30 years. The letter had "gone missing" for some time until it was rediscovered by Donald Rumbelow, a former police officer in London and author of several Ripper books. It would appear, however, that Rumbelow would not say just how this piece of evidence came into his hands. It would seem that even after more than 112 years, some people prefer to keep secret some tales of Jack the Ripper. Nevertheless, if history is any judge, "London's Bloody History" will continue.

Appendix 1

Table: Victims of the Thames Torso Killer

France

Possible! Paris November 1886	Unknown Young woman	Torso of woman with head, right arm and legs cut off and removed. *Right breast and uterus removed and missing.* Head never found.

England

May 1887	Unknown In her twenties 5'4"	Torso of woman with head, arms, and legs cut off. Head never found. *Parts missing. Breasts removed.*
c. August 20, 1888 (Central Ripper time frame)	Unknown Young woman (25–30) Plump, 5'8/9"	Torso of a woman with head, arms, and legs cut off. One leg and head never found. *Lower torso was ripped, parts missing.* Found October 2, 1888.
c. June 2, 1889	Elizabeth Jackson 24 years old Plump, 5'5"	Torso cut into sections, head, arms and legs cut off. Several smaller *sections disposed of* in many areas. (She was pregnant when murdered.) Head never found. *Parts missing.*
c. September 8, 1889	Unknown	Torso of a woman with head and

229

	around 33 years old 5'3"	legs cut off. *15" gash in abdomen.* Body was bruised. Head never found. *Death by ripped throat!*
June 1902	Unknown 25–30 years old 5'0"	Torso of a woman with head, arms and legs cut off. Backbone had been sawn in half. Head and other body parts were boiled in water or roasted in an oven. Dumped in a single pile. Scalp, hands and feet were never found. Several front teeth missing.

Note: Italicized descriptions indicate similarities to Ripper murders.

Appendix 2

Chronology of Death

1886

November 1886   Torso discovered at Montrouge Church in Paris, France.

1887

May 11, 1887   First London Torso Murder, the Rainham Mystery torso
                     discovered.

June 5, 1887   Portion of a leg is found in Thames River near Temple Pier.

June 23, 1887   Parcel containing human remains found near Thames River.

June 30, 1887   Two legs wrapped in bundle found floating on Thames.

August 13, 1887   Rainham Mystery inquest verdict is "Found dead."

August 23, 1887   Isreal Lipski of Whitechapel is executed for murder.

1888

February 25, 1888   Annie Millwood attacked in Spitalfields by stranger with a
                     knife.

March 28, 1888   Ada Wilson is attacked in Mile End, knife wound in the
                     neck.

August 7, 1888   First generally recognized Ripper victim, Martha Tabram,
                     is stabbed to death in George Yard Dwelling.

c. August 20, 1888   Murder of a woman, second torso victim, who would be
                     discovered in Whitehall on October 2, 1888.

August 31, 1888   Second Ripper victim, Mary Ann "Polly" Nichols, is
                     murdered in Buck's Row.

September 8, 1888   Third Ripper victim, Annie Chapman, is murdered in
                     backyard of 29 Hanbury Street.

September 10, 1888   Mile End Vigilance Committee is formed to search for Ripper.

September 11, 1888   Woman's arm found on Thames River Embankment.

September 27, 1888   First letter received at *Central News Agency* using the name "Jack the Ripper."

September 30, 1888   Fourth Ripper victim, Elizabeth Stride, is murdered in Dutfield's yard just off Berner Street, before 1 A.M.

September 30, 1888   Fifth Ripper victim, Catherine Eddowes, is murdered and badly mutilated in Mitre Square, before 1:45 A.M.

October 2, 1888   Second Torso victim discovered on New Scotland Yard building site in Whitehall Torso Mystery.

October 5, 1888   Ripper letter sent denying involvement in Torso Murders.

October 13–18, 1888   The Great Ripper Search is conducted in the East End of London.

October 17, 1888   Human leg of Whitehall victim discovered at worksite.

October 22, 1888   Whitehall Mystery verdict: "Found dead."

November 9, 1888   Sixth Ripper victim, Mary Jane Kelly, is murdered in her room off Dorset Street; great amount of mutilation on body.

November 10, 1888   Dr. Thomas Bond issues his medical report on the Whitechapel murders. Suspect profile.

November 10, 1888   Murder pardon issued for one Ripper murder, accomplice only.

December 20, 1888   Possible Ripper victim, Rose Mylett, is strangled by a cord.

1889

January 18, 1889   Final report on Rainham Murder Mystery is written.

c. June 2, 1889   Third Torso victim, Elizabeth Jackson, is murdered (the only victim in the series to be identified).

June 4, 1889   Body parts, including a leg, are pulled from Thames.

June 6, 1889   Female trunk found in Battersea Park; neck, shoulder and other parts found off Copington's Wharf.

June 7, 1889   Leg found near Wandsworth Bridge in Fulham; body parts found off West India Docks in Thames; flesh discovered on Riverbank at Palace Wharf.

June 8, 1889   Partial limb with hand found off Bankside in Southwark; torn body parts fished out of Thames by River Police; piece of woman's thigh found along Chelsea Embankment.

June 9, 1889   Small liver found floating in Thames off of Wapping.

July 1, 1889   Elizabeth Jackson inquest brings in verdict of "Wilful murder against some person or persons unknown."

July 17, 1889   Possible Ripper victim, Alice "Clay Pipe" McKenzie, is murdered in Castle Alley.

September 10, 1889   Fourth Torso victim discovered on Pinchin Street.

September 11, 1889   Chief Police Commissioner Monro sends confidential report on torso murder to Home Secretary, sealed for 101 years.

September 24, 1889   Pinchin Street Torso inquest brings in verdict of "Wilful murder against some person or persons unknown."

October 5, 1889   Pinchin Street Torso buried in special sealed container.

1891

February 13, 1891   Last possible Ripper victim, Frances Coles, is murdered in Swallow Gardens, alive when found.

February 27, 1891   Final Ripper murder inquest verdict: "Wilful murder against some person or persons unknown." (No one would ever be tried for murder in any Ripper case.)

1892

May 23, 1892   Serial killer Frederick Deeming is hung in Melbourne, Australia.

November 15, 1892   The Lambeth Poisoner, Dr. Thomas Neill Cream, goes to the gallows. "I am Jack the...."

1897

April 3, 1897   Severin Klosowski purchases poison and begins his murder spree on three "wives."

December 25, 1897   First Borough Poisoner victim dies—Mary Spink.

1901

February 13, 1901   Second Borough Poisoner victim dies—Bessie Taylor.

December 1901   Klosowski attempts to burn down Monument Public House for the insurance money.

1902

June 8, 1902   Fifth Torso victim discovered in Salamanca Alley—last victim.

October 22, 1902   Third and final Borough Poisoner victim dies—Maud Marsh.

1903

April 7, 1903   The Borough Poisoner, Severino Antonovich Klosowski, is given a drop of 6'6" and executed at Wandsworth Prison.

Appendix 3

The Ripper Letter

Old boss you was rite it was the left kidney i was goin to hopperate agin close to your ospitle just as i was goin to dror mi nife along of er bloomen throte them cusses of coppers spoilt the game but i guess i wil be on the job soon and will send you another bit of innerds jack the ripper

O have you sun the devle with his mikerscope and scalpul a lookin at a kidney with a slide cocked up

Jack the Ripper letter re-released to the general public in 2001.

Note by Chief Inspector Frederick George Abberline

44

Why I did not write my Reminiscences When I retired from the Metropolitan Police.

I think it is just as well to record here the Reason why as from the various cuttings from the newspapers as well as the many other matters that I was called upon to investigate - that never became public property - it must be apparent that I could write many things that would be very interesting to read.

At the time I retired from the service the Authorities were very much opposed to retired Officers writing anything for the press as previously some retired Officers had from time to time been very indiscreet in what they had caused to be published and to my knowledge had been called upon

Above and next page: This is the *only* written explanation ever given by the officer who had charge of the Ripper investigation (F. G. Abberline) as to why he did not write or grant any interviews on the case.

45
upon to explain their conduct and
in fact they had been threatened with
actions for libel.

Apart from that there is no
doubt the fact that in describing
what you did in detecting certain
crimes you are putting the criminal
classes on their guard and in
some cases you may be absolutely
telling them how to commit crime.

As an example in the Finger-
Print detection you find now the
expert thief wears gloves.

                                    F. G. Abberline

Bibliography

The Press

The *Times* of London
    May 16, 1887 — Inquests
    June 13, 1887 — The Rainham Mystery
    July 21, 1887 — The Rainham Mystery
    August 23, 1887 — Execution of Lipski
    August 10, 1888 — The Murder in Whitechapel
    August 24, 1888 — Inquests
    September 1, 1888 — Another Murder in Whitechapel
    September 3, 1888 — The Whitechapel Murder
    September 4, 1888 — The Whitechapel Murder
    September 10, 1888 — The Whitechapel Murders
    September 11, 1888 — The Whitechapel Murders
    September 15, 1888 — The Whitechapel Murders
    October 8, 1888
    October 9, 1888 — Drowned in the Thames
    November 10, 1888 — Another Whitechapel Murder
    June 5, 1889
    June 7, 1889
    June 8, 1889
    June 12, 1889
    June 13, 1889
    June 17, 1889
    September 11, 1889 — Another Murder and Mutilation in Whitechapel
    September 20, 1889
    June 19, 1902 — The Discovery of Human Remains at Lambeth
    April 8, 1903 — Execution — Severino Klosowski
    December 28, 2000
    December 29, 2000

March 3, 2001
March 7, 2001

The *New York Times*
   September 1, 1888 — A Terribly Brutal Murder in Whitechapel
   September 9, 1888 — Whitechapel Startled by a Fourth Murder
   October 1, 1888 — Dismay in Whitechapel
   October 2, 1888 — London's Awful Mystery
   October 3, 1888 — London's Record of Crime
   October 5, 1888 — The Whitechapel Murder Mysteries
   November 10, 1888 — Exciting London Events
   December 11, 1888 — Is this Jack the Ripper
   July 18, 1889 — The Whitechapel Crime
   July 21, 1889 — Gossip of the Day Abroad
   September 11, 1889 — Another London Murder
   February 13, 1891— Jack the Ripper Again
   February 14, 1891— The Whitechapel Mystery
   February 1, 1892 — A Brutal New Jersey Murder
   February 4, 1892 — The Murder of Mrs. Senior

East London Advertiser
   March 10, 1888
   August 11, 1888
   August 18, 1888
   September 8, 1888
   October 13, 1888
   October 27, 1888
   November 10, 1888

The *Weekly Herald*
   August 17, 1888 — A Mysterious Murder
   August 20, 1888
   September 7, 1888 — Horrible Murder of a Woman
   September 14, 1888 — Another London Tragedy
   October 5, 1888 — London's Horrors
   November 16, 1888 — A Woman Fiendishly Mutilated
   December 7, 1888 — The Whitechapel Fiend

Daily Telegraph
   October 4, 1888 — The Whitehall Murder
   October 5, 1888 — Whitehall Tragedy

The Illustrated Police News
   August 24, 1888
   September 8, 1888 — The Murder in Whitechapel
   October 20, 1888 — Fresh Evidence
   November 17, 1888 — Intense Excitement in the East-End

The Star
    August 31, 1888 — A Revolting Murder
    September 8, 1888 — Horror Upon Horror
    October 19, 1888

The News
    July 6, 1665

The London Gazette
    Septemb 3–Septemp 10, 1666

Evening Standard
    March 7, 2001— Ripper Fears as Another Body Is Found in the Thames

Essex Times
    June 8, 1887 — The Rainham Mystery

South London Observer
    November 1, 1902 — Southwark Poisoning Mystery
    November 2, 1902 — Publican Charged with Murder

The South London Press
    June 14, 1902 — Gruesome Discovery
    November 2, 1902 — Publican Charged with Murder
    March 21, 1902 — Southwark Murder
    April 11, 1903 — The Southwark Poisoner

South London Chronicle
    June 14, 1902 — Official Description of the Remains

Pall Mall Gazette
    November 10, 1888
    December 31, 1888
    November 4, 1889
    April 8, 1892
    March 24, 1903
    March 31, 1903

The Daily Chronicle
    March 23, 1903

East London Observer
    January 14, 1888
    February 4, 1888
    February 11, 1888
    March 10, 1888

March 17, 1888
March 24, 1888
April 21, 1888
May 19, 1888
June 3, 1888
June 9, 1888
June 21, 1888
June 23, 1888
December 22, 1888

The Writers and Researchers

Adam, Hargrave L., ed. *Trial of George Chapman*. London: William Hodge, April 1930.

Altick, Richard D. *Victorian Studies in Scarlet*. New York: W. W. Norton, 1970.

Begg, Paul, Martin Fido and Keith Skinner. *The Jack the Ripper A to Z*. London: Headline Book Publishing, 1994.

Evans, Stewart P., and Keith Skinner. *The Ultimate Jack the Ripper Companion*. New York: Carroll & Graf, 2000.

Fabian, Robert. *London After Dark*. London: The Naldrett Press, 1954.

Fido, Martin. *Murder Guide to London*. London: George Weidenfeld & Nicolson, 1986.

Fishman, W. J. *East End 1888 — Life in a London Borough Among the Laboring Poor*. Philadelphia: Temple University Press, 1988.

Gordon, R. Michael. *Alias Jack the Ripper — Beyond the Usual Whitechapel Suspects*. Jefferson, N.C.: McFarland, 2001.

Holmes, Ronald H., and Stephen T. Holmes. *Serial Murder* (Second Edition). Thousand Oaks, Calif.: Sage, 1998.

London, Jack. *The People of the Abyss*. Sonoma State University, California: Joseph Simon Publisher, 1980 (1903).

Mearns, Andrew. *The Bitter Cry of Outcast London*. New York: Leicister University Press, 1970.

Nash, Jay Robert. *Almanac of World Crime*. Garden City, N.Y.: Anchor Press/Doubleday, 1981.

O'Donnell, Elliott. *Great Thames Mysteries*. London: Selwyn and Blount, 1928.

Sugden, Philip. *The Complete History of Jack the Ripper*. New York: Carroll & Graf, 1995.

The Symphonette Press. *Crimes and Punishment — Vol. 1 & 2*. Paulton, England: BPC Publishing, 1973, 1974.

Wilson, Colin. *A Casebook of Murder*. New York: Cowles, 1969.

_____. *Unsolved Mysteries, Past and Present*. Chicago: Contemporary Books, 1992.

_____, and Patricia Pitman. *Encyclopedia of Murder*. London and Sydney: Pan Books, 1961.

The Reference and Research Locations

The Directorate of Public Affairs and Internal Communication (DPA). General

Enquires Desk, New Scotland Yard, 8 Broadway, London, SW1H 0BG England.

London Metropolitan Archives. Research Enquires Desk, 40 Northampton Road, London, EC1R 0AB England.

Metropolitan Police Service. Southwark Division, 323 Borough High Street, London, SE1 1JL England.

Public Record Office. Research Enquires Desk, Chancery Lane, 1 Myddelton St., London, EC1R 1UW England.

_____. Research Enquires Desk, Ruskin Avenue, Kew, Richmond, Surrey, TW9 4DU England.

Southwark Local Studies Library. 211 Borough High Street, London, SE1 1JA England.

The Documents

Dr. Thomas Bond's medical letter. Report on the Whitechapel murders, November 10, 1888.

Inspector Frederick George Abberline — note. Explanation for not writing his reminiscences on Ripper and other cases (reproduced by permission of the Police Museum, London).

Letter to Clerk to the Vestry — Parish of Whitechapel. E. Leigh Pemberton, October 6, 1888.

Letter to Henry Matthews. J. Whittaker Ellis, October 3, 1888.

Letter to Mr. Ruggles Brise. Reference to Ripper search, October 4, 1888.

Personal Documents held by Severino Antonovich Klosowski.
  — Birth Certificate, December 15, 1865
  — Magistrate Conduct Certificate, November 16, 1882
  — Surgical Pupil Registry Receipt, November 22–December 3, 1882
  — Apprentice Certificate, June 1, 1885
  — Instruction Certificate, April 29, 1886
  — Klosowski Personal Biography, November 15, 1886
  — Passport, November 24, 1886
  — Junior Surgeon Degree Petition, December 1886
  — Junior Surgeon Degree Acceptance, December 5, 1886
  — Hospital Fees Receipt, February 28, 1887

The Official Files

Public Record Office, Kew
Metropolitan Police:
  — MEPO 3/140 — Whitechapel Murder Files
  — MEPO 3/142 — "Jack the Ripper" letters
  — MEPO 3/153 — Post Mortem — Mary Kelly, "Dear Boss" letter, Pinchin Street News report, Murder Pardon — Kelly murder
  — MEPO 3/155 — Whitechapel Murder Victims — Photos
(Material in the Public Record Office is the copyright of the Metropolitan Police and is reproduced by permission of the Commissioner of Police of the Metropolis.)

Home Office:
  — HO 144/221/A49301 F — Mary Kelly murder
  — HO 144/221/A49301 K — Pinchin Street Torso murder
  — HO 144/680/101992 — George Chapman Poison Case

Public Record Office, Chancery Lane:
  — CRIM 1/84 — George Chapman Poison Case, Depositions
  — CRIM 4/1215 — George Chapman Poison Case, Indictments

Index

Numbers in **bold** refer to photographs and illustrations.